Learn
Windows XP

Sunrise Midday Sunset

In a Weekend

Sunrise Evening Sunset

Learn Windows XP

Sunrise · Midday · Sunset · In a Weekend · Sunrise · Evening · Sunset

Katherine Murray

Premier
Press

The Premier Press logo, top edge printing, related trade dress, and In a Weekend are trademarks of Premier Press, Inc. and may not be used without written permission. All other trademarks are the property of their respective owners.

Publisher: Stacy L. Hiquet

Marketing Manager: Heather Buzzingham

Managing Editor: Sandy Doell

Book Packager: Justak Literary Services

Project Editor: Amy Pettinella

Editorial Assistant: Margaret Bauer

Technical Reviewer: Keith Davenport

Copy Editor: Rebecca Whitney

Interior Layout: William Hartman

Cover Design: Christy Pierce

Indexer: Sherry Massey

Proofreader: Lara SerVaas

Microsoft, Windows, Internet Explorer, Notepad, and ActiveX are trademarks or registered trademarks of Microsoft Corporation.

Important: Premier Press cannot provide software support. Please contact the appropriate software manufacturer's technical support line or Web site for assistance.

Premier Press and the author have attempted throughout this book to distinguish proprietary trademarks from descriptive terms by following the capitalization style used by the manufacturer.

Information contained in this book has been obtained by Premier Press from sources believed to be reliable. However, because of the possibility of human or mechanical error by our sources, Premier Press, or others, the Publisher does not guarantee the accuracy, adequacy, or completeness of any information and is not responsible for any errors or omissions or the results obtained from use of such information. Readers should be particularly aware of the fact that the Internet is an ever-changing entity. Some facts may have changed since this book went to press.

ISBN: 1-931841-75-6

Library of Congress Catalog Card Number: 2001099834

Printed in the United States of America

02 03 04 05 RI 10 9 8 7 6 5 4 3 2

"I hear and I forget.
I see and I understand.
I do and I learn."

Chinese proverb

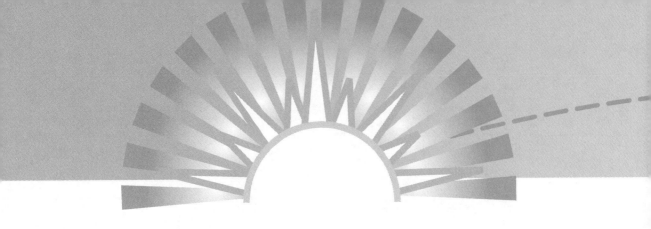

Acknowledgments

Once upon a time, writing a book took months, if not years. A writer gets an idea, thinks about it a while, makes a few notes, and lets it grow and ferment and finally hatch into something that can be talked about with a publisher. After that initial discussion, the process can take many more months as the writer and publisher plan the project and pull all the pieces together.

But sometimes a writer is lucky enough to work with that rare person who thinks the same way, knows a good idea when she hears it, and is ready to jump in—right now—and put a plan into action. That's why I like working with Stacy Hiquet and all the folks at Premier Press. The *In a Weekend* series is smart, great for readers, and fun to write. It's good, usable, friendly information put forth in a way that is easy to understand and master. We can put it together for you quickly—and by the time you hold it in your hands, many professional people have given their time and talents to make sure it is the best book it can possibly be. So, huge thank-yous go to Marta Justak, Rebecca Whitney, and Kevin Davenport for their fine-and-fast project management, editorial, and technical editing skills; and thank you to the production staff at Premier for producing such a great-looking book in such a short amount of time. And, finally, thank *you*, our reader, for allowing us to share our work with you.

About the Author

Premier Press author **Katherine Murray** has been using technology to write about technology since the early 1980s. With more than 40 computer books (and a number of parenting books) to her credit, Katherine enjoys working on projects that help readers learn new skills, uncover hidden talents, or develop mastery and efficiency in a chosen area. From books on general computer use to more specialized books on presentation graphics, Internet use, and Web animation, Katherine gets most excited about the programs that help people communicate, through print, sound, electronic, or visual expression—on or off the Web. For the past 15 years, Katherine has owned and operated reVisions Plus, Inc., a writing and publishing services company. Her company recently launched a small press, Homeward Bound Publishing (**http://www.homewardbound-publishing.com**), which published its first book, *A Different Kind of Kid: Connecting with Unconventional Teens,* in January 2002. You can reach Katherine via e-mail at **kmurray@revisionsplus.com** or visit her company on the Web at **www.revisionsplus.com**.

CONTENTS AT A GLANCE

CONTENTS

INTRODUCTION

Hello! And welcome to your fast-track weekend through Windows XP! Windows XP is the newest operating system from Microsoft, now shipping on new computers and sold in stores worldwide. If you're like many of us, you watch the Windows versions come and go, wondering which you need and which you can skip, not quite clear on the benefits of the different versions. Or perhaps you've just purchased a computer and it came with Windows XP, and—guess what? It's time to take the software for a test-drive to see what it can do.

So, whether you picked up this book because you're curious about Windows XP and are thinking about installing it on your own computer, you have upgraded to Windows XP, or you have just gotten a new PC that comes with the system preinstalled, you've come to the right place. In one weekend, you'll learn all the important tasks, tips, and techniques you need to know to get a running start with Windows XP.

What This Book Is About

Unless you've always been a diehard Macintosh fan or you've somehow resisted the flash and sparkle of the Microsoft logo for the past 20 years, you are probably familiar with Microsoft Windows, arguably the most popular graphical operating system in the world. Microsoft Windows—now in its current incarnation, Windows XP—is the friendly face that greets you when you power up your computer in the morning and the last gleam you see when you power down at night. This book helps you learn—at a fast, need-to-know pace—the primary tasks and features you'll enjoy as a Windows XP user.

Windows XP has a number of features that set it apart from other Windows versions, such as Windows Me, Windows 2000, and the old Windows 98 and Windows 95. Easy-to-use multiuser settings, improved media tools (for better sound, video, pictures, and more), and streamlined Internet features make the system easier, faster, and more fun to use than ever. The improved Help system makes getting unstuck an easier experience as well. You'll find out how to make the most of these new capabilities—and learn some extra tips along the way—as you follow along with the sessions in *Learn Windows XP in a Weekend*.

Who Should Read This Book

Learn Windows XP in a Weekend is meant for you if you want to learn what Windows XP can do for you, and if you have a limited amount of free time and the tenacity and focus to tackle the topic all in one weekend. (Or even if you don't—you can put the book down and pick it up *next weekend* and nobody will know.) By the time you work through all the sessions in this book, you'll understand all the basics about Windows XP—from the Internet features to the file organization structure to the setting of personal preferences and the handling of multiple user accounts—all in one weekend. Got the time for some fast-and-friendly exploring? Sure, you do.

What You Need to Begin

You don't need to gather many essentials as you prepare for your weekend with Windows XP. The following items are helpful (but not absolutely necessary if all you want to do for now is read about the software):

- ✿ Your computer, with Windows XP installed
- ✿ A printer connected to your PC to play with printing
- ✿ A modem to get online
- ✿ A 3½-inch disk for backing up files
- ✿ This book as your guide
- ✿ A weekend (or a reasonable facsimile) with plenty of time for learning

Because *Learn Windows XP in a Weekend* highlights all the most important features of Windows XP and provides step-by-step exercises you can follow to explore the various aspects of the program, you'll find techniques that require the use of the printer, fax, modem, and, later, a camera, scanner, microphone, and more. If you don't have one of the items, don't worry about it—just read through the information you need and leave the rest for later. The order in which you work through the book is also, of course, up to you, but the way in which I've arranged the topics is meant to lead you from "most-need-to-know" (like the basics and online techniques) to "maybe-I'll-use-this-sometime." Learning anything is easier if you really want to learn it, so my advice is to start with the things that make your eyes sparkle and then pick up the more mundane topics at a later time.

How This Book Is Organized

Let's take a look at the way this book is organized. The *Learn in a Weekend* series, published by Premier, provides a terrific modular format for learning just about anything. In a specific period of time, you focus on one issue of a program or task and go through exercises and techniques designed to help you integrate what you've read about. *Learn Windows XP in a Weekend* is a perfect fit for this series in that the types of tasks you need to learn are fairly straightforward and easy to master—and they fit nicely into work sessions geared around a specific use of the software. The sessions for *Learn Windows XP in a Weekend* look like this:

Friday Evening: Getting Started with Windows XP jumps right in with both feet by exploring the basics of Windows XP: You begin with a first look at the Windows XP desktop and an exploration of new features in Windows XP. From there, the chapter moves into practical techniques you'll use most often—launching and exiting programs, printing and faxing, adding new hardware and software, and doing a quick virus check. This chapter also includes something very important: knowing how, when, and where to yell "Help!" and discovering what to do if and when your computer locks up.

Saturday Morning: Ready, Set, Online! gets you into the important stuff quickly by giving you a bird's-eye view of the improved Windows XP Internet features and showing you how to get connected using the Internet Connection Wizard. After you're online, you learn about the new and improved Internet Explorer, Outlook Express 6, MSN Explorer (the Microsoft answer to AOL), and Windows Messenger, the addictive little pop-up instant communicator that can keep you in instant touch with family and friends. In this session, you also learn how to add other Internet services to your connection options and find out what it means to connect to other computers in your own house or office. Finally, this chapter wraps up the online discussion by exploring the Web Publishing Wizard, a tool that helps you create and post to the Web pages you create for business or just for fun.

Saturday Afternoon: Handling Files and Folders settles into the less-exciting-but-much-needed discussion of handling files and folders in Windows XP. One of the key features of an operating system is its file management capabilities: How will you store the files you create? Where will you put them? What will you name them? How will you be able to find them later? This session helps you think through the best organization scheme for your computer and plan for room to grow. You also learn what to do with those files—move, copy, delete, and rename them. You learn how to take out the trash ("Honey, would you please get that?") and discover how to compress those huge files so that they take up less space on your hard disk.

Saturday Evening: Now the Fun Part: Media! brings back the excitement with an adventure into media. Want to hear the new Britney Spears release? Oh, okay—how about Wynton Marsalis? You can listen to CD clips, watch movies trailers online, download new songs, capture your own pictures, make your own music, and more using Windows Media Player 8.0. The new Media bar and the streamlined interface of the player make it easier than ever to whistle while you work. Nobody wants to do drudge work on Saturday night—so you can crank up the music while you work through this session!

Sunday Morning: Working with Windows XP Accessories starts your last day with practical matters. Windows XP comes with a full set of system tools that help you keep an eye on your system, return your system back to its original settings (this is good to know in case you *really* mess something up!), clean off your hard disk, remove file fragments, and run diagnostics (to make sure everything is healthy in there). You can also automate certain tasks so that you don't even have to think about it next time—and you learn how to do that in this morning's session.

Sunday Afternoon: Sharing and Personalizing Windows XP wraps up the book with how-tos on setting up your version of Windows for use with multiple users. Tired of fighting with your 15-year-old about logon passwords and favorite files? Setting up a different user account for her will solve the problem. Additionally, you can create your own, personalized workspace (so that you don't have to look at her pictures of Ricky Martin), add your own screensaver, and manage and control passwords.

The book ends with a few helpful resources that provide additional Windows XP helps. **Appendix A: A Windows XP Install-and-Update Guide** explores what *installation* means and shows you how to do it yourself. Even if you purchased your system with Windows XP already installed, knowing how to reinstall or restore the original Windows XP settings is a good safeguard. **Appendix B: Windows XP Troubleshooting Tips** lists some of the most common headaches new users experience with Windows XP and tells you what to do—besides "take two aspirins"—to solve the problem and get back to the task at hand. Finally, the **Glossary** finishes off the book by listing the definitions of what may be new, unfamiliar, or cryptic terms that puzzle you.

Special Features in This Book

You'll find that the format of *Learn Windows XP in a Weekend* helps you move through the work sessions easily—exercises are easy to spot in their numbered lists, and illustrations and captions stand out so that you can grasp what's going on quickly. The book also includes a number of special elements that call attention to extra bits of information as you work through the sessions:

TIP   Tips give you quick-look, shortcut information that help you save time and keystrokes in order to carry out common tasks.

NOTE   Notes provide some extra information that goes along with the topic at hand.

That pretty much spells out what you can expect from your weekend with Windows XP and this book. If you're ready, willing, and eager (okay, just *willing* is enough!), let's get started and *Learn Windows XP in a Weekend.*

Hello! And welcome! It's Friday evening, and you've finished dinner, cleaned up the dinner dishes, and helped the kids with their homework, and now it's your turn to sit down and learn something new. Get yourself a cup of tea and let's start exploring this new operating system you're interested in finding out more about.

What's Windows?

Microsoft Windows is the operating system on your computer—the program that helps the programs you use to write and send e-mail, look at photos, create spreadsheets, and more... to do what they need to do. The operating system works on a number of levels, both running the processes of the hardware and controlling the operations of the application programs. In addition to working with your hardware and software, the operating system works with *you* to help you accomplish the following tasks in your application programs:

- Run your programs
- Add new hardware and software
- Print documents
- Send e-mail and faxes
- Save, rename, delete, and organize files
- Check for viruses
- Listen to music online

The sections that follow tell you a little more about Windows features and how they help you get things done. You also learn specifically about Windows XP and find out how it is different from previous versions of Windows.

A (VERY) LITTLE WINDOWS HISTORY

When Microsoft Windows first appeared on the PC scene, it was a revolutionary—if somewhat clunky—product. Windows was the first program for the IBM PC that enabled PC users to work with the mouse, a now-common pointing device that was previously unavailable to anyone who didn't use a Macintosh computer. Windows also brought PC users the first **graphical interface**, a screen that enabled users to work with programs and folders by simply clicking icons on the screen. Before Windows, PC users (who were working with an operating system called DOS) were forced to type commands to get their computers to do anything.

Windows has gone through a number of incarnations—from the earlier Windows 3.1 (way back in the 1980s) to the Windows 2000 (of you guessed it, year 2000) to the Windows XP of today. Each new version has made the operating system easier to use, faster, and more powerful. Windows XP (the XP stands for experience, by the way) is the culmination of many years of improved technology, increased efficiency, and enhanced reliability. And, just to keep this from sounding like a marketing piece for Microsoft, we can throw in the reality that some versions of Windows have been buggier than others—earlier versions crashed more and had limited functionality; later versions (with the possible exception of Windows Me, which got less-than-sterling reviews) have made significant improvements in speed, security, connectivity, and more.

Take Care of the Basics with Windows General Accessories

So, you probably realize by now that Windows XP is not only the program you work with as you start other programs that help you do stuff—such as Microsoft Word for Windows or e-mailing using Outlook Express—but it's also a collection of utilities that help you take care of all kinds of general computing tasks. Here's a brief overview of some of the true-blue Windows accessories you're likely to use. Note that you learn more about these tools in the sessions that deal specifically with their use:

✿ **Address Book**. Where would we be, in this day and age, without our e-mail address books? These files store the e-mail addresses of everyone we know—work, school, friends, and family (see Figure 1.1). The Windows Address Book goes beyond simple e-mail addresses, however, offering you the ability to store names, addresses, phone contacts, personal information, and more, all in one convenient file (that you need to back up regularly).

Figure 1.1

The Windows Address Book stores your important contact information and makes it available to any Windows program you're using.

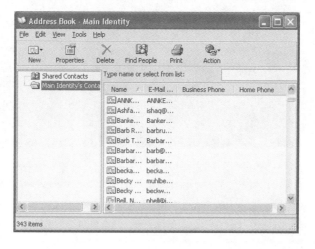

- **Calculator**. The Windows Calculator is a simple, handy tool that enables you to compute things quickly and paste the result in an active document if you choose. No terrific bells and whistles, and you have to dig to find scientific notation—but if what you need is fast figuring, Windows has the tool to help.

- **Notepad**. Windows Notepad is another accessory that has been around since early Windows. It is a simple text editor you can use to compose letters, write macros, create Web pages in HTML, and perform other simple text-editing tasks.

- **Paint**. Windows Paint is the standard graphics utility that enables you to add a little art to your work—whether you want to create a new logo, paint a picture, touch up a photo, or scan something (see Figure 1.2).

Figure 1.2

Windows Paint allows you to create, import, edit, and save graphic files in several popular formats.

NOTE For step-by-step practice on working with favorite Windows accessories—such as Notepad, Paint, and Calculator—see Sunday morning's session, "Mastering the Windows XP Tools and Accessories."

- **Program Compatibility Wizard**. This "troubleshooting" wizard, new in Windows XP, walks you through the process of testing and fixing problems that may occur when you try to use programs that worked fine with previous versions of Windows but are not working well under Windows XP.

- **Synchronize**. When you are working on a network—whether it is a local-area network or a connection via the Internet—you always run the risk of not having the most current version of a file on your computer. If you worked with something at work via a terminal server, for example, do you have the most up-to-date version on your laptop? Synchronize helps you make sure that the files are, well, *synchronized*, so that both versions match, and you don't accidentally turn in an old report.

- **Windows Movie Maker**. This fun utility, first introduced in Windows Me, enables you to literally make digital movies on your PC. If you've got the digital camcorder (or if you download clips from the Web), you can become a movie maker. See Saturday evening's session, "Now the Fun Part: Media!" for details.

- **Windows Explorer**. Windows Explorer is the tried-and-true file management system that has been around since the early days of Windows 95. Now in its most attractive and functional state, Windows Explorer uses a tree structure to display the folders and files on your hard disk (see Figure 1.3). To get comfortable working with Windows Explorer, see Saturday afternoon's session, "Handling Files and Folders."

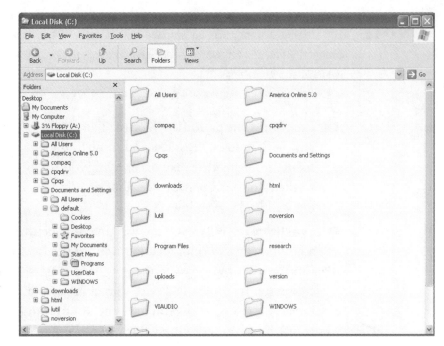

Figure 1.3

Windows Explorer
is the tool you use
to manage folders
and files.

Communicate Easily with Connectivity Tools

Connection is everything these days. Windows XP includes the tools you
need to connect with people and information in just about every possible
electronic way:

NEW IN ▶
WINDOWS XP

- ⚙ You can use Internet Explorer to browse the Web, shop, make travel plans, research, play games, chat, and more.

- ⚙ You use Outlook Express 6 to send and receive e-mail, read and post newsgroup messages, and track your Windows Messenger contacts.

- ⚙ You use Windows Messenger to trade instant messages with friends and coworkers in your contact list.

- ⚙ You can use Microsoft NetMeeting to hold a virtual meeting in cyberspace.

- ⚙ You can use Phone Dialer to make voice-to-voice and video phone calls.

NOTE

NEW IN ▶ WINDOWS XP

The connection tools also give you wizards galore—a number of wizards help you take care of all kinds of configurations. The New Connection Wizard (which replaces the Internet Connection Wizard from previous versions of Windows) helps you set up a new Internet connection; other wizards enable you to establish home or remote network settings. You can also take advantage of Microsoft NetMeeting, a program that enables you to meet with others online in a virtual meeting room, to share thoughts, review documents, view video, or even draw on a virtual whiteboard together.

NOTE

Definition: A **wizard** is an automated feature that walks you through a specific process by asking you a series of questions. You answer the question (usually by clicking an option) and click Next to move to the next step in the wizard. Windows XP uses wizards to help you set up many different elements—including Internet connections, automated tasks, home networks, and more.

HyperTerminal, which now seems like an old-fashioned connectivity tool, is a utility you can use to connect directly to other computers, bulletin board services, and more. HyperTerminal is a text-only transmission, however, so if you want the flash and fancy of the Web, Internet Explorer is your tool of choice.

Additionally, Phone Dialer lets you set up and make voice-to-voice phone calls, video calls, and even conference video calls using your computer. You can also receive calls, whether or not you have a videocamera, as long as Phone Dialer is active.

NOTE

For more about getting online with Windows XP, see Saturday morning's session, "Ready, Set, Online!"

WINDOWS FOR EVERYONE—OVERCOMING ACCESSIBILITY ISSUES

A program used as widely as Microsoft Windows needs to make it a priority to reach all kinds of users in all kinds of life situations—and not everyone can sit at a computer for hours on end, typing and clicking to their heart's content. Some people have limited vision; others have mobility challenges. Windows XP includes a number of accessibility tools that help users of all kinds to work successfully with the program:

- The Accessibility Wizard walks you through setting up Windows XP to fit your needs. The wizard offers a number of selections based on sight, hearing, and mobility needs.

- Magnifier enables you to magnify the screen display in a window above the primary screen area. You can set the level of magnification up to nine times the current display, and you can also control whether the display follows the cursor, the keyboard focus, or text-editing operations.

- The Narrator program reads aloud menu commands, announces events on-screen, helps you position the pointer, and knows what options are available. The program is installed with only one voice—Microsoft Sam—but you can use Windows XP voice-recognition features to add your own, if you prefer.

- The On-Screen Keyboard feature displays a small keyboard that enables mobility-restricted users to use a joystick or other pointing device to type on-screen.

- Utility Manager gives you an easy way to manage all the different accessibility devices easily without activating and exiting each one separately.

For more about special Windows considerations and setting up your workspace to fit your needs and style, see Sunday afternoon's session, "Personalizing and Sharing Windows XP."

Turn Up the Volume with Windows Sound Accessories

One big spotlight of Windows XP shines on the media enhancements that enable you to—among other things—download and play (and burn) your favorite CD selections; watch real-time video clips (from CNN— my favorite!); capture, print, and send digital images; and listen to Web radio while you work. Some tools that assist you in those fun activities are these:

- **Sound Recorder.** This simple little utility enables you to record your own voice, sounds, special effects, and more. If you have a microphone attached to your computer, you can simply fire up Sound Recorder and make your own noise.

- **Volume Control.** The Volume Control setting gives you both a master volume control, which controls the volume of sound for all applications, and individual controls for specific uses.

- **Windows Media Player.** Windows Media Player, new in Windows XP, is actually a big addition, or perhaps *improvement* is a better word, over the media offerings of previous Windows versions. The player combines the functionality of the CD Player with a hip design (for which you can choose your own skins) that offers continual live music, a media guide, a Web radio tuner, media library, and more (see Figure 1.4).

NOTE All about media is the focus of Saturday night's session, "Now the Fun Part: Media!"

Figure 1.4

The new Windows Media Player blows the old one away with a complete redesign and vastly enhanced features.

Find Out about Your Computer Using the System Tools

The last stop we make on this feature tour is one of those ho-hum topics that everyone needs sooner or later: the care of your computer. How do you know what's stored where? How can you change the way your screen looks, the way your mouse works, the way your program starts? What should you try if your programs start crashing and your files get lost? Knowing how to use the system tools gives you a heads-up on the tools you'll need one day in the not-too-far distant future:

🖸 The My Computer icon, on your desktop, opens a window that enables you to work with folders and files and get system information about your computer.

🖸 Control Panel enables you to add and remove hardware and software as well as set up things like screen colors, mouse-click speed, passwords, and more.

✪ Clipboard Viewer enables you to see what you've copied to the Windows Clipboard (which can be up to 24 different items, depending on the size of the clips).

✪ Disk Cleanup runs a utility that cleans up files you no longer need that are taking up space on your hard drive.

✪ Disk Defragmenter is a utility that consolidates files that have—because of additions and deletions over time—become scattered around various locations on your hard drive.

✪ The Files and Settings Transfer Wizard launches a wizard that helps you move files and settings from your old computer to your new one. For best results, you should have a connection between the two computers (either via a computer-to-computer connection or over a network) before running the wizard. This program updates files for Internet Explorer and Outlook Express as well as other commonly used program settings.

✪ Scheduled Tasks enables you to schedule routine maintenance tasks—such as synchronizing your Palm address book; backing up weekly data; running Disk Cleanup; or even checking for e-mail with an online service.

✪ System Information displays information you need to know about your specific computer system. Windows XP tells you about the hardware, software, Internet settings, and application settings you have selected.

✪ System Restore is a feature that was introduced in Windows Me and improved in Windows XP, enabling you to reset your system settings to their factory-original settings.

Seen so many features that they're making your head spin? Don't worry—you'll have a closer look at many of these different tools by the end of this weekend. Before we start exploring the Windows workspace, let's take a couple of minutes and find out what Windows XP is particularly adept at doing.

What's New in Windows XP?

Microsoft Windows XP is the newest version of Windows and, true to form, introduces both behind-the-scenes improvements and enhancements you can see on your desktop and experience in performance. For example, among other things, Windows XP is:

⚙ **Safer than ever.** It ensures your privacy whether you are shopping online or chatting with friends.

⚙ **More reliable.** It includes crash-recovery features and improved help.

⚙ **More flexible.** Now you can capture, publish, and e-mail digital photos and video clips online.

⚙ **More personal.** You can set up multiple accounts, giving each person her own desktop look and feel.

HOME OR PROFESSIONAL? WINDOWS XP VERSIONS

As you may be aware, Windows XP has two versions: a Home Edition and a Professional Edition. If you have purchased a computer for your home and you're sitting at your kitchen table (or computer desk now) reading this book, chances are that you have Windows XP Home Edition. (If you want to be sure, you can find the name of the edition you're using just beneath the title of the Help and Support Center window. To display it, click the Start button and choose Help and Support Center from the Start menu—or simply press F1 when you're not in a specific program.)

Windows XP Professional Edition is used, as you might expect, in businesses. This version of XP includes all the items you find in the Home Edition and adds extra security measures as well as some business features from Windows versions 98 and 2000. For more information on what Windows XP Professional Edition has to offer, you can check out the Microsoft Web site at **http://www.microsoft.com**.

The sections that follow describe some of the features—new and improved—you find in Windows XP.

New Workspace

If you've worked with Windows before, notice that the new display is a kinder, gentler interface. The menus are brighter and more rounded; the icons are easier to see and read; and the menu selections on the Start menu are organized so that you can quickly find the application, task, or Help item you need (see Figure 1.5).

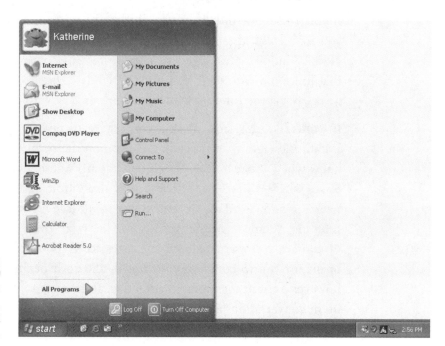

Figure 1.5

The menu system has a new, friendlier look and feel.

If this is your first experience with Windows, you should find the program fairly simple to figure out and use. The desktop is designed to function in a way similar to a real-world desktop on which you place folders to store documents, photos, and other items related to specific projects or applications. The point of power—the Start button—is in the lower-left corner of the desktop; that's where you start working with all the programs and tools in Windows XP.

NOTE For a tour of the Windows XP desktop, see the section "A Look Around," later in this session.

The New Web Messenger

If you're the type of person who likes to be up-to-date and in the know, you may enjoy the instant-messaging feature available in Windows XP. Now, Windows Messenger—a pop-up instant communication channel that links you with your best online friends—enables you to send quick messages via the Internet while you work or play with other applications.

It works like this: You create a contact list of people you want to trade instant messages with. They include you on their contact list so that they know when you're online. When you log on, Windows Messenger checks to see whether any of your contacts is also online and displays the Messenger window so that you can see the result (see Figure 1.6). If someone is online, Windows Messenger lets you know, and you can click the name of contact you want to send messages to. A pop-up message window opens for you to compose your note—and so it begins. Be forewarned, however: Instant messaging is addictive, and you can find yourself caught up in conversations about the latest fashions on the E channel instead of focusing on tasks at hand.

NOTE For more about setting up and using Windows Messenger, see Saturday morning's session, "Ready, Set, Online!"

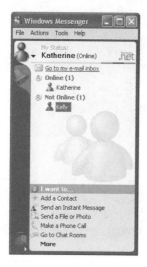

Figure 1.6

Windows Messenger is fast, friendly—and addictive.

The Digital Image

Are you into digital photography? Most people today—if they haven't already purchased a digital camera or at least borrowed one from a friend or from work—are interested in the instant-and-good photos to be captured by even a simple $200 digital camera. The digital image—whether it is captured in an electronic file by a scanner, video camcorder, or digital camera—gives you something your ordinary 35mm camera cannot: graphic images you can use on your Web pages, place in your documents, and send via e-mail. Taking our own photos—and sending them around the world—has never been easier. And Windows XP capitalizes on both this opportunity and the increasing interest of computer users everywhere.

As the costs of digital video equipment drops, users are looking for new ways to capture, organize, and work with digital images. Windows XP takes a big step in this direction by making it easier than ever to find, store, and work with digital images. Windows Messenger, the online insta-chat feature you learned about in the preceding section, includes an option strictly for sending digital photos. And the new Windows Picture and Fax Viewer enables you to easily display and page through photo after photo (see Figure 1.7).

Figure 1.7

The Windows Picture and Fax Viewer makes it easy to look at your favorite things.

NOTE The Saturday evening session—"Now the Fun Part: Media!"—explores the exciting possibilities of working with sound, video, photos, and more.

Help Improvements

Everybody needs a little help now and then. Windows has always had a pretty good Help system, but it is strengthened even more in Windows XP. The new Help and Support Center gives you a number of different ways to find the help you need. Here are a few:

○ Pressing F1 when you are working with Windows XP displays the Help and Support Center, and you can choose your task from there.

○ You can use the Remote Assistance feature to ask a friend for help if that friend is also online while you're working. Your friend can view your screen and even use his mouse and keyboard to help you solve whatever problem you're having. This feature is similar to the Windows Messenger feature and opens up an instant chat channel.

The only drawback is that your friend also must be running Windows XP.

○ You can read one of the many task-specific articles stored in the Windows XP Help system.

○ You can access a newsgroup specifically created for Windows XP users or search the Web to find the answer you need.

If you are working with a Windows XP utility, such as Paint, when you press F1, Windows assesses what you're working with and displays the Help window for that utility.

For more information about working with the Windows XP Help system, see the section "Getting Help," later in this session.

Setting Up Multiple Users

Gone are the days when only Mom or Dad used the family computer. Now, your 14-year-old daughter stands behind you while you check e-mail, impatiently tapping her foot and wanting to get online and meet her friend to play Scrabble. Your 8-year-old bugs you about checking out Cartoon Network's latest games, and your 17-year-old wants to research muscle cars. How can you solve this traffic jam of users without buying each person her own PC?

Windows XP makes it possible—and easy—to set up multiple user accounts on one system. Now you can set up a user account for each person who will be using the computer—for kids or adults (or even talented pets). You can serve as the system administrator, the Keeper of the Password Control, and the general overall boss of the PC. But each person can save his own favorites (important for lots of Web enthusiasts), screen savers, desktop themes, Windows Messenger contacts, and more.

NOTE Sunday afternoon's session, "Personalizing and Sharing Windows XP," is the time we talk about setting up and working with multiple user accounts.

Personalizing Your Workspace

We all want things the way we want them. I like the curtains open; you may like them closed. She wants a picture of your grandkitty on the desktop; you like that picture you took on vacation last summer (see Figure 1.8). Wouldn't it be nice to have a program that lets each of us have our "druthers"? Windows XP has come a bit closer to doing that—at least in the PC realm—by enabling different users to personalize their own workspaces. With Windows XP, you can have both the kitty *and* the giraffe.

Figure 1.8

You can put your own pictures on the Windows desktop.

What kind of things can you change? Just about everything involved with the look and feel of Windows XP:

- The appearance of the desktop itself
- The way your icons look
- The colors used for backgrounds, text, icons, menus, and more
- The fonts used for menus, file names, and window titles

You can change other functional items, too, such as the responsiveness of the keyboard, the action time of the mouse or touchpad, the display resolution of the monitor, whether you can use voice-activated commands and handwriting recognition, and so on. We have lots to talk about when it comes to personalizing Windows XP. That's also covered in Sunday afternoon's session.

Basic Navigating 101

Knowing how to find your way around Windows XP—which mouse button to click, which key to press, which menu to select—is a pretty simple matter after you get going. The procedures for working with your mouse or other pointing device (you may have a trackball or touchpad instead of a mouse) and the techniques for keyboard shortcuts are the focus of this section. You wind up with a quick lesson in Windows basics and then get busy exploring Windows XP on your own.

Mouse Basics

A mouse is what's called a *pointing device*, a little tool about the size of your hand (or smaller, if you have a laptop mouse) that you push around on the desktop in order to move the little arrow on the screen (called, surprisingly enough, the *pointer*). The purpose of a mouse is to give you a way to point to things on the screen and select them. Chances are that you're already familiar with the mouse and know how the thing works and what to do with the buttons. But just in case you're new to the pointing-device idea, Table 1.1 lists the basic mouse operations you use as you work with programs, files, and folders in Windows XP.

TIP

Some people fuss over the responsiveness of their mouse—that is, the amount of time the computer takes to respond to the mouse movement on-screen, the way the buttons are configured (you can switch the function of the mouse buttons, if you like), the shape of the pointer, and so on. If you want to change some things about the way your mouse operates, learn how to change them in "Personalizing and Sharing Windows XP," in the Sunday afternoon session, "Personalizing and Sharing Windows XP."

TABLE 1.1 THE MOST IMPORTANT THINGS YOU DO WITH A MOUSE

Action Name	What It Means	Why You Do It
Click	Press and release the left mouse button once.	To open a menu, select a folder, choose a command, select an option
Double-click	Press and release the left mouse button twice, quickly.	To launch a program, open a folder
Drag and drop	Press and hold the left mouse button down; then drag the item to the new location.	To move an object (such as a folder, file, or program icon) to a new location
Right-click	Position the pointer on the item you want; then click the right mouse button. A submenu appears.	To work with the object in some way—to print, edit, open, or check properties, for example; to open a context menu, which is a menu that varies its content based on the task at hand

Note that different systems have different kinds of pointing devices these days. The basic operations—clicking, double-clicking, dragging, and right-clicking—hold true whether you're using a trackball, touchpad, or stylus. If you're unsure how the actions of the mouse translate to, say, your touchpad, review your system documentation for specific instructions.

Keyboard Basics

The keyboard is pretty passé when it comes to commands and menu selections. Sure, we've got to type with it, but why even use it when you need to open menus, choose commands, selection options, and the like?

Many computer users prefer working with the keyboard only to switching back and forth between mouse and keyboard. If they know a quick key (also called a *keyboard shortcut*) that enables them to display a menu and choose a command, they use that procedure rather than taking their hands off the keyboard and reaching for the mouse so that they can point and click.

Luckily, Windows tries to accommodate all kinds of people and all kinds of preferences, and you can use a number of keyboard shortcuts to perform tasks quickly, if you choose. A quick note first: Keyboard shortcuts are two or more keys pressed in combination—that is, you press and hold one key while pressing another. For example, to use the Alt+F4 shortcut key combination to close an open window, you press and hold the Alt key and then press F4. Then release both keys, and the open window closes. Table 1.2 lists some of the more common shortcuts that apply to most Windows programs.

The various programs you use as you work with Windows have their own shortcut keys that apply to the features in the individual program. Check your program documentation or online Help system to find out about the shortcut keys unique to individual programs.

TABLE 1.2 KEYBOARD SHORTCUTS

Pressing This	Does This
Alt+F4	Closes the selected window
Alt+F	Selects the File menu
Alt+E	Selects the Edit menu
Alt+V	Selects the View menu
Alt+A	Selects the Favorites menu
Alt+T	Selects the Tools menu
Alt+H	Selects the Help menu
Alt+D	Selects the Address line entry
Alt+Shift+Tab	Cycles through all open windows, one at a time
Alt+Tab	Toggles the display between two open windows
Ctrl+A	Selects all objects in the current window
Ctrl+C	Copies selected object to Clipboard
Ctrl+V	Pastes selected object
Ctrl+X	Cuts selected object
Ctrl+Z	Undoes last operation
Delete	Deletes selected object
Enter	Selects an object or finalizes an operation
Esc	Cancels an operation or closes a dialog box

TABLE 1.2 CONTINUED	
Pressing This	**Does This**
F1	Displays the Help and Support Center
F2	Renames selected object
F3	Searches for a folder or file
F4	Displays the Address bar
F5	Refreshes the selected window
F6	Cycles through open windows
F10	Activates the menu bar
PrtSc	Copies the image of the screen to the Clipboard
Tab	Moves the highlight through selections in a window

TIP Mouse preferences aren't the only concerns that get voiced when you ask a new computer user what she thinks of her system: She may tell you about the keyboard, too—things like how slow the letters seem to appear on the screen or how lightning-fast the cursor blinks. You can change these settings, too, to make the keyboard work at the same speed you do. The steps for making changes are given in Sunday afternoon's session, "Personalizing and Sharing Windows XP."

Take a Break

How are you doing? The ideas and techniques presented thus far in this session are pretty basic—nothing too straining on the brain. But knowing what Windows XP is capable of, having an idea about the types of features you want to try first, and understanding the simple techniques for finding your way around provide an important foundation for the rest of our whirlwind weekend together. So go ahead and take a 15-minute break, grab a cup of coffee (or herbal decaffeinated tea, if it's getting late), check on the kids, and come back for the rest of this evening's session. You'll try your hand at navigating Windows XP on your own and learn about launching programs and yelling for help.

A Look Around

Now that you've been through a little Windows XP theory, you're probably ready to begin exploring for yourself. In this section, you take a look around the Windows XP desktop and learn some basic navigation techniques that apply to everything you do in Windows.

 NOTE If you planning on upgrading your computer from Windows Me to Windows XP and you haven't yet done it, you may want to take a few moments and follow the instructions in Appendix A, "Installing, Upgrading, and Restoring Windows XP," so that you can follow along with the steps in this session. Go ahead—we'll wait.

One other point—if this is the first time you've fired up your computer, you are most likely taken through an automated process that welcomes you to your PC, walks you through setting up certain components, and invites you to register online. The process is different from computer to computer. After you finish the start-up phase, you are deposited at the relatively bare Windows desktop. You see a few icons and perhaps the Taskbar, stretched across the bottom of the screen. That's where we want to begin.

Know Your Screen Elements

The Windows desktop is designed to be simple and uncluttered. You are supposed to feel that you are the master of your fate, the captain of your ship, as you survey the information and icons you place on your desktop.

With that said, however, when you first launch Windows XP, you may find already on the desktop lots of icons that are links to more information about products you haven't bought—such as an "AOL Free Trial! Icon" or a "Try McAfee Now!" icon. These items, whether you choose later to use them or not, are part of the screen landscape we need to explore.

Figure 1.9 shows you the lay of the land.

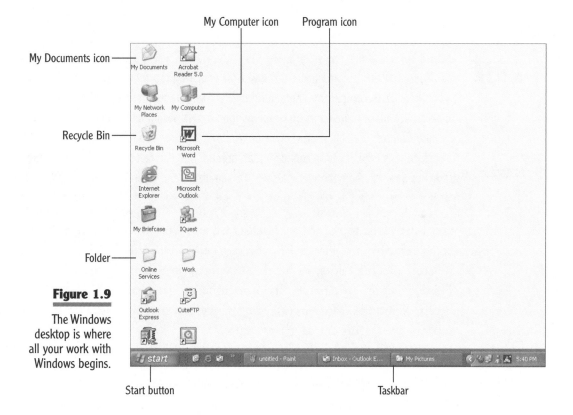

Figure 1.9

The Windows desktop is where all your work with Windows begins.

The first items you see on your Windows XP desktop, and the ones we talk about first, are these:

✪ My Documents folder

✪ My Computer icon

- My Network Places icon
- Recycle Bin
- My Briefcase
- Program icons
- Folders
- Taskbar
- Start button
- System tray

NOTE The icons that are automatically displayed on your desktop may differ from the ones shown here. Each computer manufacturer has its own arrangement with Microsoft—and some groups place more icons on desktops than others. Additionally, some manufacturers, like Compaq, set up your version of Windows to have a background showing the manufacturer's logo. If you're cool with that, great. If not, you can find out how to change it in your Sunday afternoon worksession, "Personalizing and Sharing Windows XP."

Let's start at the top of this sample screen and work our way down. In the upper-left corner of Figure 1.9, you see the My Documents icon. It shows a picture of a file folder, with a document supposedly being placed inside. This icon stores, by default, all the documents you create in programs you run in Windows XP—unless you change the default folder or choose another one during the save procedure.

NOTE **Definition:** The **default folder** is the folder a program stores files in—unless you specify otherwise.

The next group of icons includes My Computer, My Network Places, and My Briefcase. Each of these helps you organize your system, set up and maintain your network, and move files successfully from place to place. The Recycle Bin is where your files go after you press Delete to delete them; they aren't actually wiped away completely until you choose Empty the Recycle Bin to do the trick. (For specifics on deleting files, see Saturday morning's session, "Handling Files and Folders.")

Checking Out the Taskbar

The Taskbar, at the bottom of the window, is worth a closer look. This small, unassuming area of the Windows workspace provides you with lots of information and the means to switch among programs, start other applications, launch utilities, check the time, control the volume of the CD you're playing, and more. Consider the various parts of the Taskbar, as identified in Figure 1.10.

Figure 1.10

You use the Taskbar to switch among programs, start utilities, and more.

Quick Launch area   Open programs   Notification area

In the next section, you learn how to launch programs using the Start menu, so we will save that discussion for another moment or two. To the right of the Start button, you see three small icons in the *Quick Launch* area. These icons—which show the active desktop, launch Internet Explorer, and launch Outlook Express when you click them—are installed automatically and placed in the Taskbar for you.

TIP

You can add your own favorite programs to the Quick Launch bar. To add a program, simply begin in the My Computer window or Windows Explorer and drag the program icon to the Quick Launch area. The icon appears in miniature in the Quick Launch bar, and you can start the program with a single click.

Moving toward the center of the Taskbar, you find blocks that represent any open programs you've got running. In this example, Windows Paint and Windows Messenger are both being used. To switch to a program, you simply click its block in the Taskbar. That program then becomes active. When you want to switch to the other program, simply click it.

On the far right side of the Taskbar is the notification area. In this area, you see different icons that notify you of happenings with your computer. In the example shown in the figure, the small icon showing two computer monitors means that the computer is online. The little human shape to the right of the connection icon is the icon letting you know that Windows Messenger is loaded. Additional images in the notification area include an America Online Free Trial button (how did *that* get there?) and the system clock.

TIP The small round < button to the left of the system tray enables you to display icons that are hidden. To see additional icons, such as Volume and Automatic Updates, click the button once. To hide the icons later, click the button a second time.

Taskbar Exercises

Ready to exercise your knowledge a little? Let's work a bit with the Taskbar. You can do a number of things to tailor the Taskbar to suit your needs. You can change the display of applications, make the Taskbar larger, and change where the Taskbar appears on the screen.

Stretch the Quick Launch Area

You can try a few simple techniques to discover some of the ways you can change the Taskbar. For example, to make more room in the Quick Launch area, follow these steps:

1. Find the divider between the Quick Launch area and any open programs showing in the Taskbar. The divider looks like two vertical dotted lines.

2. Position the mouse pointer over the divider. The pointer changes to a double-headed arrow, indicating that you can drag the divider left or right.

3. Drag the divider to the right, making more room for Quick Launch icons. If you have additional icons that weren't being displayed, they now appear in the Taskbar.

NOTE If you can't seem to do anything with the Quick Launch area of the Taskbar, the area could be locked on your machine. To solve the problem, right-click on the Taskbar to display the context menu and click the Lock the Taskbar option to deselect it.

Enlarge the Taskbar

Next, make the Taskbar larger (giving you more room to display Quick Launch icons, open program blocks, and system tray icons), by following these steps:

1. Position the mouse pointer on the top edge of the Taskbar. Again, the pointer changes to a double-headed arrow, this time pointing vertically.

2. Drag the pointer upward toward the Windows desktop area and release the mouse button. The Taskbar is made larger, and additional information is displayed in the notification area (see Figure 1.11). If you want to return the Taskbar to its earlier size, simply drag the top edge back down to its former height.

Figure 1.11

You can enlarge the Taskbar area to display more programs and icons, if you don't mind giving up the real estate on-screen.

Move the Taskbar

Finally, try moving the Taskbar to a new position on-screen by following these steps:

1. Position the mouse pointer in a blank area of the Taskbar.

2. Press and hold the mouse button and drag the Taskbar to the right side of the Windows desktop.

3. Release the mouse button. The Taskbar moves to the side of the interface, positioning the Start button at the top, the Quick Launch icons next, the open programs following that, and the system tray icons at the bottom of the bar (see Figure 1.12). If you want to return the Taskbar to its bottom-edge location, simply drag it back down to where it was.

Figure 1.12

You can move the Taskbar to other locations on the screen—to the side, to the top, to the other side of the window.

Change Taskbar Preferences

When you first install Windows XP, the Taskbar is always visible so that you can get to it easily. As your experience with Windows grows, you may want to hide the Taskbar when you're not using it. You also might want to lock the Taskbar the way you set it up so that other members of your family or work team don't feel compelled to change it. Follow these steps to review and maybe change your Taskbar settings:

1. Right-click in an open area of the Taskbar. A small pop-up menu appears.

2. Click Properties. The Taskbar and Start Menu Properties dialog box opens (see Figure 1.13).

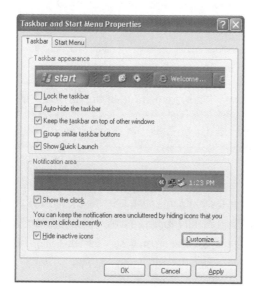

Figure 1.13

You can control how the Taskbar is changed and when it appears and disappears by setting the Taskbar Properties.

3. Click the item you want; a check mark appears in the box preceding the choice to show you that it's now selected. Table 1.3 gives you a quick overview of the function of the Taskbar settings.

TABLE 1.3 CHOOSING TASKBAR PREFERENCES

Option	Description
Lock the taskbar	Keeps you or others from making additional changes to the Taskbar
Auto-hide the taskbar	Hides the Taskbar whenever the mouse pointer is moved off the Taskbar area
Keep the taskbar on top of other windows	Displays the Taskbar whenever multiple windows are open on the screen
Group similar taskbar buttons	Puts buttons together if they are related to the same program (for example, if you have three e-mail messages open, groups them together in a list that pops up when you point to one of the items)
Show Quick Launch	Displays the Quick Launch area
Show the clock	Displays the system clock on the far right side of the Taskbar
Hide inactive icons	Hides icons you have not recently used

TIP You can customize the Taskbar notification icons by clicking the Customize button in the Taskbar and in the Start Menu Properties dialog box. For more information about customizing the icons in the notification area, see "Personalizing and Sharing Windows," in the Sunday afternoon session, "Personalizing and Sharing Windows XP."

Windows Basics

When you first double-click a folder icon or launch a program, the folder or program is displayed in a window. Every window has something in common with all the others—many things, in fact. Windows all share a similar frame, similar menus, and similar control buttons. Most windows you work with—with the exception of some application program windows—have all the basic elements you see in Figure 1.14.

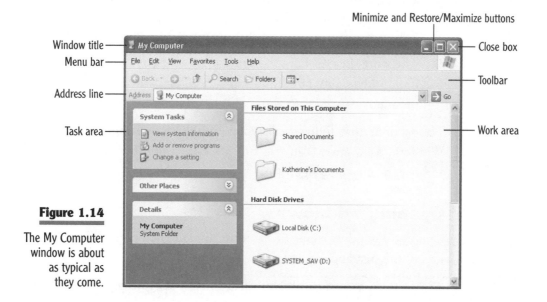

Window title

Menu bar

Address line

Task area

Minimize and Restore/Maximize buttons

Close box

Toolbar

Work area

Figure 1.14

The My Computer window is about as typical as they come.

The window elements you find yourself working with over and over again are these:

- ○ The title of the window is displayed in the upper-left edge of the window.

- ○ The Minimize and Restore/Maximize buttons appear in the far right edge of the window title bar.

- ○ The Close box, also in the upper-right corner of the window, enables you to close the window with the click of a button.

- ○ The menu bar houses six different menus, each with options related to the specific menu topic. For example, the File menu contains commands you use to open, save, rename, and delete files.

- ○ The toolbar provides you with navigational and search tools (in traditional Windows windows, anyway—application programs offer their own tools) so that you can find what you need.

- The Address line enables you to enter a URL or a folder or drive destination to move to.

- The task area offers possible actions and resources geared around what you're trying to do. In the My Computer window, one set of tasks appears; in the Control Panel window, a different set appears.

- The work area displays files (or components, as shown in the figure), folders, programs, and more. You select the files, folders, or programs you want to work with by clicking them.

The sections that follow walk you through some simple but necessary Windows techniques. You will find yourself using these procedures over and over again, so let's go through them quickly.

Opening Windows

Opening a window is one of the most fundamental of all Windows techniques. It's just about as easy as it gets:

- To open a window, double-click the folder or program icon on the desktop.

  or

- Right-click the icon on the desktop and, when the pop-up menu appears, choose Open.

The window opens on top of the Windows desktop. You can reposition the window as needed by simply clicking in the title bar and dragging it. If the window appears full size, you may want to reduce its size by clicking the Restore/Maximize button to create more room to work on-screen.

Minimizing Windows

Minimizing a window is the task of reducing a window to the Taskbar. The program is still running; however, the window is hidden and only the program block appears on the Taskbar. To minimize a window, click the Minimize button (the first button on the left in the upper-right corner of the window). The program window closes and appears to "shrink" down to the Taskbar.

Maximizing Windows

Maximizing a window means giving it the largest possible amount of screen real estate it can possibly have. This process enlarges the window to fill the entire Windows work area. When would you want to maximize a window? Here are a few possibilities:

○ When you are working on a document and don't want to have to scroll to see all the text

○ When you are looking for a file in a window and want to have as many file icons on-screen at one time as you can

○ When you simply want to have the largest workspace possible and don't need to have any other windows displayed in the work area

To maximize a window, you simply click the Maximize button, just to the left of the Close box in the upper-right corner of the window. The window enlarges to completely fill the screen.

Restoring Windows

When you want to take the window out of hiding, simply locate it on the Taskbar and click the program block. The window opens to its former size.

Restoring windows can also take on another meaning, after you have maximized it. After you have maximized a window, the Maximize button changes to the Restore button. This button image shows two screens, a larger one in the background and a smaller one in the foreground, indicating that clicking it reduces the maximized size of the screen to a smaller window. This is, in fact, what Restore does. When you click the Restore button, the maximized screen is dropped down to the size it was before it was maximized. Now you can work with other open windows on the screen at one time.

Closing Windows

The final common windows procedure we cover here is the simple task of closing a window. The big X in the red box in the upper-right corner of the window is the Close box. You can't miss it. Click it once to close the window, and you're done.

Getting Help

Earlier in this session, you had a small glimpse of help in the form of the Help and Support Center, a major overhaul of the Help system in Windows XP. That is a good thing. Previous versions of Windows had adequate help—you could find it by entering a specific word you were wondering about, searching for a task, and so on. But the new look and feel to the Help system in Windows XP is worlds better than the system offered before. Now you have multiple avenues of help, all on one screen (see Figure 1.15).

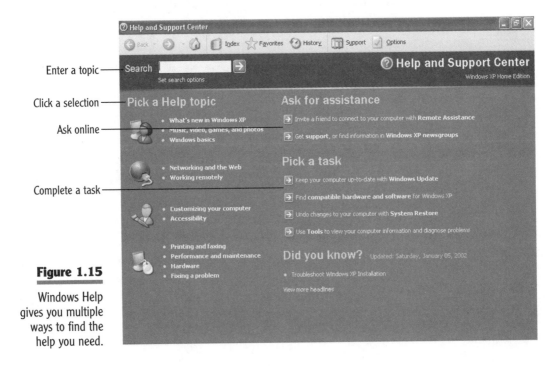

Figure 1.15

Windows Help gives you multiple ways to find the help you need.

An Overview of Help Offerings

Searching for help is a subjective thing—some people like to type a word or phrase, others like to read through a list of topics, and still others just want someone (anyone!) to tell them what to do so that they can get back to work. The Windows XP Help system offers help in several different ways so that you can find the help you need in the way you're most likely to receive it:

✪ Search enables you to type a word or phrase and pull up all sorts of help information related to the information you entered.

✪ Pick a help topic lists Windows features by category (such as what's new, music, games, networking, and printing) so that you can go right to the area that's causing you trouble.

✪ Ask for assistance enables you to go online to either use Remote Assistance (a cool feature covered in the sidebar later in this section) or take your chances with Windows XP newsgroups to see what the experts have to say about your issues.

✪ The Pick a Task area is a task-oriented approach, helping you identify the procedures you need in order to get unstuck.

✪ Finally, the Did you know? section provides the topics of the most recently displayed help topics in Windows XP.

Searching for Help

One of the easiest ways to get help in Windows XP is to simply type a search word or phrase in the Search box in the upper-left corner of the window. Let's try it out:

1. Click in the Search box.

2. Type **digital camera**.

3. Click the Go arrow or press Enter. Windows XP starts searching—you might need to wait five seconds or so—and then the Search Results window appears.

4. The task area on the left gives you a number of choices to narrow your search. The list of tasks in the Pick a Task list lets you choose what you're trying to accomplish, and Windows walks you through the process. Or, if you don't see what you want there, scroll down by dragging the scroll bar on the right side of the task area and read through the Overviews, Articles and Tutorials section.

5. Click an item you want to see, and the work area displays the specific information related to the selected help item, as Figure 1.16 shows.

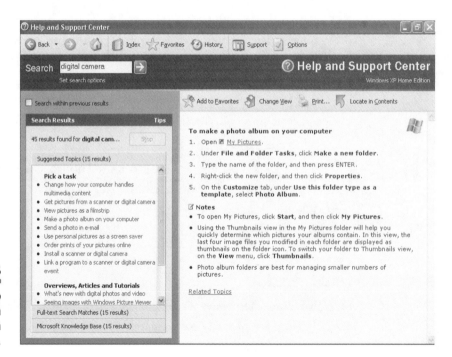

Figure 1.16

Searching for help gives you a wealth of information in different forms.

TIP After you find the help you want, you can print it quickly by clicking Print in the work area just above the Help information. That action displays the Print dialog box, and you can choose your specs (how many copies or to which printer, for example) and click Print to get your hard copy of the Help info.

If you decide that you really prefer the old Windows-style Index, with its keyword entries and odd phrasing, don't despair: Index is available in the Windows XP Help system, too. Now it's tucked away in the toolbar at the top of the Help and Support Center window. To display the Index, click the Index button. In the task area, the Index appears, complete with the keyword-entry box and the long, long list of who-da-thought-of-that? keywords.

USING REMOTE ASSISTANCE

Have you ever heard of **shadowing**? It's a phrase used to describe the process of one person watching while another person works—whether that's job shadowing or computer shadowing. If you are having trouble with your system—perhaps your computer keeps crashing or a certain application is giving you fits—you have the option of asking someone to look over your shoulder and tell you what's going wrong. The wild thing is that the person doesn't even have to be in the same state to look over your shoulder and help with your computer.

The Remote Assistance shadowing utility is somewhat similar to the Windows Messenger instant communication feature. Using Remote Assistance in the Help and Support Center, you can invite someone to come help you. If that person is using the same operating system and happens to be online at the moment, she can trade instant messages with you, find out what's going wrong, and even watch you work on your screen and take over control of your computer (with your permission, of course).

Remote Assistance walks you through the process of inviting your knight in shining armor to come help. It also keeps track of the invitations you've made and records their status so that you know when it's time to delete those no-shows.

Launching Programs

The final task—and it's a big one—that we tackle in this first session is launching an application program, the type of program you use to actually do things with Windows XP. An example of an application program might be Microsoft Word, or even Paint, or Calculator, or something else as simple. Whether it's a big, involved $700 program or a little shareware game, the process of launching is built on the standard action: Point and click.

Actually, the way in which you launch a program depends where in Windows you're working. For example, consider these ways of launching a program:

✿ If the icon of the program you want to launch appears on the desktop, you can launch the program by double-clicking it.

✿ If you don't see the icon of the program you want to launch, you need to select it by using the Start menu.

✿ If you are working in Windows Explorer, the file management tool included with Windows XP, you can launch the program file from there.

Starting from the Start Menu

As you've worked your way around the Windows desktop—from the folder icons to My Computer to the Taskbar—you've gotten closer and closer to the Start button. Now it's time to click it and see what it's hiding. When you click Start, the menu displayed in Figure 1.17 appears.

The Start menu is organized according to what Windows XP thinks you might want to do. The left side of the Start menu shows the programs you are likely to use. (How does Windows XP know? It pays attention to the programs you've most recently used.) Above the divider line, you find the Internet offering of MSN Explorer (note that this is not Internet Explorer—for more about the MSN Explorer online service, see Saturday morning's session, "Ready, Set, Online!") and others. Below the divider line, you see a collection of programs specific to your use of your computer.

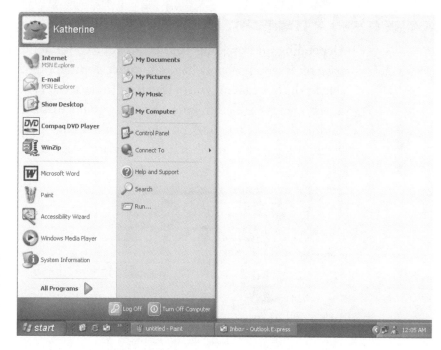

Figure 1.17

All the programs installed on your computer are available from the Start menu.

Your Start menu may appear different from the one shown here because Windows XP customizes the Start menu for each individual user. This means that if you recently worked with a specific program—such as Notepad—that program now appears in the lower-left section of the Start menu on your computer. As you can see from the figure, I've been working with Microsoft Word, WinZip, and Paint, as well as others. Also, your name (not mine) appears as the username at the top of the menu.

On the right side of the Start menu, you see a listing of folders you can look into (My Documents, My Pictures, My Music, and My Computer), as well as the Control Panel (an important offering if you ever want to change any of the settings and preferences in your system). The Connect To offering enables you to establish an online connection; Help and Support gives you—as you know—help and support; Search lets you search for specific files and folders; and Run displays a pop-up dialog box that enables you to launch a program by choosing its filename and clicking OK.

Viewing All Programs

Depending on how long you've had your computer and how much you have on it, you probably have a number of programs that are still not visible in the Start menu you're viewing. To see a full list of all programs and accessories available on your computer, point to the All Programs selection in the Start menu. A pop-up list of available programs scrolls to the right, going into two columns if necessary (see Figure 1.18).

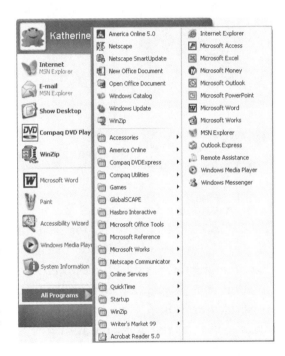

Figure 1.18

When you point to All Programs, a listing of all available programs on your computer is displayed.

Even this long list of programs doesn't quite display everything. Some entries show small arrows to the right of the product name, which means that additional choices are in a submenu related to those items. Display one of the submenus by pointing to the program selection; when you see the program selection you want, click it. That action launches the program and opens it in a window on your screen.

TIP Do you have to go through this point-point-and-click method each time you want to launch a program? Not if you don't want to. If you want to load the program into the Quick Launch area so that you can start it with a single click, you can do so from Windows Explorer (see Saturday afternoon's session, "Handling Files and Folders," for more information about that). You can also add a program icon to your desktop by right-clicking, choosing New, and creating a program shortcut. For steps on adding a program icon to your desktop, see Appendix A, "Installing, Upgrading, and Restoring Windows XP."

Shutting Windows Down

You don't need to start Windows when you first start your computer in the morning because it launches automatically. But when you are ready to turn in for the night—and it has been a long day, hasn't it? I'm ready to catch some zzz's myself!—you need to go through the proper steps to make sure that Windows XP is shut down correctly. When you're ready to turn your computer off, close Windows by following these steps:

1. Close all open programs.
2. Click Start. The Start menu appears.
3. Click Turn Off Computer, in the lower-right portion of the Start menu. The Turn Off Computer option box appears, as Figure 1.19 shows.

Figure 1.19

Shutting Windows down turns your computer off for the night.

4. Choose Turn Off to shut down your system and say goodnight. Stand By puts your computer in Hibernate mode (which conserves power), and Restart simply clears the computer's memory and begins again.

After 10 to 15 seconds, Windows XP retires, your computer closes down, and all is quiet for the night.

What's Next?

Congratulations! You've made it through your first Windows XP work-session. We've covered lots of ground, from a beginning discussion of what Windows is to the specifics of Windows XP, to you-try-it exercises on working with Windows components, like the Taskbar, windows, and programs. Finally, you learned how to shut Windows down as you power off your computer. The next session makes the jump into cyberspace with the online capabilities of Windows XP. See you in the morning!

Ready, Set, Online!

ood morning! And welcome to one of my favorite sessions in the book! The Internet is everywhere you look these days—and it's coming closer, bringing a diverse and complicated world to our home computers, television screens, even cell phones. We see Web addresses on billboards and cereal boxes, and we e-mail friends, family, and coworkers—communicating instantly and consistently instead of waiting for weeks (or months or years) to find the time to write that letter we've been putting off. We can meet virtually anywhere as long as we have access to the Web; we find tools of all sorts, ready to help us browse the Internet, trade messages with clients, chat with friends, or publish our own pages on the Web.

An Overview of Windows XP Internet Features

This session helps you learn the ins and outs of working with the Windows XP communications tools. As you learned in the preceding session, Windows XP puts a high priority on connectivity—as the world grows smaller, it's important to be able to give people quick and easy access in a way that suits their personal preferences. Toward that end, Microsoft packaged the following Internet features with Windows XP:

✿ Internet Explorer 6.0 is the Web browser that comes with Windows XP. A *Web browser* is a program that enables you to display and work with Web pages—this program is the one you use to "surf" the Internet. Internet Explorer, as you see in the sections that follow, enables you to do much more than simply look at Web pages—you can save, print, and e-mail Web pages—and collect your favorites in folders you can return to later.

✿ Outlook Express 6.0 is the e-mail program installed with Windows XP. You use Outlook Express to send and receive e-mail and read and post messages to newsgroups. Outlook Express is a "lighter" version of the larger program Microsoft Outlook (that program also includes a calendar, scheduler, note feature, and more), which is part of Microsoft Office XP.

✿ MSN Explorer is the online service offering from Microsoft. Similar in function to America Online (AOL), MSN Explorer offers a fully integrated Web experience, with Web-based e-mail, traditional browsing, chat, discussion groups, and more.

✿ Windows Messenger is the instant-messaging utility that pops up over your work so that you can trade quick messages with friends. Windows Messenger is also integrated into MSN Explorer and Outlook Express so that you can launch the program and send messages to your online buddies without leaving those other programs.

✿ NetMeeting is a program included in Windows XP that enables you to hold real-time meetings in cyberspace. By gathering in a virtual "conference room" and having an online chat, you can meet with coworkers, clients, or peers to discuss projects, proposals, strategies, and more.

You get a chance to experiment with each of these online tools as you work through this morning's session. So get yourself a cup of coffee, let the dog out, and settle in to explore the wide world of cyberspace with Windows XP.

Getting Connected

Before you can begin surfing the Web, you have to make sure that you have an Internet connection. Getting connected requires two important things: hardware and software. The hardware is the modem; the software is the utility you use to get online—whether that software is provided by Microsoft Network (MSN), AOL, or an Internet service provider (ISP). If the distinction is unclear to you right now, don't worry—you learn about the various ways to connect as you work through this session.

Your computer connects to the Internet using a device called a *modem* (which, back in the golden age of computers, authors were sure to define as a *modulator-demodulator*, describing the process the device uses to turn data into sound and then back into data again). Years ago, modems were blocky devices that sat outside the system unit of your computer; although some people still use external units, now they are usually tucked away inside your computer whether you're working on a desktop or laptop system. You plug your typical phone cord into the cord plug along the side or back of your computer, fire up the software, and go!

Checking Out Your Modem

It's not a bad idea to take a look and make sure that your modem is working properly. You use the Control Panel to check things out. Here are the steps:

1. Click the Start button on the Taskbar. The Start menu opens.
2. Choose Control Panel, in the right side of the Start menu. The Control Panel opens, filling your screen.

NOTE   Some manufacturers set up the Control Panel to open as a list rather than provide a link, as I mention here. If your computer works a bit differently than described, don't fret. The option you're looking for is Printers and Other Hardware.

3. In the Pick a Category area, choose Printers and Other Hardware. *Another* Control Panel screen appears.

4. Click Phone and Modem Options in the Pick a Control Panel Icon area. The Phone and Modem Options dialog box appears.

5. Finally, click the Modems tab. You see your modem listed, along with the speed of the modem and the port it is set to use.

6. To run a quick check of your modem, click the Properties button. Windows XP tests the device quickly to make sure that it is working properly. When the test is finished, you see a window similar to the one shown in Figure 2.1.

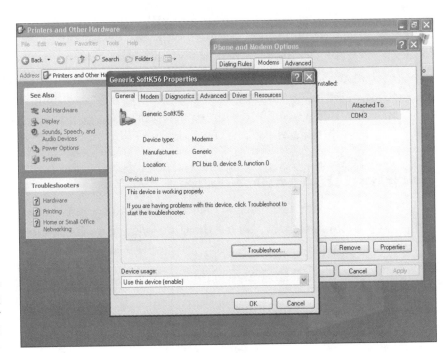

Figure 2.1

You can run a quick check on your modem by using the Control Panel.

TIP

If your modem doesn't seem to be working the way it should, click the Troubleshoot button in either the General tab or the Diagnostics tab and click Query Modem to run a diagnostics check.

THE BIG DEAL ABOUT BANDWIDTH

What's the deal about bandwidth? You're probably hearing a great deal these days about narrowband and broadband—these terms get batted around at dinner parties when people talk about cable companies offering Internet hookup and new Web-based television technologies. What is bandwidth, broad or narrow, and what does it have to do with your modem?

Bandwidth, in general, is the width of the data channel that can pass data to and from your computer. A PC hooked up to the Internet via a regular phone line is considered a narrowband. Higher-level technologies, like T-1 lines, offer very wide data channels, which enables the data to move much faster and in much larger chunks. The larger the bandwidth, the faster the transmission. The narrower the band, the slower the connection.

NOTE Anticipating the pull of the future, Microsoft has joined the ISP business by offering MSN Broadband—a "lightning-fast" online offering that uses Microsoft's IntelliSpeed technology. You sign up for service (a one-year commitment), and you get a high-performance connection, do-it-yourself installation, the use of a DSL modem, the software, and service—10 free hours of dial-up service per month. The cost is $39.95 per month. You can find out more about MSN Broadband at the **http://www.resource-center.msn.com/access/broadband/FAQ.asp** site.

Finding Someone to Connect You

So, assuming that you've got a modem and it's working, how do you make the connection and get online? The answer is simple: You need someone to call. An *Internet service provider*, or *ISP*, is a company that sells access to the Internet. You sign up and agree to pay anywhere from $19.99 to $39.99 a month (or more, if you're signing up for high-speed connectivity, like DSL or T-1 capability), and in return you get a user ID, a password, and the phone number your computer needs to call to get online. Your ISP also provides you with a unique e-mail address and perhaps some Web storage space, in case you want to post your own Web page on the Web. (Not all ISPs offer free Web space, however.)

Where do you find an ISP? You'll find providers in your local area (the Yellow Pages is a good place to start), and you'll also find national ISPs. One of the perks of going with a national ISP is that if you travel and need to log in from different parts of the country, you can use an 800 number for dial-up (or download a list of local access numbers in various regions). If you use a local provider, your service may be just as good; but when you travel, you have a long-distance number to dial when you need to get online.

TIP   What makes a good ISP good? When you're asking friends, family, and coworkers about which ISP you should try, look for the following endearing qualities: reliability, good technical support, little or no downtime (periods when you can't get online), and few bump-offs (accidental disconnections). Most ISPs can provide statistics about the number of service interruptions they've had in the past month or so. If the reliability of your service is important to you, take the time to find the answers you need.

Creating a New Connection

The actual dial-up happens after you've set up a new connection using the New Connection Wizard. Windows XP walks you through the process of putting all the numbers in the right places and choosing the settings you need to get online successfully. If you have set up an account with an ISP and you are ready to create a new connection, follow these steps:

1. Click Start to display the Start menu.

2. Select Control Panel. The Control Panel window opens.

3. In the Pick a Category area, click Network and Internet Connections.

4. In the Pick a Task list, click Setup or change your Internet connection. The Internet Properties dialog box appears (see Figure 2.2). The Connections tab is automatically displayed.

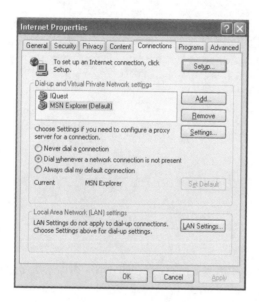

Figure 2.2

You can check your current Internet connection—and set up a new one—starting with the Internet Properties dialog box.

5. Click the Setup button at the top of the dialog box. This step launches the New Connection Wizard, which leads you through the process of establishing the new Internet connection. Read the opening screen and click Next.

6. The first screen of the New Connection Wizard asks whether you want to set up a connection to the Internet, a network, a home network, or an advanced connection. Leave the first option, Connect to the Internet, selected and click Next.

7. The Getting Ready page asks you to decide how you want to set up your connection. You can choose from the following three choices (see Figure 2.3):

   ○ Choose from a list of Internet Service providers (ISPs)

   ○ Set up my connection manually

   ○ Use the CD I got from an ISP

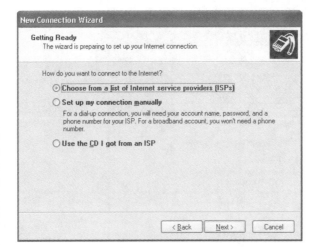

Figure 2.3

In the Getting Ready page of the New Connection Wizard, you can choose how you want to create your connection.

Each of these items starts you down a different path. If you select the first option, you are given the choice of selecting MSN as your provider; you can choose other well-known services, too, such as AOL and Prodigy. The second option is the one you choose if you already have an account with an ISP; the third option is the one you want if you have your own ISP account and someone there has sent you a CD with the software you need to use to connect to the Internet. For our use here, select the second option and click Next.

8. On the Internet Connection screen, you choose whether you want to use a dial-up modem (which is what most home users have), a broadband connection you connect with occasionally,

or a broadband connection that is always open. Make your choice and click Next again.

9. Next, enter the name of the ISP you are using. Click Next.

10. Type the phone number your modem dials to access the ISP. Your ISP gives you this number when you sign up. Click Next.

11. In the Internet Account Information screen, enter the username and password the ISP gave you. You need to retype the password in the Confirm Password box.

NOTE By default, the Make this the default Internet connection check box is selected. It makes this connection your default connection (so that whenever you want to go online, this connection is used). If that's all right with you, leave the box selected. If you plan on using this connection only occasionally and don't want it to be the default selection, click the check box to deselect it.

12. Click Next to display the last page of the wizard. The wizard displays a short list of options you've selected for this connection. If you want to add the connection icon to your desktop, click the Add a shortcut check box; then click Finish.

The wizard is done, and you're all set to connect to the Internet!

Making the Call

Assuming that you placed the new connection icon on your desktop, to start the call you need only to point at the icon and double-click it. The Connect dialog box opens, as you see in Figure 2.4.

NOTE If you have not placed an icon on the desktop, the Connect dialog box opens when you attempt to launch an Internet application, such as Internet Explorer or Outlook Express.

Figure 2.4

When you double-click the new connection, the Connect Vision dialog box opens with all you need to connect.

The information you provided to the New Connection Wizard plugs in the username and password for you. Check the Dial number to make sure that the computer will be dialing correctly and then click Dial. You hear the computer dialing the number shown, and then, after a minute, you may hear a high-pitched electronic sound, and then…silence (although some newer modems are silent).

Unless you see an error message pop up on your screen, that silence means that the connection has been established and you are online. Congratulations! The Connect window shrinks down to a small icon and appears as a small image in the notification area of the Taskbar.

Now that you're online, you're ready to begin exploring. Internet Explorer is a good place to start!

The New, Improved Internet Explorer

Internet Explorer (IE) is your doorway to the Web. You use Internet Explorer to find information, shop, chat, read articles, buy stocks, search for new sandals, get a map to Des Moines, research colleges, look for jobs—the list goes on and on and on.

The Web, or *World Wide Web,* as it was originally called, has grown from something a few geeky scientist-like people use to something everyone, from Baby Sam in preschool to Aunt Edna at the retirement village, knows about. Your kids may have known about the Web before you did. Whether you feel behind the times or on the cutting edge, here's your chance to start surfing.

Starting Internet Explorer

After you've established your Internet connection, you can launch Internet Explorer in one of two ways:

✪ Click the Internet Explorer icon in the Quick Launch area of the Taskbar.

✪ Click Start, All Programs and select Internet Explorer. The Internet Explorer window opens fully over the Windows desktop.

NOTE You don't have to establish your Internet connection before you attempt to launch Internet Explorer or any other Internet application. When you select the icon to start the program, Windows XP knows to display the Connect dialog box so that you can get online and start the program. Logic follows, though, that you need to have made the connection before you can begin surfing or e-mailing online.

The first Web page you see may have all kinds of information (see Figure 2.5). Depending on the manufacturer of your computer and the vendors with whom they made arrangements, you may see MSN as your "home" page, your ISP's home page, or the home page of your computer manufacturer.

As you can see from this one page, you can do lots of things on the Web. The sections that follow introduce you first to the tools you use to get around in Internet Explorer and then present the various ways you can navigate the Web.

Buy something   Chat with other people   Search for information

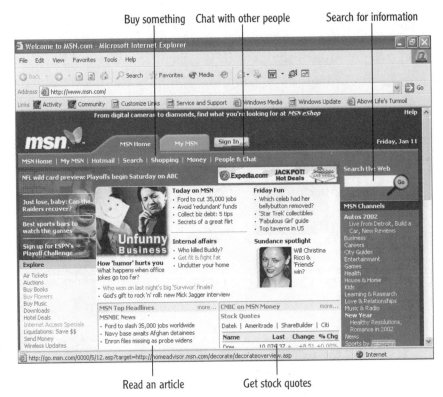

Figure 2.5

What can you do
on the Web? Almost
anything you want.

Read an article   Get stock quotes

NOTE   **Definition:** The **home page** in your browser is the page on which your worksession starts.

Learning IE Tools

No matter what your level of Web experience, you'll find it easy to reach what you need in the Internet Explorer window (see Figure 2.6).

The window is designed to put all the tools you need within reach— you'll soon know how to surf like a pro. The Internet Explorer window includes the following elements that help you navigate the Web:

- The title bar includes the name of the current page and the Minimize, Maximize, and Close buttons.

- The menu bar shows six menus: File, Edit, View, Favorites, Tools, and Help. You use the commands in these menus to save and print Web pages, copy and paste information, change the display of toolbars and text, collect your favorite pages, use mail tools, and get help.

- The toolbar includes the tools you use to move from one Web page to another. Table 2.1 lists the various tools on the IE toolbar.

- The Address bar enables you to type the URL of the Web page you want to see.

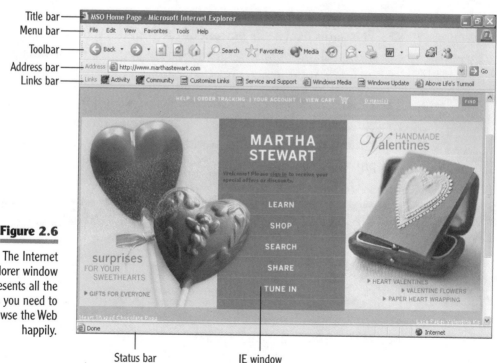

Figure 2.6

The Internet Explorer window presents all the tools you need to browse the Web happily.

Title bar

Menu bar

Toolbar

Address bar

Links bar

Status bar

IE window

NOTE **Definition: URL** is an acronym for Universal Resource Locator, the technical term for "Web address." A typical Web address is **http://www.microsoft.com**. It is also known as the site's URL.

⚙ The Links bar displays special sites that are already saved as quick-link buttons. By clicking one of these links, you can move right to the page. These links may be preset by your manufacturer, or you can add your own

⚙ The IE window is the main area of the page—where you see the Web page displayed. The window is bordered with scroll bars so that you can move up and down and from side to side on the Web pages you visit.

⚙ The status bar, at the bottom of the window, often displays information about the page, the link you're pointing to, or the next steps you need to take in an operation.

The Internet Explorer tools stretched across the top of the window give you almost everything you need to move from one page to another—across the Web and across the world. Table 2.1 shows each of these tools and provides a brief description of each one's function.

	TABLE 2.1 IE TOOLS	
Tool	**Name**	**Description**
◄	Back	Moves to the last page you viewed
►	Forward	Moves to the next page
⊠	Stop	Stops the loading of the current page

TABLE 2.1 CONTINUED		

Tool	Name	Description
	Refresh	Refreshes the display of the current page
	Home	Displays the page that is set as the home page for your system
	Search	Opens the Search Companion so that you can search for specific information
	Favorites	Displays the Favorites panel so that you can add and manage your favorite Web site
	Media	Opens the Media panel so that you can sample music, radio, movies, and more
	History	Displays the History panel so that you can visit Web pages you've previously seen
	Mail	Displays a submenu so that you can send a page via e-mail
	Print	Prints the displayed Web page
	Edit	Opens a text editor so that you can view and edit the source code of the current page (Your icon may look different, depending on which editor you use.)
	Discuss	Displays a Discussion toolbar at the bottom of the screen so that you can discuss the page with other people
	Messenger	Displays the Windows Messenger pop-up window over Internet Explorer

Exploring the IE Window

After you begin looking around the Web, you find all sorts of sites. Some pages want to sell you something; others give you information; still others enable you to play games; and others offer a whole slew of experiences, all in one place. Different sites show links, text, buttons, or images that enable you to move to other pages—in different ways. Consider the Microsoft Windows home page, for example. You'll find text links, graphic links, and tabs waiting for your click (see Figure 2.7).

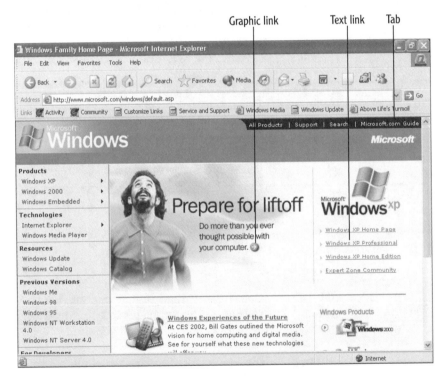

Figure 2.7

Sites show you where the clickable areas are—that's how you know how to move from page to page.

When you find something on a page that interests you and you want to see more, what do you do? Simply click a link to move to the next page of information. Two different kinds of links are typically used on the Web:

- A *text link* can be a word, a phrase, a menu item, or other text that is usually highlighted or underlined to show that it's a link.
- A *graphics link* can be a photo, a drawing, a graphic created in an art program, or some other image.

> **TIP**
>
> If you aren't sure whether an item on a Web page is linked to something else, position the mouse pointer over it. If the pointer changes to a hand pointer, the item is a link. If the pointer stays in the same arrow shape, the item is not linked.

Moving to Another Page

Of course, you didn't come to the Web to look at just one page and then get off—you want to explore a little! When you're ready to move from one page to another, you can do so in several different ways:

- Click one of the links on the page to move to a different page.
- Click in the Address bar and type the URL of the new page you want to move to.
- Use the navigation buttons (Back, Forward, or Home) in the tool-bar to move to another page.

> **TIP**
>
> If you accidentally move to the wrong page (perhaps you typed the URL incorrectly), you can stop the page from loading by clicking the Stop button in the IE toolbar. The page stops loading, and you can then click in the Address bar and type the URL you meant to type in the first place.

Moving Back Where You Came From

Suppose that you move to a new site and then think "Wait a minute—I forgot to check something on that last site." You don't have to look up the URL and enter it again; instead, just click the Back button. Internet Explorer takes you back where you came from.

After you've jumped around a while, the Back button offers subchoices you can display when you want to return to a previous page. Simply click the down-arrow on the right side of the button, and a menu of past pages opens up (see Figure 2.8). To move to the page you want, just click it.

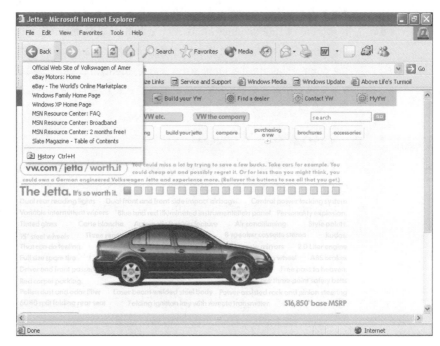

Figure 2.8

The Back button keeps track of other pages you've visited in your current work session and lets you choose which one to return to.

You Can Go Home Again

The Home button in the Internet Explorer toolbar doesn't take you back to the home page of the current site, as new users often think. Instead, it returns you to the home page that is set up on *your* computer. The *home page* is the Web page your computer starts with when you first log on and fire up Internet Explorer. Although the manufacturers of your computer set the home page for you at first, you can change it to begin on whatever your heart desires.

If you want to change the place you start out on the Web in the morning, follow these steps:

1. Make sure that Internet Explorer is open; then click Tools in the menu bar. The Tools menu opens.

2. Select Internet Options. The Internet Options dialog box appears (see Figure 2.9). The General tab should be displayed by default. If it's not, click it to bring the General options to the forefront. The Address line in the Home page section of the tab should be highlighted. If not, highlight it and press Delete. This action deletes the current page.

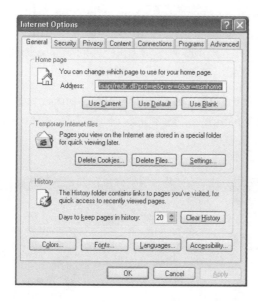

Figure 2.9

You change your home page selection in the General tab of the Internet Options dialog box.

3. Type the URL for the page you want to use or choose the button that fits what you want to do:

   ○ If you're now displaying the page you want to use as your home page, click Use Current.

   ○ If you want to return to the system default (which is unlikely because you probably haven't changed it yet), click Use Default.

   ○ Click Use Blank if you want Internet Explorer to display no Web page—only a blank HTML page.

4. Click Apply to apply the changes.

5. Click OK to close the Internet Options dialog box and return to the Web. The next time you launch Internet Explorer, it displays the new home page by default.

Searching on the Web

The Web is so vast—is there anything you can't find out there somewhere? With such a huge collection of available data, you need some sane method of searching for and finding what you want. Luckily, Internet Explorer builds a search feature into Internet Explorer so that you can click a button, type a phrase, and find what you're looking for. Here are the steps:

1. Click the Search tool in the Internet Explorer toolbar. The Search Companion panel opens to the left of the IE window (see Figure 2.10).

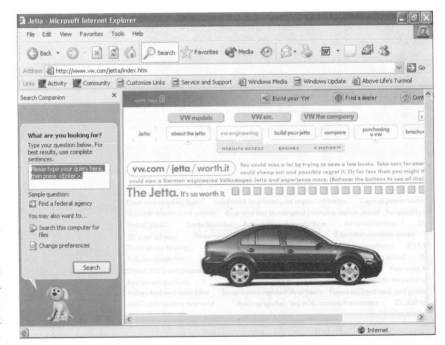

Figure 2.10

The Search Companion panel opens to the left of the browser window so that you can enter the topic you're looking for.

2. Type a phrase that tells IE what you're looking for. You can search for anything—Steve Martin movies, vacation homes in St. John, pictures of otters—whatever.

3. Click Search or press Enter to start the process. Windows XP, or rather, the Search Companion, begins scouring the Web for pages with the information you're looking for. The results are displayed in the IE window, as you see in Figure 2.11.

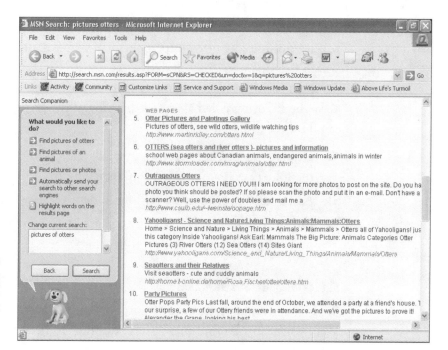

Figure 2.11

The result is a list of links that are likely to have what you want—if not, try again.

TIP Another quick-search method: Just click in the Address bar, type the search word or phrase, and press Enter.

TIP If you didn't quite find what you were looking for, you can use the Search Companion to refine your search a bit. Sometimes, thinking of new ways to refer to the subject can help you locate the information you seek. Click one of the Search Companion choices or enter a new search.

Collecting Your Favorite Sites

After you locate all these wonderful sites, what will you do with them? You need some way of collecting them so that you don't have to use the Search Companion over and over again to find them. That's where Favorites come in. Clicking the Favorites button in the IE toolbar displays the Favorites panel along the left side of the IE window. There, you can do three different tasks:

✿ Display one of your favorites by navigating to the site you want in the folders that are displayed and clicking it.

✿ Add a new favorite to an existing folder or a new folder you create.

✿ Organize your favorites, deleting pages you no longer want and moving pages to new folders if necessary.

Adding a Favorite

With the seemingly infinite amount of information out there on the Web, you're sure to find many sites you want to be able to refer to later. You keep track of these sites by adding them to your Favorites folders. This process starts in the Favorites panel. To add your Web page favorites, follow these steps:

1. Navigate to a Web page you want to keep. Click Favorites in the IE toolbar. The Favorites panel opens.

2. Click Add at the top of the panel. The Add Favorite dialog box appears, as Figure 2.12 shows.

3. Click the folder in which you want to save the new favorite and click OK.

NOTE If you don't see a list of folders in the Add Favorite dialog box, click the Create in button. The dialog box enlarges and the list of folders is displayed beneath the Name box.

4. Or, if you don't see a folder that will work for your new page, click New Folder, and the Create New Folder dialog box appears. Type the name for the new folder and click OK. Now you can save the favorite in the new folder by selecting it in the list and clicking OK.

TIP Want to be able to look at this site later, when you're offline? Simply click the Make available offline check box before you click OK in the Add Favorite dialog box, and Internet Explorer takes care of the rest.

Organizing Your Favorites

Organizing your favorites is another matter. After you collect a few dozen favorites, what will you do with them? I hope that you've been creating folders and organizing them as you add them—if you haven't, you can use the Organize option to put the favorites in their proper place. To start organizing your favorites, follow these steps:

1. In Internet Explorer, click the Favorites button. The Favorites panel opens on the left side of the window.

2. Click Organize. The Organize Favorites dialog box appears, as you see in Figure 2.13.

Figure 2.13

Getting organized may not be the most fun thing you do on the Web— but if you want to know how to find the places you like most, it's a necessity.

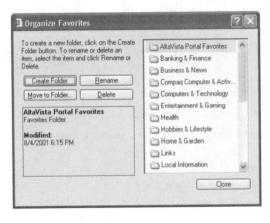

3. Now you can click the button that reflects what you need to do to get organized. Choose one of the following:

   ✿ **Create Folder.** This option enables you to create a new folder for storing favorites.

   ✿ **Move to Folder.** Use this option to move favorites to the new folder you just created.

   ✿ **Rename.** You can use this option to rename favorites or the folders that store them.

   ✿ **Delete.** Use this option to remove sites you no longer need or folders you don't use.

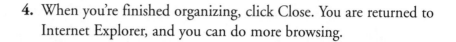

4. When you're finished organizing, click Close. You are returned to Internet Explorer, and you can do more browsing.

NOTE Note that you don't need to be online to organize your favorites. Because Internet Explorer saves the links to the pages and not the pages themselves, you do not need to be connected in order to move favorites around.

Saving Web Pages

Even though you know how to save a Web page in your Favorites folders, you may want to save the file on your hard disk. That's as simple as saving any other file. Here are the steps:

1. Navigate to the Web page you want to save.

2. Click File in the menu bar. The File menu opens.

3. Choose Save As. The Save Web Page dialog box appears, as Figure 2.14 shows.

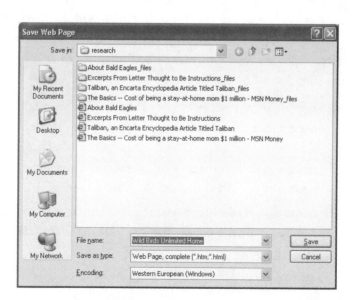

Figure 2.14

You can save Web pages to use, print, or refer to later.

4. Choose the folder in which you want to save the page by clicking the down-arrow to the right of the Save in box; click your choice.

5. Enter a name for the page in the File name box if you want to change the default.

6. Click Save. The Web page is saved to your hard drive in the folder you specified.

When you open the Web page in the future, Internet Explorer automatically opens to display it. If you would rather save the file as a text file (which means that you don't save the digital images on the site), you can click the Save as type down-arrow in the Save Web Page dialog box and choose Text File as the format for the saved file. Then click Save as usual.

Working with Media

NEW IN ▶
WINDOWS XP

Who can resist media? Sure, you're supposed to be working, but what harm will a little music do while you're at it? Or maybe a movie trailer. Hey, have you seen *Harry Potter* yet? (Okay, who hasn't?)

The Windows Media Player is a feature that, at the click of the IE Media button, gives you a choice for online media in the Media panel, to the left of the browser area. You can search for the media item you want—CD clips, video trailers, and more—and play them as you browse. Here are the steps:

1. While you're online, display Internet Explorer and click Media in the toolbar. The Media panel opens along the left side of your work area (see Figure 2.15). At the top of the Media panel, you see today's offerings from WindowsMedia.com—suggesting moving segments or videos you might want to see.

2. Scroll down the Media panel by dragging the scroll bar along the right edge of the panel. You see four main choices:

- ✿ Music
- ✿ Movies
- ✿ Radio
- ✿ MSN Music

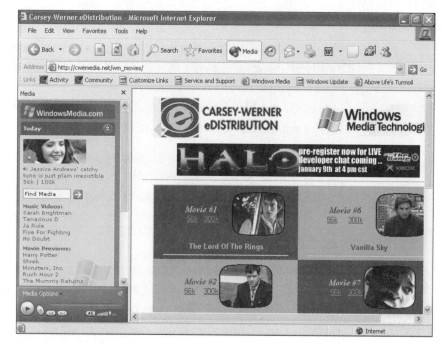

Figure 2.15

The result is a list of links that are likely to have what you want—if not, try again.

3. Each of these choices gives you a different selection for the type of media you can experience or download. To display the choices, click the double down-arrow to the right of the media type. You'll find Editors Picks as well as Featured Stations (or Releases); to see or hear the one you want, simply click it.

When you're finished playing around with the Media bar, simply click the Close button in the upper-right corner of the Media panel to close it and get your full-screen browser window back. (For more about working with the Media bar and other Windows XP media features, see tonight's session, "Now for the Fun Part: Media!")

TIP   If you like to visit certain sites every day, you can add them to your Link bar (just beneath the Address bar, at the top of the IE window). To add the site quickly, just highlight the URL and drag it from the Address bar to the Links bar; then release the mouse button. IE puts the icon and the page name on the bar, and you can click the icon to move to the site quickly.

Checking Your History

Okay, so suppose that you were surfing last week and visited a whole bunch of interesting pages that you didn't think you would need again. But now you want to know where you've been. You can use History to find out. Click the History button, and the History panel shows you a listing of sites you've visited today, yesterday, last week—up to two weeks ago.

Just click the folder that you think has the best shot of containing the page you want to see and look for the page name. When you find it, click it, and the page appears in the browser window.

Printing Web Pages

Here's another simple task. Assuming that you have a printer that is hooked up to your computer and stocked with paper, you can crank out a printout of that cool Web page by clicking the Print button in the IE toolbar. There's no other step—no dialog box to respond to. The page just goes to your printer. End of story.

Someone to Watch Over Me

The Content Advisor is the final stop we make on this whirlwind tour of Internet Explorer. (We've got to get on to other online tools! There's so much to see!). The Content Advisor is the Internet Explorer offering for those homes and offices that need a ratings feature—for those of us who would rather avoid obscene, frightening, or threatening information. To put the advisor in a position to keep an eye on the Web content you and your family members (or officemates) view, follow these steps:

1. Click Tools in the IE menu and choose Internet Options. The Internet Options dialog box appears.

2. Click the Content tab. In the Content Advisor area, click Enable. The Content Advisor dialog box opens, as shown in Figure 2.16.

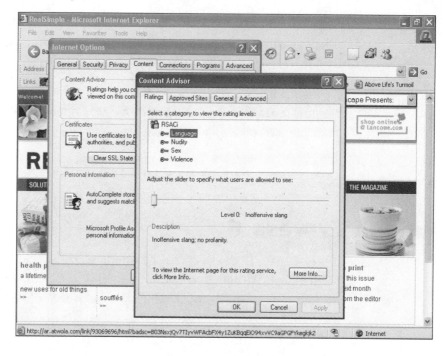

Figure 2.16

The Content
Advisor helps you
limit the amount of
bad language,
nudity, sex, and
violence you view
online.

3. Start by choosing the category you want to set the controls for
(Language, Nudity, Sex, or Violence).

4. Move the slider to reflect the level of control you want to exercise
(drag the slider to the right to raise the allowable level; drag the
slider to the left to decrease the allowable level).

5. Repeat steps 3 and 4 for each of the category areas you want to set.

6. Click Apply to save the controls. The Create Supervisor Password
dialog box appears, asking you to provide (and confirm) a password
so that other people can't undo the controls you've set. Enter the
information and click OK to continue. A message appears, telling
you that the Content Advisor has been activated. Click OK.

7. Click OK to close the dialog box and return to browsing.

If you decide later that you want to change the settings or do away with
the Content Advisor, go back to the advisor by choosing Tools, Internet
Options and clicking the Content tab. Click either Disable (to fire the

advisor) or Settings (to change the allowable levels). Either way, you're asked to enter your password. After you enter your password, Internet Explorer carries out the commands as you request.

TIP   Be sure to remember to keep your Content Advisor password in a safe place—and don't lose it. The Advisor is a by-the-book kind of tool and doesn't accept any excuse for a lost password.

Outlook Express 6

On to e-mail! If you've ever used online services, chances are that you've tried e-mail. Although you can use many different e-mail programs—including Web-based e-mail, which you learn about later in this chapter—Outlook Express is the best one I've found for the money. Of course, it's packaged free with Windows XP, but it's a great, easy-to-use e-mail utility that can do just about everything you would want in an e-mail program.

NOTE   Outlook Express is a "light" version of Microsoft Outlook, a larger program that includes scheduling features, a calendar, journaling, and more. The latest version of Microsoft Outlook is available with Microsoft Office XP.

In this section, you start the program and explore the Outlook Express window, compose and send an e-mail message, learn how to check for incoming messages, and keep track of your contacts with the Windows Address Book.

Starting Outlook Express

When you're ready to launch e-mail, begin by connecting to the Internet. After your connection is established, start Outlook Express by using one of these three methods:

- ✿ Click the Outlook Express icon in the Quick Launch area of the Taskbar.
- ✿ Double-click the Outlook Express icon on the Windows desktop.
- ✿ Click Start to display the Start menu and then choose All Programs, Communications, Outlook Express.

The Outlook Express window opens, and you can begin your e-mail adventure.

Taking a Walk around the Outlook Express Window

Outlook Express is another program that packs lots of information in one screen. Notice the familiar window organization: title bar on top, menus next, toolbar following that. Outlook Express includes a number of different functions, however, that enable you to see all the different aspects of e-mail on-screen at one time (see Figure 2.17).

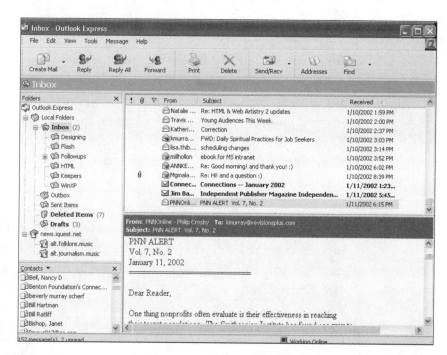

Figure 2.17

The Outlook Express window has four panels: Folders, Contacts, messages, and content. New messages appear in bold in the message window.

Here are the components you'll be most interested in:

- In the upper-left panel, the folder area displays all the folders you've created in Outlook Express and some that were created for you. The program comes with Inbox, Outbox, Sent Items, Deleted Items, and Drafts folders just awaiting your use.

- In the lower-left corner, the Contacts panel lists the contacts now in your Windows Address Book.

- The upper-right panel shows the messages in the selected folder.

- The lower-right panel shows the contents of the individual message selected in the upper-right panel.

Using Outlook Express Tools

As you might expect, Outlook Express has its own set of unique tools. Table 2.2 lists the tools you work with as you create, send, receive, and respond to e-mail messages.

Receiving Messages

When you first created the connection that allows you to get on the Internet, the New Connection Wizard asked you for both ISP information and e-mail account information. That information is automatically plugged into your Windows XP information, so Outlook Express already knows whom to call. When you fire up the program for the first time, Outlook Express should be able to check for and retrieve your e-mail without a hitch.

The program automatically checks for messages when you first open the program; any received messages are displayed in your Inbox. New messages appear in bold type in the message panel. To open and read a message, you simply double-click it, and it opens in its own window (see Figure 2.18).

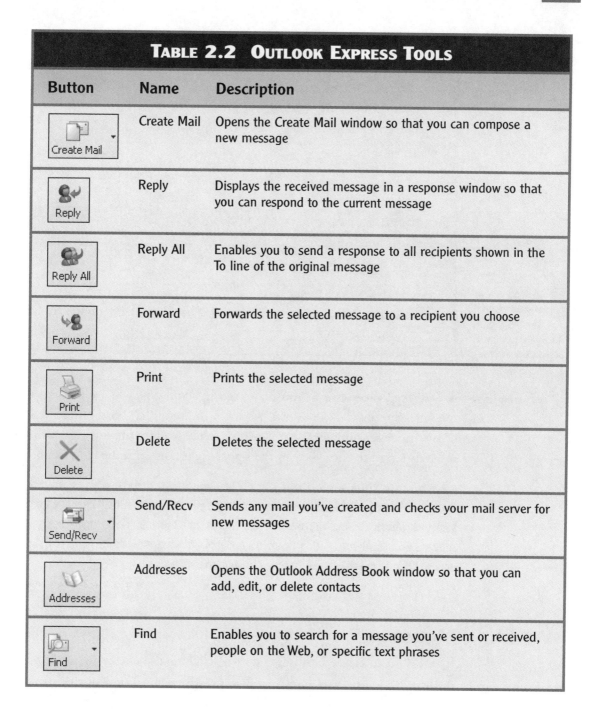

TABLE 2.2 OUTLOOK EXPRESS TOOLS

Button	Name	Description
Create Mail	Create Mail	Opens the Create Mail window so that you can compose a new message
Reply	Reply	Displays the received message in a response window so that you can respond to the current message
Reply All	Reply All	Enables you to send a response to all recipients shown in the To line of the original message
Forward	Forward	Forwards the selected message to a recipient you choose
Print	Print	Prints the selected message
Delete	Delete	Deletes the selected message
Send/Recv	Send/Recv	Sends any mail you've created and checks your mail server for new messages
Addresses	Addresses	Opens the Outlook Address Book window so that you can add, edit, or delete contacts
Find	Find	Enables you to search for a message you've sent or received, people on the Web, or specific text phrases

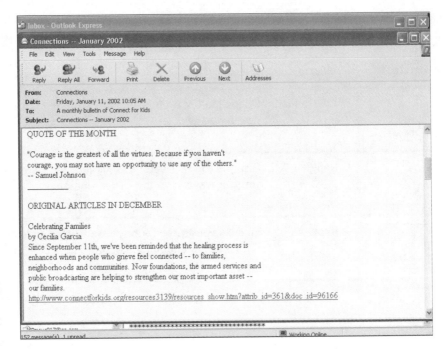

Figure 2.18

Double-click a
message to view it
in its own window.

As you read the message, you may need to scroll down to see the entire
message. Simply click the down-arrow in the scroll bar on the right side
of the message window. When you're finished reading the message, close
it by clicking the Close box in the upper-right corner of the window.

TIP   Want to build up your Address Book quickly? When you receive an e-mail message from
someone whose address you want to capture in your Address Book, right-click the
sender's e-mail address. A pop-up menu appears, showing the Add to Address Book
option. Click it, and the sender is added to your contact list.

Writing a Message

If you want to create a message, start by clicking the Create Mail button
in the Outlook Express toolbar. The New Message window opens.

Your tasks at this point are to answer three basic questions:

- ✪ Whom do you want to send the message to?
- ✪ What's the message about?
- ✪ What do you want to say?

NOTE You can write messages online or offline. After you finish composing your message, open the File menu and choose Send Later. Outlook stores the message until the next time you go online.

You answer these questions by following these steps:

1. Click in the To: line of the New Message window. If you know the e-mail address you want to use, type it in the line.

    or

    Click the To: button to display the Windows Address book. Select the name of the person or people you want to send the message to. To do this, click a recipient in the list on the left, click To, and click OK.

TIP If you want to send a copy of the message to others, enter their e-mail addresses in the CC: (courtesy copy) line. They receive a copy but understand that the message is not addressed directly to them.

2. Click in the Subject line and type the main topic of your message. You should keep the Subject line short so that it can be read in the message panel of the Outlook Express window.

3. Type the message in the message window. You can make the message as long as you like—you can even include charts, photos, and more, if you choose. You also can attach files, such as reports, presentations, and the like. But that's the subject of the section "Send a File As an Attachment," later in this chapter.

ADD YOUR JOHN HANCOCK

If you have a favorite phrase, quote, motto, or epithet you want to add at the end of your e-mail messages, you can create a signature that is attached to all your outgoing mail. Here are the steps:

1. Click Tools in the Outlook Express menu bar and choose Options.

2. Click the Signatures tab. Click New.

3. Type your signature (the phrase, address, or what-have-you) in the Edit Signature line. Alternatively, you can attach a file with your signature by choosing File and selecting the file you want to use.

4. Click the Add signatures to all outgoing messages check box to apply the signature. Any messages you create from this point forward show the signature.

TIP You don't need to stop there—you can "fancy up" the text by changing fonts, colors, text sizes, formats, and more. The New Message window includes everything you need to change the formatting. You can change the font, size, color, alignment—even the stationery on which the e-mail is composed. All these tools are in the New Message window and affect only the e-mail you compose in that window.

Sending a File as an Attachment

In addition to sending simple e-mail messages, Outlook Express allows you to send files attached to messages. You can send a report to the office, send a cartoon to the kids, e-mail Grandma the kids' latest school pictures, and forward a presentation to your team members.

To attach a file to your e-mail message, follow these steps:

1. In Outlook Express, click Create Message. The New Message window opens.

2. Choose the recipient and enter the subject line as usual. Type the body of your message and format it the way you like.

3. Click the Attach tool in the toolbar. The Insert Attachment dialog box appears, as Figure 2.19 shows.

4. Navigate to the folder where the file is stored.

5. Click the file you want to attach.

6. Click Attach to add the file.

7. Click Send. Outlook Express begins sending the file. Depending on the size of the file, it may take anywhere from seconds to minutes to transmit the file.

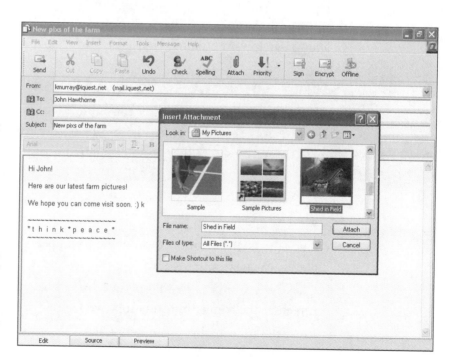

Figure 2.19

Navigate to the folder storing the file you want to attach to your email message.

TIP

As a general rule, Internet service providers have a maximum size limit for file attachments. Before sending an attachment, take its size—and the connection speed of your recipient—into consideration. Compressing large files with a file compression utility like WinZip helps reduce the size of your file attachments. Learn more about compressing files in Saturday afternoon's session, "Handling Files and Folders."

Managing Your Contacts with Address Book

You learned about the Windows Address Book in Chapter 1, but here's where the action starts. Windows Address Book is a terrific tool for storing just about every piece of information you need to store about someone: e-mail addresses, phone numbers, fax numbers, addresses—even birthdays, pet names, and anniversaries! For our purposes, we're most interested in saving and organizing recipient addresses. When you get time to explore all the features in the Address Book, however, do so—a little organization can go a long way toward building your little black book.

Adding Someone to Your Address Book

Have you ever come home from a convention with a pocketful of business cards? You should capture those e-mail addresses before they go through the wash—here's how to enter them into your Windows Address Book:

1. In Outlook Express, click the Addresses tool. The Address Book window opens.

2. Click the New button. A drop-down list appears so that you can choose to create a new contact, group, or folder.

3. Click New Contact. The Properties dialog box opens so that you can enter the contact information (see Figure 2.20).

4. Enter the information as needed. Click OK to close the dialog box when you're finished.

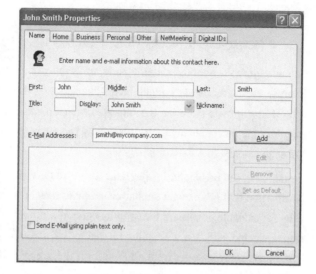

Figure 2.20

E-mail addresses are just the start of the data you can gather in your Address Book.

Using Your Existing Address Book

What if you've been using Outlook Express on another computer—or someone has at work an address book they want you to use—and you don't want to type in 150 new contacts? Luckily, Outlook Express includes a feature that enables you to import address books. To import a contact list, follow these steps:

1. In Outlook Express, click the Address Book tool. The Address Book opens.

2. Click File in the menu bar and click Import. The Import dialog box appears, giving you three options:

   ✪ Address Book (WAB)
   ✪ Business Card (vCard)
   ✪ Other Address Book

3. Assuming that you want to import another address book, select the first option; then click Import. Outlook Express then imports your contacts and merges them with the current Address Book.

NEWSGROUPS: A BIT ROUGH AROUND THE EDGES

The newsgroup is another e-mail-type offering you can use in Outlook Express. Newsgroups are bulletin board-like lists that focus on different topics. Newsgroups are often unmoderated, which means that no one monitors the messages. As a result, you may see many inappropriate messages posted to a newsgroup listing.

Newsgroups can be helpful in situations where you are looking for information that others with similar experiences may be able to provide; for example, if you are trying to install a new program and you're having trouble with it, a newsgroup related to that software product might have some answers from other users who have experienced the same thing. Beyond that type of use, however, newsgroups may be more trouble than they're worth. If you choose to use the newsreader feature in Outlook Express, you can set it up as follows:

1. Click Tools in the menu and choose Accounts. The Internet Accounts dialog box appears.

2. Click the News tab.

3. Click the Add button and choose News. This step launches the Internet Connection Wizard.

4. The wizard asks you to enter the name of your news server (you may need to get this name from your ISP). Type it and then click Finish. The news server is added to the News tab of the Internet Accounts dialog box.

5. Click Close to complete the operation. A message appears, asking whether you want to download newsgroups from the news account you added. If you want to add newsgroups, click OK; otherwise, click No.

After you set up Outlook Express to work with newsgroups, the name of your news server appears at the bottom of the Outlook Express list in the folders panel. When you're ready to subscribe to newsgroups, simply click the news server name.

Take a Break

We've covered lots of ground in this chapter! The sun must be high in the sky right now—perhaps you're feeling like you should go mow the grass or walk the dog. Now is a good time for a break. Take 15 minutes or so and check up on the kids, grab some lunch, stretch and walk around— your brain will thank you for it. When you've had a little break, come on back and we'll talk about even more online possibilities with MSN Explorer, NetMeeting, and more.

MSN Explorer

Everyone in the entire world has heard about America Online, or AOL. From television commercials to those annoying CDs that come in the mail every few weeks, AOL has the biggest marketing blitz of any online service worldwide. Those folks want you to know about AOL. They're friends with Microsoft, they'll have you know. A free AOL Trial icon may even be packaged with your version of Windows XP. (It depends on the third-party relationships established by the vendor of your computer, however.)

But what happens when Microsoft develops its *own* online service, rivaling the features offered by AOL? That's the story of MSN Explorer, the new online service that gives users Internet access (if they choose); an online community with chats, articles, experts, and more; Web-based e-mail; and smooth integration with Windows Messenger. And all this is free, for Windows XP users (if you have your own Internet service somewhere else). If you choose to go to Microsoft for the whole package, you can purchase Internet access from that company, and that takes care of all the Web features you need.

Starting MSN Explorer

Remember when you were first setting up an Internet connection with the New Connection Wizard? One choice involved using MSN Explorer as your online service of choice. If you had your own ISP, chances are that you skipped that option then; but if you want to set MSN Explorer up at any point in the future, you can go back to that point and choose the necessary option. Here's a quick reminder of the steps:

1. Click Start and choose Control Panel.

2. Click Network and Internet Connections; then choose Set up or change your Internet connection.

3. In the Connections tab of the Internet Properties dialog box, click Setup. The New Connection Wizard starts. Click Next to get through the introductory page.

4. On the Network Connection Type page, leave the first option selected and click Next.

5. On the Getting Ready page, leave the first option, Choose from a list of Internet service providers and click Next.

6. The Completing the New Connection Wizard page gives you the option of getting online with MSN or selecting from a list of ISPs. Leave the MSN option selected and click Finish. The MSN Explorer window appears, as shown in Figure 2.21.

7. Enter your password or, if you don't yet have a password, simply click Sign In to get your account information set up with MSN.

Exploring, Uh, Explorer

You have to admit, the graphics and colors in MSN Explorer are cool. The whole experience is pretty low key, probably because it was designed in Seattle. You get one of those friendly "Good morning!" voices when you log on (a direct knock-off from AOL, but it doesn't rankle quite as much). The screen is inviting and easy to figure out.

As you can see from Figure 2.22, in the typical MSN Explorer window the tools are oversized and colorful, positioned across the top of the browser window. Tasks are placed in the column to the left of the browser window, enabling you to check your calendar, see how your stocks are doing, chat with friends, or play around with your digital photos without leaving the main window.

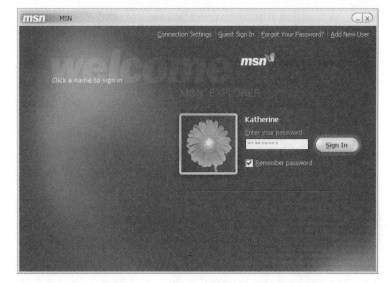

Figure 2.21

MSN Explorer displays its welcome screen so that you can sign in and log on.

Figure 2.22

The MSN Explorer window is colorful and easy to understand.

A look around the screen shows you the elements you've come to expect from any online service worth its salt:

⚙ Help & Settings, in the upper-right corner of the MSN window, takes you to the Member Center, where you can customize your MSN Explorer settings.

⚙ The toolbar shows you the way to the Web, e-mail, chat, buddies, shopping, and more.

⚙ The Address bar gives you the means to jump to that Web page you're looking for.

⚙ The browser window shows the current Web page. It's here you find text, graphics, links, and more as you move from page to page.

⚙ The My Stuff column on the left provides links to four areas that MSN thinks you'll want easy access to: My Calendar, My Stocks, My Communities, and My Photos.

⚙ A search box enables you to look quickly for that topic you want to research online.

⚙ The small media player positioned in the lower-left corner of the MSN Explorer window gives you your own, private sound system. When you click Play, you are taken to the Music page so that you can select the type of music you want to hear.

Checking Out the MSN Tool Set

The tools in MSN Explorer are pretty easy to figure out, but Table 2.3 runs through them just the same.

TIP

One extra feature of the MSN Explorer tools is that they let you know when people or messages are waiting. Both the Buddies tool and the E-mail tool display a number if any of your contacts is online or if you have e-mail messages waiting. This feature lets you know to go into those areas sooner rather than later to visit with friends or check your mail.

TABLE 2.3 MSN EXPLORER TOOLS

Button	Name	Description
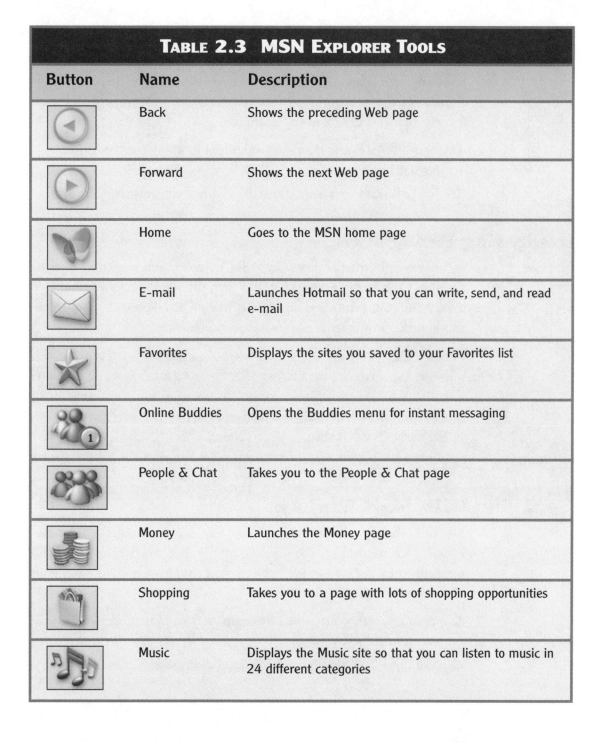	Back	Shows the preceding Web page
	Forward	Shows the next Web page
	Home	Goes to the MSN home page
	E-mail	Launches Hotmail so that you can write, send, and read e-mail
	Favorites	Displays the sites you saved to your Favorites list
	Online Buddies	Opens the Buddies menu for instant messaging
	People & Chat	Takes you to the People & Chat page
	Money	Launches the Money page
	Shopping	Takes you to a page with lots of shopping opportunities
	Music	Displays the Music site so that you can listen to music in 24 different categories

Knowing Your Links

By now, you should know what you're looking for when you watch for links on a Web page. The pages displayed in MSN Explorer are no different from the ones you see in Internet Explorer—or any other browser, for that matter. Here's a quick reminder:

✿ Text links are usually underlined, often in a different color from regular text.

✿ Image links might be pictures of products, drawings, or buttons.

Navigating Web Pages

You navigate in the usual way in MSN Explorer. You might start off by typing a URL in the Address bar and then use the Back tool to move to a previous page. Another time, you might click Forward to move to another page in the sequence you've been following.

TIP   When you find a page you want to keep, click the Favorites tool in the MSN Explorer toolbar. Click Add to Favorites, and a pop-up dialog box appears. Enter a name for the page and click OK. MSN Explorer saves the page so that you can later display it by simply clicking the Favorites button.

E-mailing with MSN Explorer

E-mail is slightly different with MSN Explorer because it's *Web-based e-mail.* That means that the messages stay online, resident in the server maintained by the service itself. Here are a couple of great things about Web-based e-mail:

✿ You can access your e-mail from anyone's computer, anywhere you can connect to the Web.

✿ You don't have to use your own hard disk space to store messages.

A couple of things aren't so great about Web-based e-mail:

○ It's a bit harder to look something up quickly—you have to go online, find the message, and so on.

○ If you can't get online for one reason or another, you can't work with your e-mail. (Even if you are stuck offline for a while with a traditional e-mail program, if you have an e-mail program on your computer, you can compose and respond to messages that you'll send later.)

Reading Your Mail

As soon as you sign on to MSN, you know whether you have mail. You know because the E-mail button in the MSN Explorer toolbar displays a small number if new mail has been sent to you. To read your mail, simply click the E-mail tool in the toolbar. The Hotmail window opens, as you see in Figure 2.23, and your new messages are listed in the My E-mail tab.

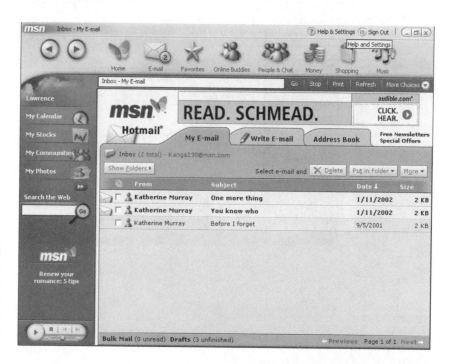

Figure 2.23

The E-mail notification lets you know you have mail. Click the My E-mail tab to see it.

Three options are presented to you at this point—even before you open the message:

○ You can just pitch the message by selecting it and clicking Delete.

○ You can file it away for later in the appropriate folder by clicking Put in Folder.

○ You can click More to perform additional mail-type tasks, such as Check Mail or Organize Folders, or block the person who sent the message to you in the first place.

To read the new message, click the text in the From or Subject columns. The new message opens in the Hotmail window (see Figure 2.24).

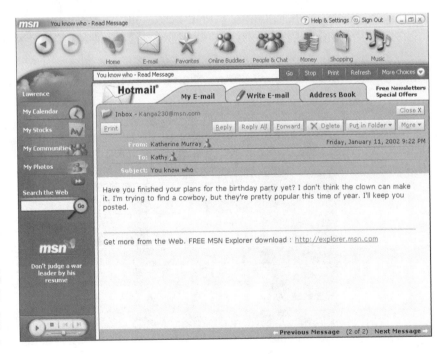

Figure 2.24

Web-based e-mail lets you read, write, and leave your mail online.

"Okay, I Read It—Now What?"

After you open and read the message, you have to figure out what to do with it. MSN Explorer (with the help of Hotmail) gives you the option of printing, replying, forwarding, deleting, or filing the message. Here's a quick overview of these different mail management tasks:

- To print the message, click Print, choose whether you want to print the current frame (in which the e-mail message is displayed) or the whole screen, and then click Print.

- To reply to it, click Reply, type your message, and click Send. If you were one of many people who received the message, you can click Reply All if you want to send a response to everyone who got the first one.

- To forward the message to someone else, click Forward, and choose the recipient from your Address Book. If you want to add a message at the top of the forwarded message, click and type it—then click Send.

- To file the message in a folder, click Put in Folder. Then choose whether you want to save the message online or on your hard disk.

- To delete the message, select it and click Delete.

- To close it, just click Close. MSN Explorer leaves the e-mail messages in your My E-mail tab forever, until you do something with them.

Writing E-mail

The process of writing a message with MSN Explorer is as simple as reading one. First, click the Write E-mail tab. A blank e-mail window appears, listing your Address Book entries on the right side of the screen—a nice convenience (see Figure 2.25).

Click someone in your Address Book to add the name to the To: line or type the e-mail address directly in the line. Next, type a topic in the Subject line. Change the look of the text, if you want, by changing the font,

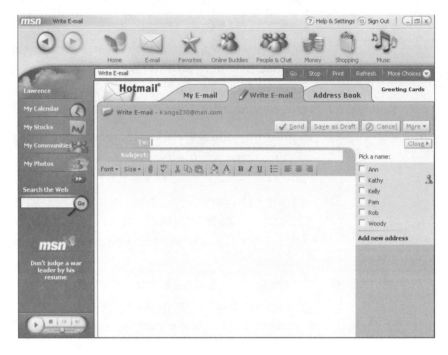

Figure 2.25

Writing e-mail online with MSN Explorer.

size, color, style, and alignment options. Then simply type your message and click Send. MSN Explorer displays a message saying that your message has been sent.

TIP Your message might not be ready to send right away—you can save a draft of the message to send later, if you like. Just click Save as Draft to save what you've done so far. MSN displays a message box telling you that the message will be saved in your Drafts folder.

Adding People to Your Online Address Book

As you've seen, the MSN Explorer Address Book displays names to the right of the message area when you're working in the Create E-mail tab. That's a nice feature. You can easily add to and organize the names in your Address Book by clicking the Address Book tab (see Figure 2.26).

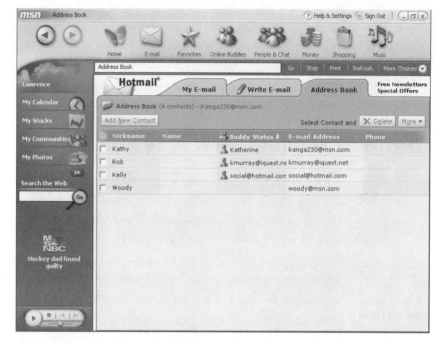

Figure 2.26

Even the Address
Book is online
when you're
working with
Web-based e-mail.

You can add a new entry in your Address Book by following these steps:

1. Click the Add New Contact button. A dialog box pops up on the screen so that you can add information.

2. Enter the nickname of the person you want to add.

3. Type the e-mail address.

4. If you want the new contact to be available through Online Buddies, click the Add to Online Buddies check box.

5. Enter the name and phone information if applicable.

6. Click OK to save the information. Hotmail adds the name to your Address Book, and it is available the next time you begin to write a message or click the Address Book tab.

> **TIP** When you're working in the Write E-mail tab, you can add addresses quickly by clicking the Add New Address link just beneath the names from the Address Book. Simply enter the new information and click OK.

Windows Messenger, Anyone?

> **NOTE** You've probably been hearing about Windows Messenger—it's an instant pop-up messaging program that lets your friends and coworkers know when you're online and willing to receive mini-messages. Windows Messenger is well-connected; you can get it through Hotmail (**http://www.hotmail.com**), from the Windows Web site, in MSN Explorer, and probably on men's room walls. The great thing about Windows Messenger, besides the fact that it's free, is that it's simple and fast. And it's built right into Windows XP.

The Windows Messenger window is a small pop-up box that lists any online and offline buddies you may have (see Figure 2.27).

Figure 2.27

The Windows Messenger pop-up box shows you who's online and who isn't.

NOTE

When you log on, you may see that a new version of Windows Messenger is available. The newest version, version 4.6 as I was writing this book, includes add-ins for Windows Messenger from third-party developers, which can make Windows Messenger more fun and useful: e-mail; chat; mobile text messaging; create-your-own user profile; voice calls from your computer to a phone anywhere in the world;, and improved Help screens.

To send a message, you simply click one of your online contacts and a chat-like window appears. The Windows Messenger window gives you plenty of room to talk, as Figure 2.28 shows. Type the message you want to send in the box at the bottom of the window; then click Send. The message is sent to the recipient, and a notification box appears on his screen. He can then respond, and his response shows up in your message window instantly. It's almost like real-time, voice-to-voice communication.

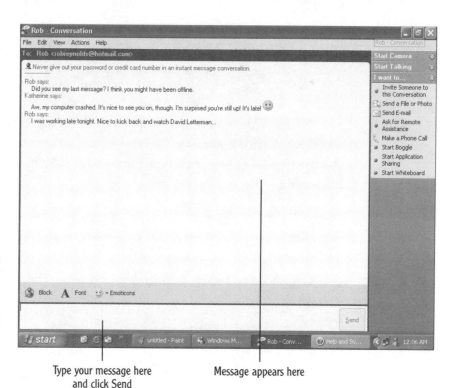

Figure 2.28

The newest version of Windows Messenger borrows the look and feel of a chat room.

Type your message here and click Send

Message appears here

Windows Messenger also enables you to use your videocamera and microphone, if you choose, and if one of the recipients is running Windows 2000, you can even launch NetMeeting from within Messenger. (Note that this capability isn't available in XP, although you can launch NetMeeting separately and hold a conference with your online buddies.)

The newest version of Messenger also supports voice-to-voice calls, application sharing, and whiteboarding (the last two features are part of NetMeeting). See some overlap here? Windows XP wants to make it as easy as possible for you to communicate—and it seems that every which way you turn, a new feature can help you do just that.

When you're ready to end your instant conversation, simply click the Close button to exit the program. The next time one of your buddies goes online, if Windows Messenger is still active on your computer, you are notified so that you can start a conversation if you choose.

We've Got to Stop NetMeeting Like This

The NetMeeting program has been around for a long time in previous versions of Windows. But it's never been as slick and easy to use as it is now. NetMeeting is a communications tool that enables you to meet with other people either over the Internet or on a company intranet to talk about projects, clients, vacation time—whatever. Using the features in NetMeeting, you can do the following:

- Talk voice-to-voice about a project.
- Sketch on a whiteboard that everyone can see.
- Share applications—for example, you can show everyone the new photo editor on your system and demo the new logo you're developing.
- Show video of yourself or a presentation.
- Send files to participants.

Starting NetMeeting

The steps for starting NetMeeting area simple. You begin at the Start menu.

1. Click Start to display the Start menu.

2. Point to All Programs. The program list appears.

3. Point first to Accessories and then to Communications. When the submenu appears, click NetMeeting.

Setting Up NetMeeting

The first time you launch NetMeeting, a wizard helps you get everything up and running so that your meeting goes smoothly. Here are the steps:

1. As soon as you start the program, the NetMeeting wizard begins. Read the introductory screen and click Next.

2. Fill in your personal information. Your name and e-mail address are mandatory—everything else is optional. After you enter the information, click Next.

3. You are asked how you want to handle the directory server. The Microsoft directory server lists people you can call using NetMeeting. If you log on, the people in the directory see your name and can call you unless you specify otherwise. If you want to log on to the server and remain anonymous, click the Do not list my name in directory check box. Click Next.

4. The next page asks you to choose your modem speed. Most likely, the speed of the modem on your current system is already selected. Click Next to continue.

5. The wizard asks whether you want to add a NetMeeting shortcut to your desktop and also put one in the Quick Launch bar. It's your choice, but it's convenient to do so. Click Next to continue.

6. The Audio Tuning Wizard starts to configure your microphone— the test plays a funky percussion beat that was enough to wake up

my cat and cause my son to call from the other room, "What was *that*?" After the test is done, click Next.

7. The next page tests the recording volume of your microphone. Make sure that your mic is plugged in and turned on and then say a few words for the people at home.

8. That's all there is to it. NetMeeting is ready for you. Click Finish to wrap things up.

Now you can launch NetMeeting by simply double-clicking the Net-Meeting icon on your desktop (or clicking the mini-icon in the Quick Launch bar). Assuming that you are still connected to the Internet, Net-Meeting launches, and you're ready to meet.

Checking Out the NetMeeting Window

The NetMeeting window is a compact screen that gives you a number of important tools (see Figure 2.29). In this window, you do all the management required in your online meeting.

Figure 2.29

NetMeeting enables you to meet with others online in real-time.

The menus across the top of the NetMeeting window enable you to do the following:

- The Call menu contains commands related to making, receiving, and managing calls.
- The View menu enables you to control what's being displayed on-screen during the meeting and how it is displayed.
- The Tools menu provides you with the means of working with video and audio and enables and disables the various features (sharing, chat, whiteboard, and file transfer).
- Help gives you—you guessed it—help.

The Name list shows the number of participants in your current meeting. Above and below the Name list, as well as to the right of the video window, are a collection of NetMeeting tools. Table 2.4 gives you a brief description of the function of those tools.

Hosting a Meeting

If you are the host of the meeting, you are the one setting things up and inviting people to join you at your computer at a certain time on a certain day. You are the one in the power seat—you get to determine which tools you want to use, whether security is required for the meeting (only those with the secret password gain entrance), and whether you want to control who gets to place and accept calls. You make all these decisions in the Host a Meeting dialog box, which you display by clicking the Call menu and choosing Host a meeting (see Figure 2.30).

The most important things about the Host a Meeting dialog box are the meeting settings. If you assign a password to the meeting, it is sent as an encrypted password to participants. Before they can join the meeting, they must provide the password. Similarly, you can require that all participants call in on a secure line by checking the Require security for this meeting check box. Granted—who among us runs such important hush-hush calls from home? But Windows XP prides itself for its increased security, so the features are in there—just in case.

TABLE 2.4 NetMeeting Tools

Button	Name	Description
	Address	Enter the address of the person you want to call
	Place call	Dials the address given
	End call	Stops the call
	Find	Allows you to locate someone in the directory
	Stop/Start video	Acts as a toggle to stop and restart video transmission
	Picture-in-Picture	Displays a small video frame in the lower corner of the larger display
	Adjust Audio Volume	Allows you to reset your audio settings as needed
	Share Program	Enables you to share a program on your computer with meeting participants
	Chat	Opens a chat window
	Whiteboard	Displays a whiteboard for participants to use
	Transfer Files	Opens a window in which participants can send files to each other

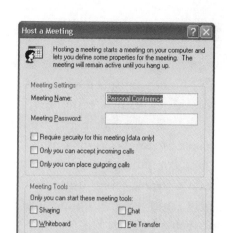

Figure 2.30

You can make hosting decisions in this dialog box.

If you decide to have a more open meeting, you can allow participants to both receive and make calls—and let those callers join in the meeting— if you choose. If you like that kind of open-door policy, leave the two check boxes in the bottom of the Meeting Settings area unchecked. If you want to be the only one who can make and receive calls in the middle of the meeting, click the check boxes to select the options.

The final group of options in the Host a Meeting dialog box has to do with who gets to launch applications and when. If you want to be the one to control whether the whiteboard is used (which isn't a bad idea if you have doodlers in the crowd), click these tool check boxes to guarantee that you're running the show. When you've set up the meeting the way you want it, click OK and you're ready to roll.

Ending a Call

When all the fun's over and you're ready to put away your dry-erase markers for another day, you simply click End Call and the connections are disabled. Close the NetMeeting window by clicking the Call menu and choosing Exit.

Home Networking 101

Why in the world would anyone want to create a home network? How about "Because you can"? It's not unusual now for the all-American home to have two or maybe even three personal computers. Dad and Mom may have the big system in the den; the kids may have the Compaq in the family room; and of course there's always the laptop to use when you get the chance. Linking those computers together—so that different members of the family can do different things using the same programs—or making it possible to play games together online or trade data from computer to computer isn't such a bad idea.

Computers on a network can share a single Internet connection so that Dad can check e-mail while Junior's getting game codes on the Web. A network connection also means that you can share other resources, like a printer or scanner, even if the printer's in the den while the computer's in the family room. Pretty cool.

You can also set up folders on the computer in a way that helps you stay organized—no more carrying a disk from one computer to another, trying to find the piece of the report you worked on last weekend. Just look in the network folders, and you're sure to find the mystery file—right where you left it.

What does it take to create a home network? A few simple things:

- Time
- Hardware
- Know-how

Windows XP offers you the software you need and helps you put the whole network together successfully. In this section, you get a quick overview of the process—just in case you're thinking of taking that next networking step.

What Do You Need for a Home Network?

Most likely, you'll create your home network in stages. The first things you need to start with are the following:

○ Two or more computers, with the primary system running Windows XP and the other system (or systems) running Windows XP, Windows Me, or Windows 98

○ The right network adapter for the type of network you want to create

NOTE **Definition:** A **network adapter card** is a device that enables the computer to be connected to a network. The card is also sometimes called a network interface card (NIC) or simply a network card.

The easiest type of network to set up in a home is the HPNA (Home Phoneline Network Adapter), which allows your PCs to simply use phone lines to connect. Using simple telephone cabling and phone jacks, you can connect your computer through the existing wiring in your house.

NOTE For more information on choosing the type of network you need and making a shopping list of the necessary hardware and cabling, click Start, choose Help and Support Center, choose Networking and the Web, and click Home and small office networking. You can then read through a series of articles on planning, assembling, and testing a home network.

After the Setup: Running the Wizard

NEW IN ▶
WINDOWS XP
After you have everything set up and ready to run, you simply run the Network Setup Wizard to configure the network adapters, set up the shared Internet connection, create the shared folders, and establish the

shared devices (such as the printer and scanner your network might share).

To run the wizard, follow these steps:

1. Click the Start button and choose Control Panel.

2. Choose Network and Internet Connections and then select Set up or change your home or small office network. This step launches the Network Setup Wizard (see Figure 2.31).

3. Follow the prompts as the network walks you through the process of configuring the various components in your home network.

Figure 2.31

The last step: Letting the Network Setup Wizard configure everything for you.

Instant Web Pages with the Web Publishing Wizard

NEW IN ▶
WINDOWS XP

The last online offering we explore in this session is the new Web Publishing Wizard available in Windows XP. Publishing information on the Web has never been easier. Want to show the world pictures of that new puppy? Have a new project you're just dying to show off? You can upload the files easily with the help of a friendly wizard. To publish a file to the Web, follow these steps:

1. Begin by opening your My Documents folder.

2. Select the file you want to publish on the Web.

3. In the File and Folder Tasks pane on the left side of the window, choose Publish this file to the Web. The Web Publishing Wizard launches. Click Next.

4. The first page asks whether you want to change your file selection (see Figure 2.32).

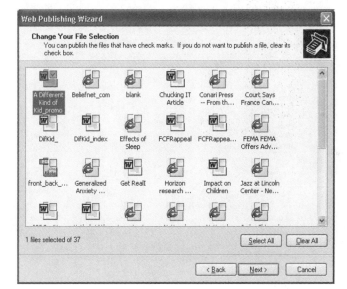

Figure 2.32

The Web Publishing Wizard asks you to double-check the file you're publishing.

5. Select the file or files you want to publish and click Next.

6. The wizard downloads information from the Internet and then asks you to choose a community to host the site (I chose MSN). The two services presented are these:

   ❖ Xdrive Plus, a community for Windows XP users

   ❖ MSN Communities

7. The wizard downloads more information and then gives you the option of selecting where you want to store the published files. You can choose one of the following:

   ✿ My Web Documents

   ✿ Create a new MSN Community

8. Next, the wizard shows you where the files will be posted online (see Figure 2.33). You can change the directories if you choose, but the default address should be fine for most uses.

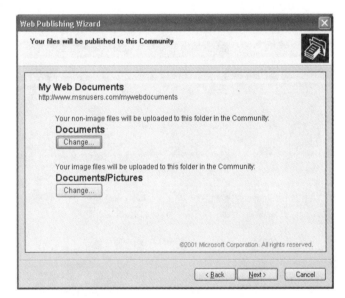

Figure 2.33

The wizard shows you where the file will be published online.

9. Click Next and the wizard begins copying the files to the destination. After a few moments, the wizard displays a notice that the upload was successful and gives you the URL for the published file.

10. Click Next and you see the final page of the wizard. Be sure to click the Open this site when I click Finish check box if you want to view the page on the Web. Click Finish.

11. Congratulations! You're now a published Web page author.

If you chose MSN Communities as the site you want to publish to, when you first go out to the Web site you see that the document is published as a link on the documents page. Click the document title and the file opens in its own Web page (see Figure 2.34).

Now you can send e-mail to all your friends to visit your new site and see those puppy pictures.

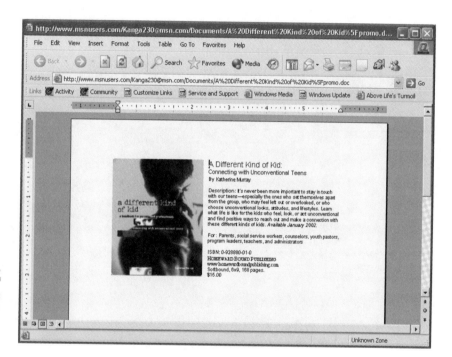

Figure 2.34

There it is, just the way you envisioned it—published on the Web.

What's Next?

Are you worn out? This chapter has covered all of cyberspace—from Web surfing to e-mail to cybermeetings to Web publishing. By now you should have a sense of what online life is all about. Although we've touched on many features, we still have many more to uncover—so take time to explore and experiment with the Web features of Windows XP.

Let's call it a morning—go do something fun (it's Saturday, after all) and I'll see you back here this afternoon, when we talk about something less exciting but equally important: organizing your files and folders.

Handling Files and Folders

- ✿ Windows, folders, and files—an overview
- ✿ Working with My Documents
- ✿ Using Windows Explorer to manage files
- ✿ Taking out the trash
- ✿ Compressing and extracting files

The way you handle the files you create in the programs you run under Windows XP may not sound like an exciting topic. And I won't kid you—it's not nearly as fun or as mind-bending as online topics or as pulse-pounding as media. But file management is one of the more important issues at the core of your computer experience—if you don't know how to keep track of and take care of the items you create on your computer, what good is it? This session shows you how to organize, find, and work with the files you create, download, or inherit. Windows XP has made some good strides in making files and folders easier to manage.

NOTE Notes are scattered throughout this session in the old-fashioned Q&A format, answering common questions about file and folder management issues.

Windows, Folders, and Files—an Overview

Once upon a time, in order to manage the files and folders you created in Windows, you needed to use Windows Explorer, a program that simply makes it easy for you to see and work with the file structure you create on your computer. The problem with Windows Explorer is that it's not as user-friendly as some folks would like and, in earlier versions of

Windows, it wasn't as integrated with applications as they would have liked. If someone wanted to do something simple and fast—like change the name of a file—working with Windows Explorer seemed cumbersome. Today's Windows Explorer, as you see later in this session, is easier to use and works more flexibly with your applications. But the My Documents window, which existed in other versions of Windows but really shines in Windows XP, makes quick file-management tasks easier and more intuitive than ever.

You can also work with files in My Network Places, which becomes important if your computer is part of a local-area or home network. You work with My Network Places to view files on not only your computer but also the other computer connected to the network.

NOTE   "Where do I store files?" When you first begin creating and saving files, the files are placed in the My Documents folder on your Windows desktop. This single folder stores all the files you create—so you never have to go far to find them when you want to work with them again.

File Management Basics

Before we get down to exploring the various tools for managing files and folders in Windows XP, let's take a moment and talk about the basics of file management and learn about some of the tools you use to manage those files. Some definitions and introductions are in order:

○   **File**. A file is, of course, a collection of data you save on your computer disk. A file could be anything—a letter to your mother, a spreadsheet table for your accountant, a listing of your favorite CDs, a résumé, a section of your dissertation, a photo from your digital camera, a cut off the new Wynton Marsalis album, or the video trailer of *Lord of the Rings*, for example. You create your own files *and* use files other people create.

NOTE One of the issues you need to deal with when you use files other people create on their computers is the unfortunate reality of computer viruses. See Sunday morning's session, "Mastering Windows XP Tools & Accessories," for more information on protecting your computer against viruses.

❖ **Folder**. A folder is similar to a file folder in a filing cabinet in that it enables you to group and store similar files. You might create a folder, for example, to store all the documents in your dissertation. Or you might create a folder to save the music samples you download from the Web. However you choose to create folders, the keys are to store them where you'll find them later and name them in such a way that the topic is clearly identified. For more on naming and organizing folders, see the section "Working with Folders," later in this session.

❖ **My Documents folder.** The My Documents folder is the place where all the documents you create in programs running in Windows XP are stored by default. (*By default* means that Windows XP is set to put files in your My Documents automatically, unless you specify a different place or folder on your computer where you want a file to be stored.) You can create additional folders in your My Documents folder to help organize the files stored there. My Documents is the place to work when you want to move, copy, rename, print, or delete a file quickly—if you don't need to do heavy-duty file management tasks (such as archive folders, clean off your hard disk, or reorganize multiple projects), My Documents is your place.

❖ **My Network Places.** If you are working with a computer attached to a local-area network or a home network, you will share some folders. These are called, appropriately enough, *shared folders*. In addition to storing shared folders with files that more than one computer on the network can access, My Network Places contains icons for shared devices, like a shared printer or scanner.

Recycle Bin

- ❖ **Recycle Bin.** When you delete a file or folder—whether you do the deletion in the My Computer folder, Windows Explorer, My Network Places, or somewhere else—the file is sent to the Recycle Bin. It is removed from your computer only when you choose Empty Recycle Bin. See "Taking Out the Trash," later in this session, for more about the Recycle Bin.

My Briefcase

- ❖ **My Briefcase.** Briefcase is helpful if you are working on a networked system and often move versions of files from one place to another and need an easy way of synchronizing them so that you know you're working with the most current version. (Depending on the way your system is set up, My Briefcase may not have been installed by default.)

- ❖ **Windows Explorer.** Windows Explorer is the file management program you use when you want to work with files in a bigger way. When you need to work with multiple files and see all the folders available on the computer (no matter how many users accounts you've set up), you can display the hierarchical tree structure used to display the contents and organization of your computer to make the changes you need to make. Sound confusing? It's not. In the section "Using Windows Explorer to Manage Files," later in this afternoon's session, it all becomes clear as crystal.

NOTE "How can I find my files after I've saved them?" This is the best reason for thinking through the organization of the folders you create. Finding your files—especially if you create a number of them—takes some remembering, unless you put all your documents in the My Documents folder (which is not a bad idea while you're getting used to creating, saving, and finding files). Later in this session, you learn how to search for the files you need.

File and Folder Improvements in Windows XP

One of the great changes Windows XP brings to file management is its new look. Whether you are working in the Control Panel, opening the My Documents folder, or saving a letter you just wrote in Microsoft Word, notice that things look the same—and work the way you expect them to. The File and Folder Tasks pane appears on the left side of the various windows, and the files you will be working with appear in the right pane. This arrangement is consistent throughout the program, making it easier for you to remember the steps you need to take no matter where you are in the program.

NEW IN
WINDOWS XP
In addition to the changes in the appearance of the program, Windows XP has taken steps to make certain tasks more flexible. Now you can publish to the Web or send a file via e-mail without leaving the My Documents folder. You can print a file from either My Documents or Windows Explorer. And you can share folders between users with a simple click of a mouse button.

NOTE "What if we have more than one user on this system?" Because Windows XP supports multiple users, if you have set up individual user accounts, each user will have her own My Documents folder. That allows each user to save her files in My Documents so that the files don't get mixed up. Documents can be shared so that multiple users can access the same programs and files, if needed.

The biggest file and folder improvements in Windows XP can be summed up like this:

- The new look makes managing files and folders easier than ever.
- You can perform a number of file-related tasks—print, e-mail, copy, move, and more—from within the My Documents window.
- Tasks are linked in various places so that you can perform file-management functions when you need them—you don't have to go to a specific window to print a file, for example.

- You now have new options for viewing file and folder details.
- You can make file associations more easily, assigning file types to a greater variety of applications.
- You can compress files and folders on-the-fly, saving space on your hard disk and making files easier to manage and move.

Now that you know what to expect and where to expect it, let's move on to some actual file juggling.

Working with My Documents

The My Documents folder is the place where Windows XP places by default all the files you create—unless you choose a different folder or disk when you save the file. Suppose that you've just written a letter in Word. When you go to save the file by opening the File menu and choosing Save, the Save As dialog box appears, as Figure 3.1 shows. Notice that, in this case, My Documents is the first selection in the displayed list and not the folder selected by default. To save the document in the My Documents folder, double-click it; then type a file name for the file and click Save. That saves the document to your folder, where you can find it again later.

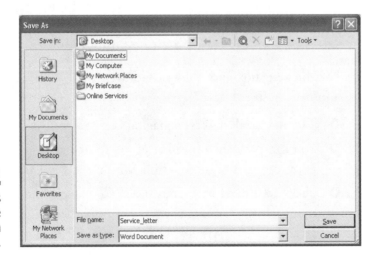

Figure 3.1

My Documents is offered in the Save As dialog box when you save a file.

NOTE

When you save picture files, the default folder offered is My Pictures; when you save media or music files, the default folder is My Music. Both My Music and My Pictures are subfolders within My Documents.

When you want to work with the files you save in My Documents, you can open the folder in two different ways (see Figure 3.2):

⚙ Double-click the My Documents on the desktop.

⚙ Click Start to open the Start menu and click My Documents. The My Documents window opens.

Click the menu selection

Double-click the icon

Figure 3.2

You can open My Documents from the Windows XP desktop or from the Start menu.

Taking a Tour of the My Documents Window

The My Documents folder opens into a full-screen window when you first open it, as Figure 3.3 shows. The display is divided into two panes: the Task pane, giving you various choices for selecting tasks and options, appears on the left; the folders and files in the My Documents folder appear in the pane on the right (see Figure 3.3).

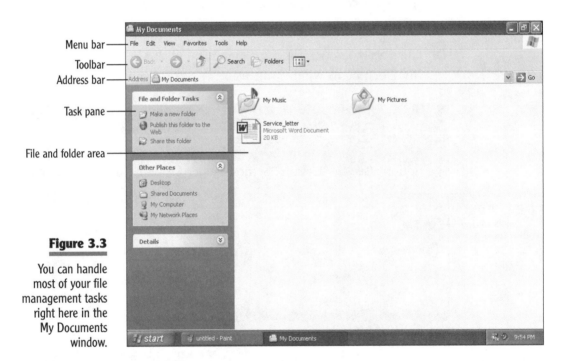

Figure 3.3

You can handle most of your file management tasks right here in the My Documents window.

A Quick Look at the Menus

Similar to other windows you've been viewing, the My Documents folder opens to a window with the familiar title bar, menu bar, and Address bar. Here's what the menus do:

○ **File menu.** Contains commands that enable you to create new files, folders, and shortcuts; delete and rename files; and check file properties.

- **Edit menu.** Includes commands that let you copy, cut, and paste files; copy and move files from one folder to another; and undo your latest operation.

- **View menu.** Enables you to display and hide elements on the screen, including the toolbars, status bar, and Explorer bar. You can also change the way files and folders are displayed by selecting the way icons are arranged and the types of icons used to represent the files.

- **Favorites menu.** The same Favorites menu you see in Internet Explorer, listing your saved Web pages and giving you the option of adding to or organizing the pages you've collected.

- **Tools menu.** Enables you to perform network tasks, such as map a network drive or synchronize files, folders, and drives. Additionally, for the non-networked, the Tools menu enables you to set folder options (see the section "Setting Folder Options," for more about this task).

- **Help menu.** Provides—you guessed it—help. You can click the Help and Support Center option to display the Help system or select an option to help you determine whether your copy of Windows XP is legal.

The My Documents Tools

Beneath the menu bar, you see some familiar tools. Table 3.1 introduces you (or re-introduces you, in some cases) to the tools and gives you an idea of what they do.

The Familiar Address Bar

The Address bar looks identical to the one you see in Internet Explorer—and it is, with one exception. Instead of moving to Web pages (which it *can* do if are you are online), the Address bar displays additional places on your computer where you might want to go. Take a look at Figure 3.4.

TABLE 3.1 MY DOCUMENTS TOOLS		
Tool	**Name**	**Description**
Back ▾	Back	Moves to the last page you viewed
➡ ▾	Forward	Moves to the next page in a sequence
⬆	Up	Displays the folder that the current folder is a part of
🔍 Search	Search	Opens the Search Companion so that you can search for files or folders on your computer or search for something on the Web
📁 Folders	Folders	Displays the Folders task pane, showing the hierarchical structure of the folders and drives on your computer (similar to the Windows Explorer view)
▦ ▾	Views	Opens a drop-down menu so that you can choose a different view for files in the current folder

When you click the down-arrow at the end of the Address bar, you see a listing of drives and major folders on your computer. To move to a new drive or folder, simply click it.

NOTE What's with the Go key? Why is Go positioned out there at the end of the Address bar if all you need to do is click the drive or folder you want to move to? Just in case you type the name of a folder or disk and don't feel like pressing Enter, you can type the phrase or folder name and click Go. Add a little variety to your tasks.

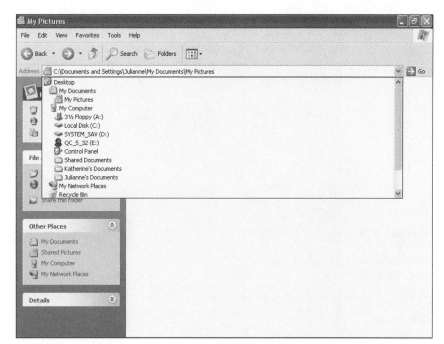

Figure 3.4

The Address bar
enables you to
jump quickly to any
other drive or
folder on your hard
drive.

The Task Pane

NEW IN ►
WINDOWS XP
You've probably noticed by now that there's a similarity among most of
the windows you open in Windows XP. The Task pane, along the left side
of the window, offers options, menu selections, categories, and more—
items you might want to use or places you might want to go while you're
working with the items in the main display area. Whether you are taking
a look at Help, working in My Documents, or opening the Recycle Bin,
notice this same task pane, ready with the helpful commands you need
for carrying out common tasks.

When you are working in My Documents, notice that the items in the
Task pane change depending on what you've selected. For example, compare the screen in Figure 3.5 with Figure 3.3, shown earlier. In Figure 3.5,
the document file is selected and the items in the Task pane all relate to
tasks you might want to accomplish with that file. Figure 3.3 simply
shows, by comparison, the My Documents folder with no specific file
selection. In this case, the focus is on possible folder activities.

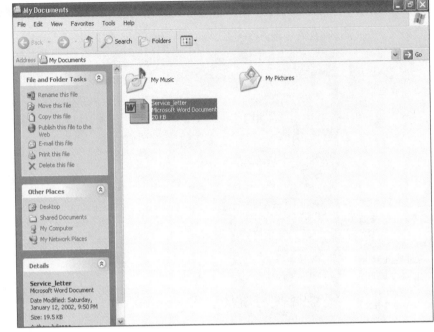

Figure 3.5

The Task pane changes to offer you tasks tailored to the type of file you're working with.

If you select a photo file instead of a document file, the title in the top portion of the Taskbar changes to Picture Tasks and the choices are as follows:

- View as a slide show
- Order prints online
- Print this picture
- Set as desktop background

NOTE For more about working with the Task pane and displaying file details, see "Viewing File Details" later in this session.

The Files and Folders Area

Finally, we come to the main reason for opening the My Documents folder in the first place: the files and folders area. In this area of the window, you see the files and folders that are stored in the My Documents folder. In this window, you can select, move, copy, delete, rename, print, and e-mail files. You can compress files to save space and publish files to the Web, if you choose. And those tasks just happen to be the focus of the next section.

Working with Files

This section walks you through the most common file tasks you'll want to do in the My Documents window. First, though, some basic selection procedures:

- To select a single file, click it.
- To select multiple *contiguous* files (the files are one beside another), click one file, press and hold Shift, and click the additional files.
- To select multiple *noncontiguous* files (files that *aren't* beside one another), click one file, press and hold Ctrl, and click the additional files.
- To select all files in the folder, either open the Edit menu and choose Select All or press Ctrl+A.

Copying and Pasting Files

You may want to copy and paste a file from one place to another when you move a file from your hard disk to a diskette. Copy and paste is actually two operations: first copy and then paste. And you can accomplish this task in two different ways—use the Task pane and *don't* use the Task pane. Here are the steps for both procedures:

Using the Task pane:

1. Select the file you want to copy.

2. In the File and Folder Tasks pane, click Copy this file. The Copy Items dialog box opens so that you can choose the place where you want to paste the copy of the file (see Figure 3.6).

Figure 3.6

When you copy an item using the Task pane, you do the copy-and-paste operation all in one procedure.

3. Click the folder in which you want to paste the copy of the file. If you want to display a subfolder, click the plus sign to the left of the folder name. If you want to create a new folder to store the file, click Make New Folder.

4. Click Copy. The file is copied and placed in the folder you selected.

Using the menus:

1. Select the file you want to copy.

2. Open the Edit menu and choose Copy. (You can instead press Ctrl+C, if you prefer.)

3. Move to the drive or folder where you want to paste the file by clicking the Address bar down-arrow and choosing the new folder for the file. (If you want to paste the file in the same folder, that's okay too.)

4. Paste the file by choosing one of these options:

⚙ Open the Edit menu and choose Paste.

⚙ Press Ctrl+V.

Moving Files

When you want to move files in the My Documents window, start by selecting the files you want to move. Then follow these steps:

1. Click Move this file in the File and Folder Tasks pane. The Move Items dialog box appears.

2. Select the folder to which you want to move the files.

3. Click Move to move the files.

TIP If you make a move and decide you've made a mistake, you can press Ctrl+Z to undo the preceding operation.

Renaming Files

Renaming files is a simple task. Just click the file you want to rename and click Rename this file in the Task pane. The name of the file is highlighted so that you can type the new name. After you enter the name, click outside the file name. Yes, it really is that simple.

Publishing Files to the Web

You learned about publishing files to the Web in this morning's session, "Ready, Set, Online!" You can start the process here, in the Task pane of the My Documents window. Select the file you want to publish and click Publish this file to the Web, in the Task pane. This action launches the Web Publishing Wizard, and, with you following along and answering questions as prompted, the wizard does the rest.

NOTE To get a play-by-play on the process of publishing files to the Web, check out this morning's session.

E-mailing Files

When you want to e-mail a file, you can do it right from the My Documents window. Simply select the file you want to e-mail and then click E-mail this file in the File and Folder Tasks area of the Task pane. This action launches your e-mail utility, and the E-mailing window appears with the file you selected displayed in the Attach box (see Figure 3.7).

In the To box, simply fill in the e-mail address of the person you want to send the file to, change the Subject line if necessary (it's already filled in for you), add text to the body of the message if you want to, and click Send.

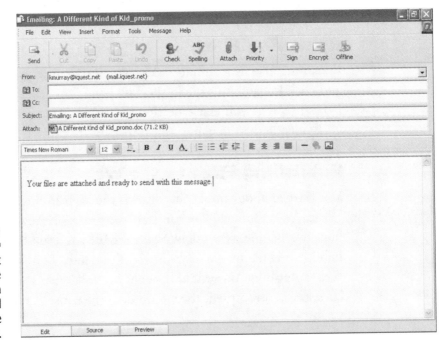

Figure 3.7

The file attachment appears in the header information of the e-mail message you're sending.

Deleting Files

Deleting files is like a two-step dance: Click the file and then click Delete this file. The file goes to the Recycle Bin where you can have all the think-it-over time you want before emptying the trash.

Viewing File Details

One final file trick that can help you work with files more effectively—when you need to check the date and size of a file (perhaps to make sure you're working with the most recent version)—is to display the Details listing at the bottom of the Task pane. Simply follow these steps:

1. Click the file for which you want to display details.

2. Click the Details down-arrow. A list of information about the selected file is displayed, giving you these bits of information:

   - The name of the file
   - The program in which the file was created
   - The date the file was last modified
   - The size of the file
   - The author of the file

NOTE You learn more about working with the Recycle Bin in the section "Taking Out the Trash," later in this session.

Changing the View

Now that you know how to do all the basic tasks in the My Documents folder, you might want to shake things up a bit and tailor the window to your liking. You can change the view by hiding and redisplaying the tool-bars, displaying the status bar, displaying the tip of the day, and adding Explorer bar panes.

Hiding and Redisplaying Toolbars

You can hide and display the various toolbars in the My Documents window—and you can even customize the existing toolbars, if you choose. By default, the standard buttons (which you saw in Table 3.1) and the Address bar are displayed in the My Documents folder window. You can also add the Links bar (which displays the default Web page links you would see in Internet Explorer).

Another item you may want to add—which can be helpful if you're into displaying file detail information—is the status bar. It gives you file or folder information along the bottom of the window.

To hide and redisplay these toolbars in the My Computer window, simply click View to open the menu and then choose the item you want to hide or display. If an item has a check mark, it is already displayed, and clicking it turns the feature off. If an item does not have a check mark, clicking it displays the item.

Turning on the Explorer Bar

Now that you're getting used to the Task pane and know what to look for in the list of commands and options you find there, you will change everything completely with the Explorer bar. This feature is new in Windows XP, part of the integrate-everything-with-the-Web philosophy that is part of the keynote of this new version.

The Explorer bar is a replacement for the Task pane, inserting instead panes you learned about when you were working with Internet Explorer (with one exception—Folders is taken from Windows Explorer, not from Internet Explorer).

To display one of the Explorer bars, simply open the View menu, point to Explorer bar, and choose the bar you want. For example, you can choose these options for the Explorer bar:

- Select Search (or press Ctrl+E) to open the Search Companion, which you can use to search for files on your computer or online.

- Click Favorites (or press Ctrl+I) to display the Favorites pane so that you can click one of your favorite Web sites or add new ones.

- Select Media to open the Windows Media Player in the side pane, along with links to your favorite online media channels.

- Choose History (or press Ctrl+H) to display the History pane and review the Web sites you've visited recently.

- Click Folders to display the Folders pane, which shows the hierarchical tree structure used by Windows Explorer to show the file and folder organization of your computer.

When you want to get rid of the Explorer bar and return to the normal Task pane display, just click the Close button in the upper-right corner of the Explorer bar pane.

Displaying the Tip of the Day

When you're first learning to work with Windows XP and are feeling your way through the My Documents window, you may want to turn on the Tip of the Day feature to get hints and reminders about basic file-management tasks. To display the Tip of the Day, follow these steps:

1. Click View to open the menu.

2. Point to Explorer Bar. The submenu appears.

3. Choose Tip of the Day. The Tip window opens at the bottom of the window (see Figure 3.8).

4. If you want to read through additional tips, click Next tip on the right side of the Tip window.

5. When you are ready to put the tips away, click the Close button to the left of the Tip area.

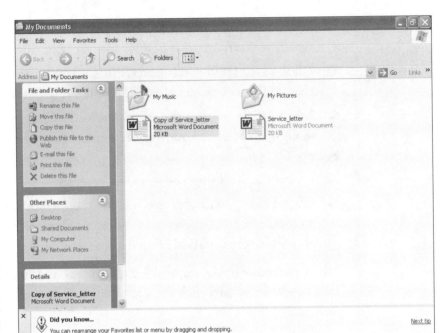

Figure 3.8

Tip of the Day
opens along the
bottom of the My
Documents
window.

Changing the Look of Files

You have only one thing left to do with files in the My Document window: You can change the way they are displayed on the screen. Until you begin accumulating a number of files, you may be fine with the display as it is—but after those files start growing in number, you may look for other ways to fit more information on a screen.

You can change the way files are displayed on the screen by either opening the View menu and choosing the view you want or by clicking the Views tool on the toolbar. Here are the different ways you can view files in My Documents:

○ **Filmstrip.** Displays images in a reduced size along the bottom of the view and shows the selected image larger in the upper-right panel of the Explorer window

○ **Thumbnails.** Shows each image in a box with the file name underneath

☼ **Tiles.** The default; displays the file or folder icon to the left of the file name and size

☼ **Icons.** Shows only the file and folder icon with the appropriate name

☼ **List.** Shows small folder and file icons, presented in list format

☼ **Details.** Uses the list form to display the icons and displays the size, type, and date the file was last modified (see Figure 3.9)

TIP

If you want to apply the look you've selected to all the folders you work with in Windows XP, open the Tools menu, choose Folder Options, click the View tab, and click Apply to All Folders; then click Apply and click OK to close the dialog box. If you decide later that you want to return the folders to their original settings, return to the View tab of the Folder Options dialog box and click Reset All Folders.

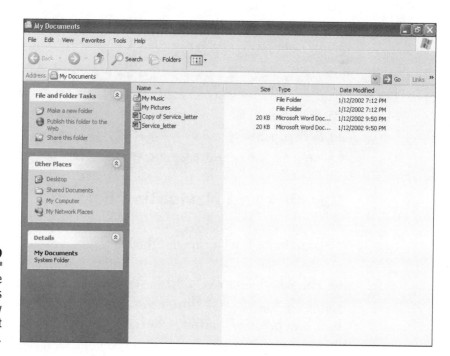

Figure 3.9

You can change the way you view files and folders to show only what you want on-screen.

Working with Folders

Part of creating a smart organization for your files and folders involves thinking through the way in which you'll use the folders you create. What will you need? Organized around what topics? Will you need subfolders—and if so, how many?

Creating folders and then deleting them, renaming them, and moving them are all simple tasks in My Documents. Lucky thing, too, because your folder needs are sure to change as your experience with Windows XP grows. This section walks you through the basic tasks you'll want to accomplish with My Documents.

Creating a New Folder

When you want to create a new folder in the My Documents window, simply click Make a new folder in the File and Folder Tasks pane. A new folder is displayed in the file and folder area, and the name New Folder is highlighted so that you can type a name for the new folder (see Figure 3.10). After you type the name, click outside the folder to deselect it.

 TIP Notice that after the folder is created, the options in the File and Folder Tasks pane change to give you the same opportunities for folder tasks—renaming, copying, moving, deleting, publishing, and e-mailing—that you had for files.

Opening and Navigating Folders

After you create a few new folders, you can move among them by using the tools in the My Documents toolbar (refer to Table 3.1 for more information on the tools, if necessary.) To open a folder, simply double-click it. The new folder area fills the window, and the name of the folder appears in place of My Documents, in the title bar. Notice also that the Back tool becomes available (see Figure 3.11).

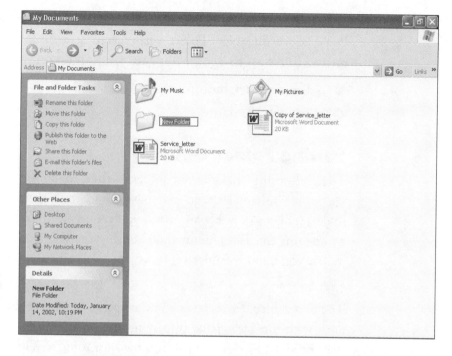

Figure 3.10

Creating a new folder is easy from the Task pane.

Click Back to return to My Documents

The address shows the parent directory

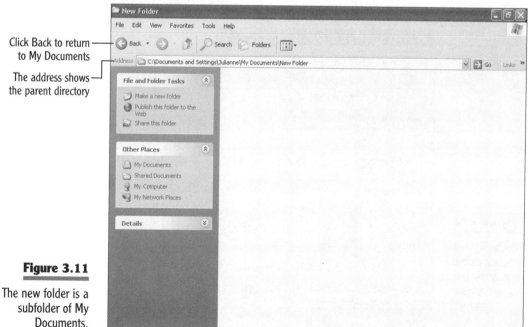

Figure 3.11

The new folder is a subfolder of My Documents.

Notice that the Address bar in the example shows the path of the folder. You can see that New Folder was created as a subfolder of My Documents. To return to My Documents, you can do one of two things:

- Click the Back button.
- Click the Up button.

Setting Folder Options

There's nothing tricky about folders—they are simply the places where you store similar files. You may have some preferences for the way your folders look and act, however, and you can make your preferences known by opening the Tools menu and choosing the Folder Options command. When you choose Folder Options, the dialog box appears, as shown in Figure 3.12.

The first choice, Tasks, gives you the option of leaving things the way they are—with the Tasks pane displaying the most common folder tasks you may need—and changing things back to a retro Windows classic look.

Figure 3.12

Folder Options gives you control over the way your folders look and act.

(In case you've forgotten, or never knew to begin with, Classic Windows simply resembles the My Documents window without the Task pane.)

The second folder option, Browse folders, controls whether the new folder you select opens the same window or a new window. The primary difference between these two options is the use of the navigation buttons Back, Up, and Forward. If you open the folder in a new window, these buttons don't function as they do when the folder is opened in the same window.

The final folder option has to do with the action you need to take in order to open an item. Do you want to single-click or double-click? Double-clicking is the default and, if you have a jumpy mouse pointer finger, that's not a bad choice—otherwise, you wind up opening folders when you really didn't mean to.

TIP If you make changes in the Folder Options dialog box and then decide that you don't like them after all, you can return the settings to their original settings by clicking the Restore Defaults button.

Understanding File Associations

You can tell a file's type by its three-character extension (the three-letter tag after the period in the file's name). Document files, for example, have the file extension .doc, and Windows XP knows that .doc files should be opened by Microsoft Word (if you have that program installed on your system—if not, WordPad can open .doc files). How does Windows know this? Word (or WordPad) creates a file association so that Windows knows that any .doc file can be opened by Word. Other file types—such as the graphic files .bmp or .pcx—are associated with other programs, such as Windows Paint.

Take a Break

Now that you've had a time of file wrangling, it's time to take a break. Try to clear your mind and not think about organizing the glasses in the cabinet or arranging the forks in order of height. After you've had a chance to relax a little—walking the dog, laughing with the kids, washing the car—come back and settle in for the rest of this afternoon's lesson, dealing with saving, importing, exporting, printing, and compressing files.

Using Windows Explorer to Manage Files

As mentioned earlier in this session, Windows Explorer is the file management utility that has been used for several Windows incarnations to enable you to copy, paste, delete, rename, and organize your files. With the great enhancements in My Documents, is Windows Explorer left out in the cold? Different users have different preferences, but people often like working with Windows Explorer when they are working with multiple files and need to do some heavy-duty file management tasks.

Starting Windows Explorer

You can launch Windows Explorer in one of two ways:

- ⚙ Click Start, point to All Programs, click Accessories, and click Windows Explorer.
- ⚙ Right-click the Start button and choose Explore.

Either way, the window shown in Figure 3.13 opens.

NOTE   Windows Explorer lists all the folders stored on your system, whether you have a single user or multiple users on the same computer.

In the Folders pane on the left side of the Windows Explorer window, you see what's known as a *hierarchical tree structure*, which shows by indenting

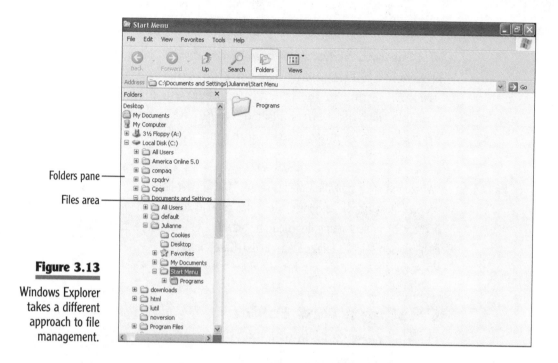

Folders pane —

Files area —

Figure 3.13

Windows Explorer takes a different approach to file management.

folders which folders are subfolders of other folders. The drives and folders are displayed in the hierarchical tree structure, and the files (and subfolders) in the selected folder are displayed on the right side of the window.

WAIT A MINUTE—THIS LOOKS LIKE MY DOCUMENTS!

If you're thinking that the Windows Explorer screen looks much like the My Documents window with the Folders pane displayed, you're absolutely right—it is one of the "seamless" features of Windows XP. If you want to work with Windows Explorer-like features in My Documents, just click the Folders tool to add the hierarchical tree structure. If you decide that you want to go back to the Task pane approach for working with individual files, simply click the Folder pane's Close box to remove it.

Working with Folders in Windows Explorer

Working with folders in Windows Explorer is a bit different from the process in My Documents. For one thing, you've got the hierarchical tree structure getting in the way. For another, you may want to work with multiple files and folders all at once. But don't fret—the process is still simple. It just requires a little more mouse action.

NOTE   "What kind of organization makes sense?" The answer here will be different for different people. Most people organize their files around topics that make sense to them—perhaps by project name, by client, by activity (for example, School, Work, Household), or by person (Mom's folder, Dad's folder, Kate's folder).

Creating a New Folder

Creating a new folder in Windows Explorer is a matter of menu selection. To create a folder, follow these steps:

1. In the Folders pane, click the folder under which you want to create the new folder.

2. Open the File menu and point to New. The submenu appears (see Figure 3.14).

3. Click Folder. The new folder is placed in the selected folders. You can see "New Folder" in the right pane of the window.

4. Rename the folder by typing the name you want to use; press Enter or click outside the folder to accept the name.

Moving Folders

Moving folders in Windows Explorer is a simple matter of dragging the folder from where it is to where you want it to be. To drag the folder, follow these steps:

1. Select the folder you want to move.

Figure 3.14

Click File, New to create a new folder.

2. Press and hold the mouse button while dragging the folder to the new location. Be sure to place the folder on the folder *under which* you want the folder to be placed. The icon and name of the folder move with the pointer so that you can easily see where to position the folder before you release the mouse button.

TIP If you accidentally move the folder to the wrong place, press Ctrl+Z to undo your changes.

Handling Other Folder Management Tasks

After you get down to the basics of cutting, copying, deleting, and renaming folders in Windows Explorer, you can use a single menu to do it all. It's a right-click menu, also called the *context menu,* available when you right-click the folder you want to work with. Figure 3.15 shows you what that menu looks like.

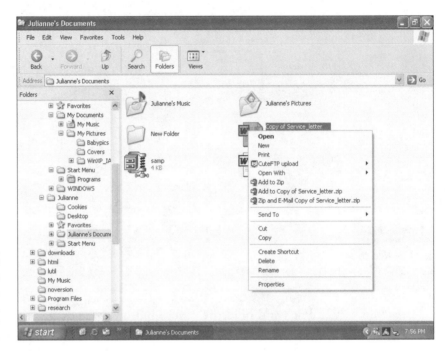

Figure 3.15

When you're working in Windows Explorer, right-click to display the menu.

If you want to copy a folder, for example, follow these steps:

1. Select the folder in the Folders pane.

2. Right-click the folder name. The pop-up menu appears.

3. Click Copy. A copy of the folder in placed on the Windows Clipboard.

4. Right-click the folder into which you want to paste the copied folder.

5. Choose Paste. The folder is pasted in the selected folder.

File Wrangling

When you are working with files in Windows Explorer, the same right-click theme applies. Although you can cut, copy, paste, and move files in Windows Explorer by using the commands in the Edit menu, you can also right-click and use the pop-up menu to help you with the operations. Let's try it:

1. Display Windows Explorer by right-clicking the Start menu and choosing Explorer, if necessary.

2. Click a folder with documents you can play with.

3. Right-click a document in the Files pane. The pop-up menu appears. You can now perform the following tasks from Windows Explorer:

   ✿ Select Open to open the file.

   ✿ Choose New to create a new file of the same type.

   ✿ Click Print to launch the file's application and print the file.

   ✿ Click Open With to choose the program to open the file.

   ✿ Choose Send To to send the file to a disk, folder, or e-mail recipient.

   ✿ Select Cut to remove the file and place it on the Windows Clipboard.

   ✿ Click Copy to copy the file.

   ✿ Choose Create Shortcut to create a shortcut for the file.

   ✿ Select Delete to send the file to the Recycle Bin.

   ✿ Click Rename to select the file name of the file.

   ✿ Choose Properties to display file details.

NOTE "How do I save a file to a 3½-inch disk?" The 3½-inch disk is shown as drive A: in Windows Explorer. You can also save a file from within an application by choosing drive A: in the Save in box before you click Save.

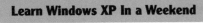

Taking Out the Trash

As you learned earlier in this session, the Recycle Bin is the place where all your files go to be deleted. After you press Delete or click Delete this file, the file is placed in the Recycle Bin until you empty the container.

Sending files to the Recycle Bin instead of deleting them instantly is a great safety net—it keeps you from deleting files you may want to hold on to.

You can open the Recycle Bin into a window just like you can any other window in Windows XP. Checking out the contents of the bin before you delete the contents is a good idea—at least until you get used to working with files and folders. To display the Recycle Bin window, go to the Windows XP desktop and double-click the Recycle Bin. The window opens, as shown in Figure 3.16.

NOTE Deleted items do not stay in the Recycle Bin forever, however. The Recycle Bin has a maximum size based on the size of your hard drive (10 percent is the default), and after this limit is reached, the oldest files are automatically deleted to make room for newer deleted items.

You can empty the Recycle Bin in two different ways:

⚙ Right-click the Recycle Bin and choose Empty Recycle Bin from the pop-up menu.

⚙ In Windows Explorer, scroll down to the Recycle Bin in the Folders pane and right-click the folder name. Click Empty Recycle Bin to erase the contents of the folder.

TIP If you decide that you would rather not delete the items in the Recycle Bin, you can click the Restore all items option in the Recycle Bin Tasks pane of the Recycle Bin window. Windows XP then asks you to confirm the change.

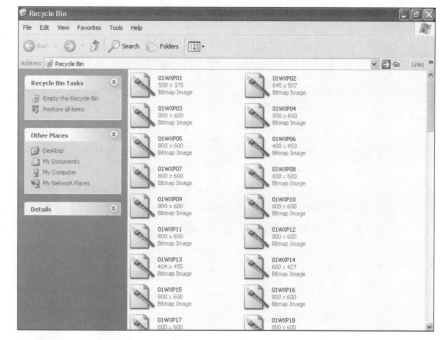

Figure 3.16

You can take a look at the Recycle Bin before you delete what's there.

Compressing and Extracting Files

NEW IN ▶
WINDOWS XP

Compressing files is the process of reducing the size of a file and compacting it to a more manageable size. The reverse process, called *extracting*, is the process of expanding the once-compressed files back to their original size.

When might you want to put your files through this kind of squeeze-me procedure? Here are a few examples:

- You want to save several photos on a disk to send to your mother.
- You have many files attached to an e-mail message that needs to be sent at once.
- You want to archive all documents that are connected with a particular project and make sure that no pieces are left out.

You can compress files in either Windows Explorer or the My Documents window. When you are using My Documents, follow these steps:

1. In the files and folders area, select the files and folders you want to compress. (Remember to press Shift or Ctrl while you click to select multiple files.)

2. Open the File menu and choose WinZip, Add to Zip. This step launches WinZip, if you have it installed on your computer. WinZip is an archive utility for Windows. An opening screen appears, letting you know that the version of the software you are using is for evaluation only. Click I Agree if you accept the conditions and go on to use the compression utility. The Add window opens so that you can add the files to a new archive.

3. Click New and the New Archive dialog box appears.

4. Enter a file name for the archive and click OK. The Add menu is redisplayed.

5. Click Add to add the selected files to the archive. The WinZip window shows you that the files have been added to the archive (see Figure 3.17).

The zipped file is placed in your My Documents window, and you can now close the zipped file and e-mail or copy the zipped file as needed.

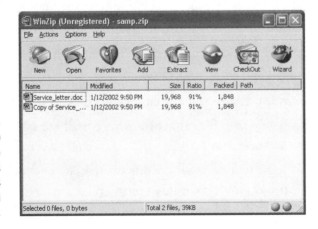

Figure 3.17

If you have WinZip installed, Windows XP helps compress your files in Windows Explorer.

TIP The process of zipping up files in Windows Explorer is similar, except that you access the Add to Zip command by right-clicking the file or files you want to add.

What's Next?

In this afternoon session, you've learned quite a bit about handling files and folders in Windows XP. You've learned about the different tools and the different interfaces you use to create and organize folders and copy, paste, move, rename, delete, e-mail, and print files. It's time to take a break and get a little exercise! When you come back this evening, we'll do a fun Saturday-night kind of session as you master the Windows Media Player in "Now for the Fun Part: Media!"

Now the Fun Part: Media!

- ✿ Imagining the possibilities
- ✿ The easiest way to play: Pop in a CD!
- ✿ A bird's-eye view of Windows Media Player 8.0
- ✿ What's in My Music?
- ✿ Test-driving the Media bar
- ✿ Making your own music
- ✿ Capturing and publishing photos and pictures
- ✿ Directing your own show with Windows Movie Maker

Computers have gotten more fun in the past few years, thank goodness. Sitting down to write a report, create an income statement, or sort a database doesn't have to be something you dread. Researching stock gains and losses, looking into new insurance providers, and copying and moving files from one place to another don't have to be tasks that make your eyes glaze.

Life is better with a sound, color, and *action!*

Now, because of the ever-increasing capabilities of our computers—and more specifically, our computers with Windows XP—we can whistle while we work, surf, chat, or play. Playing your favorite CD is as simple as inserting a disc; watching a movie trailer isn't any more difficult than finding the URL and clicking the mouse button. Whether you want to add color photos to your reports, scan your favorite CD covers, or just add some art to liven things up, Windows XP media features can help you do that. Want to find out more? You're in luck—because this fun stuff is the topic of this evening's session.

Imagining the Possibilities

If you're old enough to remember the 8-track stereo in your big brother's car, you may still be reeling from the introduction of new and smaller media, like the small cassette player, the handheld tape recorder, the Betamax and then the VHS VCR, the portable Walkman, and that odd invention, the CD. (I remember thinking when I saw my first CD player, "Nobody's going to buy those! Cassette tapes and records are all we need!")

And now, those are the old days. Technology has gotten smaller and slicker. VHS tapes are on their way out, to be replaced by DVDs (digital video discs). Our camcorders have shrunk to a quarter of their original size and weight, and we no longer record on tape—now it's all digital (electronic) files. Even our fine 35mm cameras are being traded for digital counterparts—pictures composed of electronic dots on a screen that sometimes rival high-quality prints. And our music: Our music goes with us—on CDs or mini-discs or streams over the Internet; it's real-time music that needs no device other than our computers in order to fill our rooms and our heads with sound.

This is the age of digital media: sound, video, and images that comprise electronic files, packaged and presented in a number of different forms. The benefit is that because a song is a file, you can save it and play it on a number of different devices. You can attach it to an e-mail message; you can put it on a disc. An image is not just a photo in your scrapbook, but rather a file on your hard disk that you can put in a letter, add to a Web page, or send to a friend. After media becomes digital data, its uses are almost endless.

In this session, you work with a number of tools, all geared in their own way toward helping you create, enjoy, capture, or modify digital media. These are the tools you use:

○ **Windows Media Player.** With this CD-player-meets-VCR-and-radio combination, you can watch a movie on DVD, listen to an audio CD, or tune in to any one of hundreds of worldwide Internet radio stations. In addition, you can save clips to make your own playlists and recordings from your personal computer.

○ **Media bar.** Use this feature to listen to recordings, tune to the radio, or watch video on the Internet.

- **Sound Recorder.** This built-in recorder makes the most of your plug-in or built-in microphone and enables you to add your own sounds to system events, documents, and more.
- **Scanner and Camera Wizard.** This automated utility steps you through the process of using digitized photos and images.
- **Online Print Ordering Wizard.** This tool takes you online to find a vendor to print your pictures
- **Windows Movie Maker.** This fun video program enables you to mix a variety of input to create, edit, and play movies.

As you can see, that's a great deal of fast-moving ground to cover before we break for the night. You may want to go grab yourself that last Diet Coke out of the fridge and come right back so that we can get started.

The Easiest Way to Play: Pop in a CD

The first time you ever insert a CD in your CD-ROM drive after you purchase a new Windows XP system or upgrade to the new operating system, a dialog box appears, telling you that Windows can perform the same action each time you insert a disc as you've done here (see Figure 4.1). You click the Windows Media Player option, as shown in the figure, and click the Always do the selected action check box; then click OK. The Windows Media Player launches. From now on, whenever you insert a CD in the drive, Windows Media Player launches automatically.

Some CD producers pack extra multimedia information on an audio CD. When this happens, the CD may surprise you by popping up its own interface, like the one you see. When you click the CD player button, the software will launch Windows Media Player.

Today, CDs are being created with this kind of multimedia approach in mind. But what if you pop in that Duke Ellington CD and the Windows Media Player tells you that he's an "Unknown Artist" (see Figure 4.2)? Older CDs don't always have the artist and track information that newer

CDs have. You can enter the information yourself by clicking Copy from CD, right-clicking the track you want to change, and choosing Edit.

Figure 4.1

You can have Windows Media Player start automatically whenever you insert a CD.

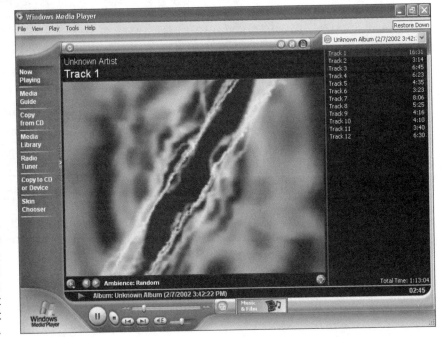

Figure 4.2

Older CDs may not show the artist and track information you want—but you can enter it yourself.

A Bird's-Eye View of Windows Media Player 8.0

The first time you take a good look at the Windows Media Player, you may wonder why the churning display looks like a lava lamp gone wrong (see Figure 4.3). This effect is called a *visualization*. The one you see at first, called *Ambience*, is only one of 12 different visualization styles. And, what's even better—you can download more from the Web. (See the section "Being Creative with Your Visuals," later in this session, for the steps on changing the screen effect.)

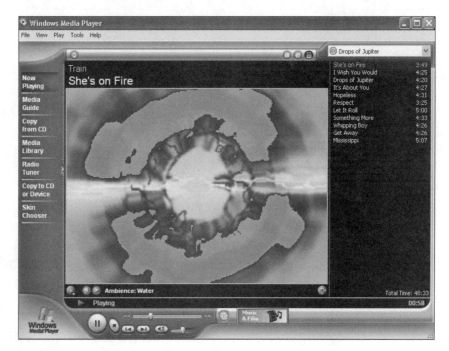

Figure 4.3

The initial display for a music CD is an electronic psychedelic effect.

This section gives you a quick walk-through with Windows Media Player features. There's more here to show—and much more for you to explore on your own. So plug your headphones in and crank up the player—and let's see what's out there for media moguls. First, you need a quick overview of the various features:

- Now Playing is the screen you watch when you're listening to music or watching a video.

- Media Guide is an online entertainment "magazine" that gives you tips on and clips of the latest happenings in entertainment.

- Copy from CD enables you to copy tracks you like from favorite CDs and place the tracks on your hard disk.

- Media Library helps you organize your media files and arrange them by album, artist, or genre.

- Radio Tuner enables you to connect to an online radio station— nearby or around the world.

- Copy to CD or Device is what you use to copy a track or clip from your hard disk to a CD or device.

- Skin Chooser enables you to select a new look for Windows Media Player.

Launching Windows Media Player

Before jumping in too far, let's back up a little and talk about how to launch Windows Media Player when you *don't* put a CD in the drive to fire up the program. If you are planning on watching a DVD, going online to see the latest movie clips, or listening to an NPR interview, you need to know how to launch Media Player on its own. Here are the steps:

1. Click Start to open the Start menu.

2. Point to All Programs. When the program list appears, click Windows Media Player.

TIP

If you are online when you launch Media Player, the Media Guide page appears automatically, providing all kinds of links for music, radio, movies, and other types of entertainment.

No matter which screen you are working with in the Media Player, certain tools are available to you at all times. Table 4.1 gives you a quick look at these tools and explains their functions.

TABLE 4.1 WINDOWS MEDIA PLAYER TOOLS		
Tool	**Name**	**Description**
	Auto hide menu bar	Suppresses the display of the Media Player title bar and menu
	Turn shuffle on/off	Enables or disables random play
	Show equalizer and settings in Now Playing	Displays balance and sound controls in the lower portion of the display window
	Hide/show playlist	Alternately hides and displays the playlist panel
Ophelia	Display playlists & presets	Lists playlists and player preset stations
	Play	Plays the inserted CD or DVD
	Stop	Stops the playing track
	Previous	Begins playing the previous track
	Next	Begins playing the next track

TABLE 4.1 CONTINUED		
Tool	**Name**	**Description**
	Mute	Mutes the sound of the playing track
	Volume	Adjusts the volume of the player
	Seek	Enables you to use a slider to seek a spot in the current song
	Switch to skin mode	Displays the player as a small desktop device
	Rewind	Rewinds current song
	Fast forward	Forwards through current song

Now Playing...on Your Computer

The Now Playing window is the one in which you watch videos or DVDs or follow along with the visualization of an audio track. When you insert a CD and the Windows Media Player launches automatically, it's the Now Playing window that presents you with the wild visualizations you see on-screen. The Now Playing window also includes a number of tools and navigation devices that help you choose the songs you want to play and create the order in which you want to play them. For example, take a look at the Now Playing screen, as shown in Figure 4.4. The artist name and CD name appear at the top of the display area (this is also where the visualizations appear); and the song, or track, names and playing times appear in the playlist area on the right side of the screen.

Figure 4.4

The Now Playing window shows you information about the CD or DVD you've inserted.

If you want to listen to the CD in the order that the songs are presented, you can simply click the Play button in the play controls at the bottom of the screen to start the CD. If you want to play a selected track, simply double-click it.

TIP By simply dragging the songs in the playlist panel to the order in which you want them to play, you can rearrange the order of the songs so that you can hear what you want to hear—when you want to hear it. You also can create your own playlist of songs you mix and match from other CDs and sources. In the "Using the Media Library" section, later in this session, you'll find out how.

Being Creative with Your Visuals

As soon as you begin playing a CD, you notice the visualizations—if you haven't already. Multihued swirls and spikes and constant movement with the flow of the music fill the Media Player window (and your entire screen, if you choose to display full-screen mode).

When the CD begins to play, a new toolbar appears beneath the images that enables you to change the visualization you've selected (see Figure 4.5). To select a different visualization style, click the Select visualization button (the first button in the toolbar), and a pop-up menu of choices appears. Click your new selection, and the screen display changes immediately. You can cycle through the different displays in the new visualization style by using the Next and Previous buttons in the visualizations toolbar.

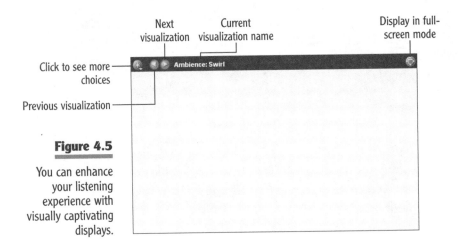

Figure 4.5

You can enhance your listening experience with visually captivating displays.

You can also display these visualizations, and discover the names of the ones you really like, by opening the View menu and choosing Visualizations. When you point to each of the visualization styles (Ambience, Bars, or Waves, for example), a submenu of individual visualizations appears. If you've got some time to play with, choose a few to see which ones you like.

TIP When you get bored with the visualizations that come with Windows Media Player 8.0, you can download more visualizations from the Web: Simply open the Tools menu and choose Download Visualizations. If you're online, the player launches Internet Explorer and takes you to a page that offers the latest and greatest visualizations. You can simply click one you like to begin the download process.

What's On Tonight? Using the Media Guide

When you want to see what's going on with the world outside your own computer, you can click the Media Guide tab of the Windows Media Player. The guide is meant to serve as a kind of electronic entertainment guide, offering you information on celebrities, movies, music, and more. You can download music, watch interviews, sample new visualizations, and more.

TIP One of the great things about the Media Guide is that you can tune in for periodic updates. To control how often you want Media Player to search for updates, open the Tools menu and choose Options. The Options dialog box appears. Click the Player tab and, in the Automatic updates section of the dialog box, choose whether you want to check for updates once a day, once a week, or once a month. The option Download codecs automatically is already enabled for you, meaning that the Media Player automatically checks and downloads the files you need.

The Media Guide, as you can see in Figure 4.6, provides you with many different options. You can search for media, if you like, by typing a phrase in the text box in the upper-left corner and clicking Go. Or, if you decide that you want to explore what's here, you can view movie clips, hear Attorney General Ashcroft's latest press conference, see moving reviews, get add-ons for Windows XP and your portable device, and much more. To move to any of the pages you see that are of interest, simply click the link you want. That action launches Internet Explorer, and you can

Figure 4.6

The Media Guide shows you what's on, what's hot, and what's downloadable.

browse to your heart's content. When you're ready to return to the Media Player, simply click the Internet Explorer Close box.

TIP One interesting thing the Media Guide presents is a link to the free Windows Media Bonus Pack. The Bonus Pack includes skins, which enable you to customize the look of your Media Player, new visualizations, PowerToys, add-ons for Windows Movie Maker, and more. To find out more, go to **http://www.microsoft.com/windows/windowsmedia/download/bonuspack.asp.**

Copying CD Tracks

Gone are the days when CDs were read-only. Now you can make copies of songs you really like—for your own personal use, of course. You use the Copy from CD selection in the player to copy selected files (or the whole album, if you like) to your computer so that you can listen to them at any time, with or without the CD. To copy songs from a CD to your computer, follow these steps:

1. Display the player's Copy from CD screen.

2. Make sure that check marks appear to the left of the songs you want to copy. Clear the check boxes of songs you *don't* want to copy by clicking them to remove the check marks.

3. Click Copy Music. Windows XP displays a warning screen about music copy protection and offers to place a security feature on the copied songs so that they cannot be copied off your computer. If you want to enable this protection, leave the Do not protect content check box cleared. If you want to remove the protection, click the check box. Click OK to continue.

4. The player begins copying the selected tracks to your computer. The status of the copy is shown in the Copy Status column (see Figure 4.7).

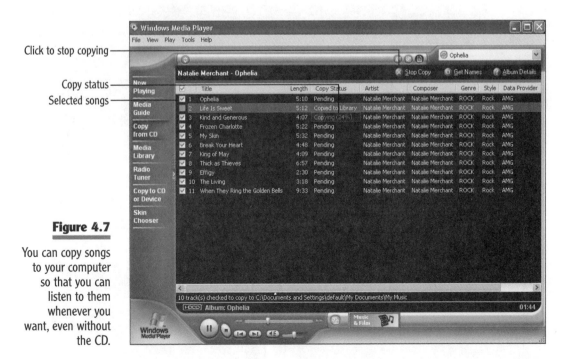

Figure 4.7

You can copy songs to your computer so that you can listen to them whenever you want, even without the CD.

TIP

■ ■

As you might expect, sound files can be **huge.** Windows XP needs to be really smart, therefore, about compressing the sound files you save on your computer—otherwise, you run out of disk storage pretty fast. You can help Windows XP economize disk space by opening the Tools menu, choosing Options, and clicking the Copy Music tab. Drag the Copy music at this quality slider to the point on the bar where you want it. At the smallest-size end, you get the poorest listening quality; at the best-quality end, you get the largest files. You may need to try out the setting a few times to determine which listening quality is right for you. Click OK to close the Options dialog box.

■ ■

The Copy from CD window also enables you to get more information about the artist and album you're interested in. When you click the Show Details button, a panel of information on the album, with links to WindowsMedia.com, appears in the bottom portion of the window (see Figure 4.8).

Figure 4.8

You can get more information about the album you're considering by clicking Album Details.

TIP Before you insert a CD you want to copy, make sure that your computer is connected to the Internet. If you are, Media Player searches for the title, track names, and even the album cover art of the CD you inserted. Most CDs, even obscure ones, are in the online database. After finding your CD, Media Player stores the title and song titles, which saves you from entering the names yourself.

Using the Media Library

You use the Media Library in the Windows Media Player to organize and store the digital music files you collect. In this window, you can save links to media you want to visit again, create and order your playlists, and arrange your music and videos by title, genre, and artist. You can also use the Media Library to download your music to a portable media device if you just can't be without your tunes.

When you click Media Library for the first time, the Windows Media Player tells you that you haven't yet done a search for all the media on your system and asks whether it's okay to do one now. Click OK and the utility searches for all your files. When the search is finished, click OK and the Media Library window appears.

In the left panel of the window, you see several types of information: Audio, Video, My Playlists, Radio Tuner Presets, and Deleted Items. Audio is selected by default. The right panel lists any tracks you have copied to the library (see Figure 4.9).

Creating and Using Your Own Playlists

Although you use the Media Library to do many things, your most common task is likely to be creating new playlists. A *playlist* is what it sounds like—a list of songs you want to play. You control the order, the artist, the album—even the genre. You can mix and match your favorite songs in

Figure 4.9

The Media Library enables you to organize the songs and videos you want to save and use.

any way you want to hear them. To create a playlist in the Media Library, follow these steps:

1. Click the New playlist button above the left panel in the player window. The New Playlist dialog box appears.

2. Type a name for the playlist and click OK. The new playlist appears in the My Playlist category in the column in the left panel.

Now that you've got the playlist, you need to add songs to it. To do that, select the songs you want to add in the panel on the right; then click the Add to playlist button. A drop-down menu appears, displaying the names of available playlists. Click the playlist you just created, and the selected songs are added to the list (see Figure 4.10).

TIP You can add songs to your playlist quickly by simply selecting them in the song panel and dragging them to the name of the playlist displayed in the panel on the left.

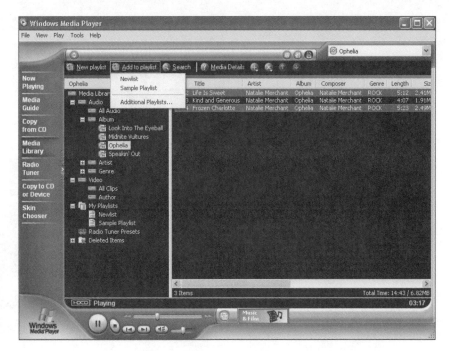

Figure 4.10

After you create a
playlist, you can
add songs to it
easily.

The only thing you need to know now is how to select and play the list
you've just created. Whenever you want to play the new list, simply click
the selection down-arrow in the upper-right corner of the Media Library
window. A drop-down list of playlists and preset stations and sites
appears. Click your playlist to select it (see Figure 4.11). The list is loaded
and begins playing immediately with the first song in the list.

TIP

If you've created a playlist for your computer and the songs aren't playing in the right
order, you may have Shuffle turned on. Shuffle selects songs at random and plays them
out of order. To turn Shuffle off, click the Shuffle button in the top edge of the Media
Player frame or open the Play menu and click Shuffle to deselect it.

This section has just touched on a few of the more common tasks you'll
try with Media Library—I could write a whole session on the features in

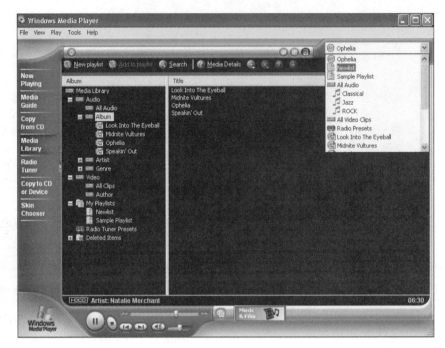

Figure 4.11

Selecting your
playlist is as simple
as point-and-click.

this one part of Windows Media Player! Be sure to come back and explore more when you have the time—you're sure to find many things that make your time at your computer more pleasant, and more musical, too.

On the Web Radio

When you select the Radio Tuner option in the Media Player, Windows-Media.com appears, bringing with it a wide selection of featured radio stations that are broadcasting on the Web (see Figure 4.12). You can listen in on what the station's playing, go to the station's Web site, or add a station to your own list of favorite stations by simply clicking your choice. (For more on setting up radio stations according to your preferences, see "Setting Up Your Own Radio Stations," later in this session.)

Figure 4.12

The Radio Tuner takes you to the world of Internet radio.

 TIP The stations shown here are only the tiniest tip of the radio iceberg. Use the Find More Stations link to search all over the world for stations that play the kind of music or host the kind of talk you want to hear.

Copying Your Media Files

The Media Player's Copy to CD or Device option allows you to download to a handheld device or a CD burner the music you've saved. If you don't have either of these devices, you can save that feature for future reference.

When you choose Copy to CD or Device, the player searches for the connected device and then prompts you to connect the device and press F5 to copy. The selected songs displayed in the left panel are copied to your device (see Figure 4.13).

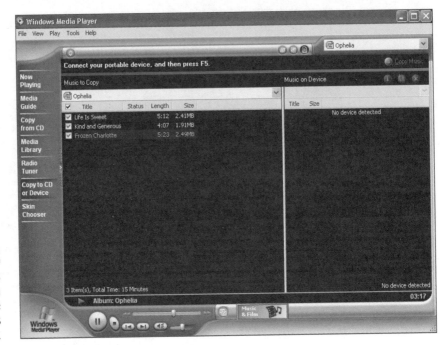

Figure 4.13

You can copy songs and video clips to a portable device using the Windows Media Player.

Choosing a New Skin

We live in a time of changing form—we are accustomed to things changing form and taking on new shapes as they are improved and enhanced. Now Windows Media Player gives you the option of doing the same thing with your media device. You can use the Skin Chooser to select the look you want for the player—whether it's full-screen or handheld size. Click Skin Chooser to see your initial selections (see Figure 4.14).

Browse through the list and choose the one you want to try. Click Apply Skin to try on the skin. The player appears on your desktop, sporting the new look (see Figure 4.15). To discover what the buttons are on the new skin, simply position the mouse pointer over them, and a name label appears. A small control box also appears in the lower-right corner of the window, displaying the Return to Full Mode button. You can minimize the display of this button box, so that only the player is displayed on-screen, by clicking the Minimize button. When you want to return to the

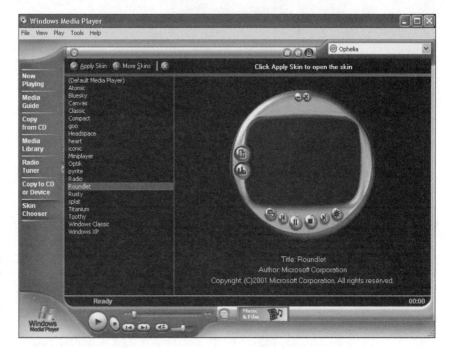

Figure 4.14

The Skin Chooser presents 15 different designs for the Media Player.

Figure 4.15

The skins are small versions of the full player, taking up less room on-screen, but still fun.

full-screen version of Windows Media Player, you can click the Return to Full Mode button on the skin (usually along the bottom) or restore the button box and click Full Mode there.

TIP Similar to the way Windows XP handles visualizations, it doesn't want you to get bored with the skin collection you've got. To get more skins, click the More Skins button in the top of the Skin Chooser window. If you are online, this click takes you to a Web page in which you can sample and download additional skins.

What's in My Music?

The My Music folder is the physical place on your computer where all your music files are stored. In this afternoon's session, you learned how to navigate the My Documents folder and discovered the different choices and commands used to work with the files and folders you create. The My Music folder is similar to My Documents, except that this is where you store music files you download, record, and copy.

You'll find My Music inside the My Documents folder. To get there, double-click My Documents; then locate My Music and double-click that icon. The folder opens on the screen, as Figure 4.16 shows.

The primary differences in the My Music folder are the options in the Music Tasks portion of the left panel. When you click a folder or song (folders are typically albums, and individual songs are tracks from an album), you see two options in the Music Tasks area: Play selection and Shop for music online.

- ✪ Click Play selection to launch the Windows Media Player and listen to the album.

- ✪ Click Shop for music online to display musical selections you can add to your collection. If you are already online, you are taken to the Shop for Music Online page, where you can search for the artist you want to find and listen to a sample of the music before you buy (see Figure 4.17).

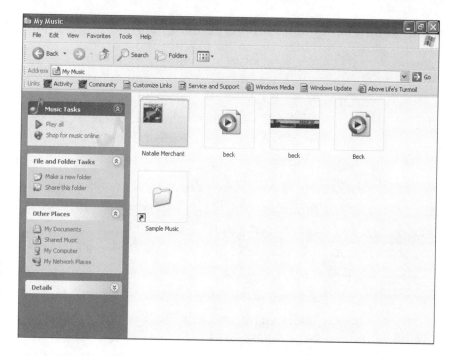

Figure 4.16

Windows XP stores all your music files in your My Music folder.

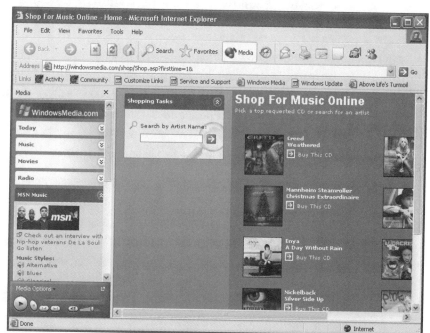

Figure 4.17

You can shop for music online from Music Tasks in the My Music folder.

Test-Driving the Media Bar

NEW IN ▶ WINDOWS XP

The new Media bar is an addition to Internet Explorer. Sing along while you surf; listen to online radio stations; watch your favorite news commentators; listen to a lecturer while you research the report you're writing—all with the simple click of a button in the Internet Explorer toolbar. When you click the Media button, the Media bar appears, as you see in Figure 4.18. The Media bar includes the following choices:

- My Music displays the My Music folder on your computer. You find a few sample files here when you first begin, but *nothing* like the samples you find on the Web.

- My Video also displays video clips you have on your machine.

- More Media takes you to the MSN.com Web site, where you can listen to music, view photos, play games, and more.

- Radio Guide opens the Radio Guide, hosted by WindowsMedia. com. You can add radio stations to your own list of radio favorites, listen in, and visit a station's Web site.

NOTE When you are listening to or watching media files online, you are experiencing streaming media. **Streaming** refers to the process of downloading a file in segments, buffering the file and playing the segments it has while downloading and buffering the rest. This process keeps you from having to wait for the entire file to download before you can experience it; streaming also makes it possible for you to have the media experience without actually storing the media file on your computer.

When Windows XP is buffering information it is receiving from a media source, the status bar in the bottom of the Windows Media Player or the Media bar lets you know what's going on. If lots of traffic on the Web causes the streaming to be interrupted and the data in the buffer runs out, you may hear a glitch in the recording or lose video transmission for just a moment. Generally, the Windows Media Player recovers on its own, however, and picks up the transmission where it left off.

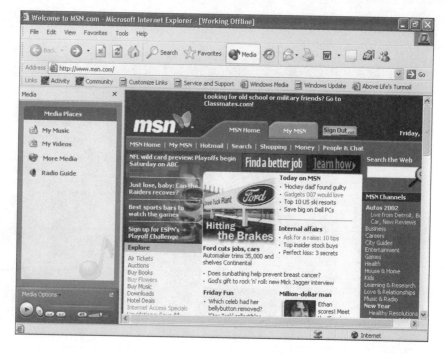

Figure 4.18

The Media bar opens alongside the browser window when you click the Media tool.

Playing a Media File

Let's try playing a file that is already saved on your computer. Eventually, after you've had a chance to scour the Web a bit, you accumulate quite a collection of favorite artists, radio stations, movie clips, and more. To use the Media bar to play a media file that is already on your computer, follow these steps:

1. With Internet Explorer open and online, click Media to display the Media bar.

2. Click My Videos. Windows XP opens your My Videos folder.

3. By default, you find one sample file in the Windows Movie Maker folder. Double-click the image, and the movie launches in Windows Media Player (see Figure 4.19).

4. To close the Windows Media Player, click the Close box.

5. To return to Internet Explorer, click the Back button in the My Videos toolbar.

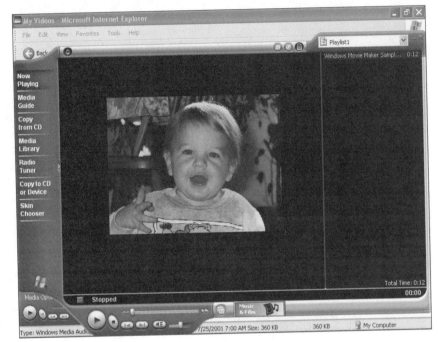

Figure 4.19

When you double-
click the video clip,
it launches in
Windows Media
Player.

Setting Up Your Own Radio Stations

Earlier in this session, you learned that the Radio Tuner in the Windows Media Player displays choices for listening to Web-broadcast radio stations worldwide. The Radio Guide option in the Media bar takes you to the same spot and enables you to choose the stations you want to hear and visit their sites or listen to their programs. Here are the steps for setting up and listening to radio stations online:

1. Click Radio Guide. WindowsMedia.com appears, with three options displayed center stage:

   ⚙ Featured Stations

   ⚙ My Stations

   ⚙ Recently Played Stations

2. Click the Featured Stations down-arrow, and the stations featured by WindowsMedia.com appear in a list.

3. Click a station you want to hear. A description of the radio station appears, as you see in Figure 4.20, giving you the following information:

   ✿ The transmission speed the radio station uses

   ✿ The format (Top 40 or Jazz, for example)

   ✿ The location of the station

   ✿ A description of the station

4. Make your choice from the following items:

   ✿ Add to My Stations

   ✿ Visit Website

   ✿ Play

5. If you want to hear a sample of the station before you add it, click Play.

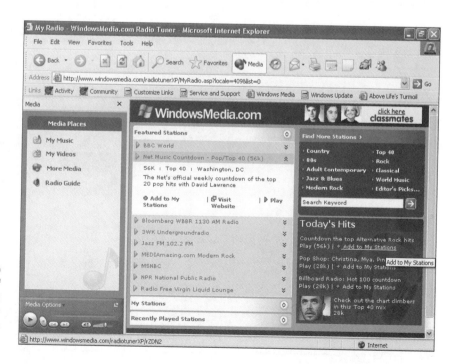

Figure 4.20

Finding and adding radio stations to your own Radio Tuner playlist.

> **TIP**
> After you add a radio station to your station list, you can go to it by simply clicking Radio Guide and then clicking My Stations and selecting the station you want.

Running the Media Bar in a Separate Window

Depending on where you browse and what you want to view, your browser window may be a busy place—you probably want to display as much as possible on your screen. You can separate the Media bar from the Media panel and allow the bar to float over the Web pages you're viewing to give you more room for the browser window. To undock the Media bar, click the Undock Player button in the bottom of the Media bar. The bar is removed from the panel, and you can position it anywhere on the screen you want. You also can go ahead and close the Media panel to get the maximum display space on-screen (see Figure 4.21).

Figure 4.21

When you double-click the video clip, it launches in Windows Media Player.

To start the player, just click the link of the item you want to hear or view. The Media bar begins playing. You can then use one of the following buttons:

○ Click Pause to pause the item.

○ Click Stop to stop the item.

○ Use Mute to turn off the sound (and click it again to turn the sound on).

○ Drag the Volume setting to increase or decrease the volume.

TIP The Previous Track and Next Track buttons are available only if you are listening to a CD with multiple tracks.

If you want to put the Media bar back where it goes, simply click the Dock button in the upper-right corner of the bar. Or, if you prefer, you can just close the bar by clicking the Close button. The next time you display the bar, it is positioned in the Media panel along the left side of the browser window.

Making Your Own Music

You aren't limited to playing only the music of world-reknowned artists in Windows XP: You can assign your own beeps and squacks; you can record your own voice shouting "Woo-hoo! I'm going to Disney World!" You can record a voiceover taken from your television, captured from the Web, or played back from your tape recorder. Whatever noise—I mean *music*—you want to make, Windows XP has some additional tools that let you further tailor the sound capability to ring your chimes.

NOTE To run sound tools on your computer, you must have a sound card and speakers installed in, or available to, your computer. Most newer computers come equipped with sound capability. If you are upgrading to Windows XP instead of purchasing a new system with Windows XP installed, you can check to make sure you have sound capability by going to Sound and Audio Devices in the Control Panel. In the Sound and Audio Devices Properties dialog box, click the Hardware tab to see which sound devices are installed on your system.

Adding Your Own Sound to Common Tasks

You've probably already noticed that your computer beeps and blips at you when you do certain things. When you log on in the morning, for example, you hear that familiar Windows chime. When you try to select an option a program doesn't want you to select, you might hear a metallic "clunk" sound. Other actions might bring up beeps or whistles or bells. Did you know that you can ditch the sounds that annoy you and come up with your own to replace them? Here's how:

First, if you want simply to add *different* sounds to the common events in Windows XP, you start in the Control Panel, with these steps:

1. Click Start and choose Control Panel. The Control Panel window appears.
2. Choose the Sounds, Speech, and Audio Devices option.
3. Click the Sound and Audio Devices options. The dialog box opens.
4. Click the Sound tab, if necessary. In the Program events list, click the name of the event you want to change.
5. Click the Sounds down-arrow, and a huge list of available sounds appears. Click the sound that you want to play when the event occurs (see Figure 4.22).
6. Test the sound by selecting it and clicking Play Sound. Click Stop to stop the sound. If you want to make a change, repeat steps 4 and 5 till you get it right.

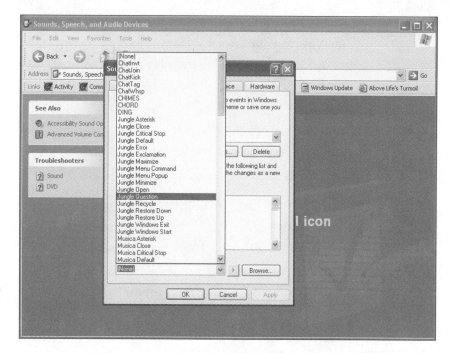

Figure 4.22

You can assign a
new sound to a
program event.

TIP

If you change a number of program events and you want to save them as a group, you can save them as a sound scheme. To do that, display the Sound and Audio Devices Properties dialog box (by opening the Control Panel and clicking Sound and Audio Devices). Start by clicking the Sounds tab and assigning the sounds you want to all the events you see. Then click Save As in the Sound scheme area. Enter a name for the new scheme and click Save. Now the sound scheme is saved, and you can apply it to your current settings by clicking Apply and then OK.

Recording Your Own Sound

Windows XP (and just about every version of Windows before this one) includes a sound-recording device called—not surprisingly—*Sound Recorder*. The Sound Recorder is a simple little device that enables you to record, edit, play, and even mix sounds. You might use Sound Recorder to record yourself saying "Congratulations!" when you send an e-mail message to your friend in Minneapolis who just had triplets. You could record the cat meowing and play it over and over again simply to taunt the dog. What you do with it is your business, but be forewarned: It's a fun and addictive tool.

You find Sound Recorder in the Accessories folder of the All Programs menu. Here's the step-by-step to get you there:

1. Click Start and the Start menu opens.

2. Click All Programs. The program list appears across the Windows desktop.

3. Click Accessories. Another submenu appears.

4. Click Entertainment and choose Sound Recorder. The Sound Recorder dialog box then appears on your desktop (see Figure 4.23).

Figure 4.23

You can easily record your own sounds using Sound Recorder.

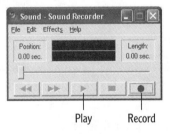

Play   Record

5. Make sure your microphone is plugged in and turned on, and, when you're ready, click Record. The slider moves to the right, showing you that you are being recorded.

6. When you're finished recording, click Stop.

7. To listen to your recording, click Rewind and then click Play.

8. If you want to save what you've done, open the File menu and choose Save. The Save As dialog box appears.

9. Navigate to the My Music folder (My Documents is shown by default), enter a name for the file, and click Save.

You can then attach the sounds you create to e-mail messages, incorporate them in documents, or assign them to program events, such as the closing of a file or the display of an error message. Be creative! Amaze your friends!

Take a Break

Well, your ears must be ringing by now. From Christina Aguilera to Snoop to Creed to Wynton Marsalis, you've had more than an earful. Hopefully, you've had a taste of the fun that's to be had in the sound offerings on both the Web and your computer. It's time to take a break and tuck the kids in or let the dog out or maybe fix your spouse a snack. After you've had a few moments to clear your mind, come on back and let's talk about games, graphics, and more.

Capturing and Publishing Photos and Pictures

Don't you *love* your digital camera? What? You don't have one? Time to check out eBay for the lowest prices—because *everybody* needs a digital camera. They're fun. They're easy. And they give you photos you can hold over your kids' heads.

And what about that scanner? How did you ever live without it? Oh— you *don't?* Well, they're down to $99 in most department stores. When you think of all the fun you can have, scanning photos and sending them to friends and family, you won't be on the fence long. Windows XP includes a number of features that make it easy to add digital images to your computer—in fact, the program pretty much does it for you, as you see in the sections that follow.

Saving Photos from the Web

Suppose that you're scouting around on the Web and you find this *great* picture of puffins you would love to make into a background for your Windows XP desktop. How do you capture it? And is it legal to use?

The easiest way to grab photos on the Web is this:

1. Find the photo you want to save.

2. Right-click on the photo. A pop-up menu of choices appears (see Figure 4.24).

3. Choose Save Picture As. The Save Picture dialog box appears, all ready to save the picture to your My Pictures folder. Change to a different folder, if you like, and click Save.

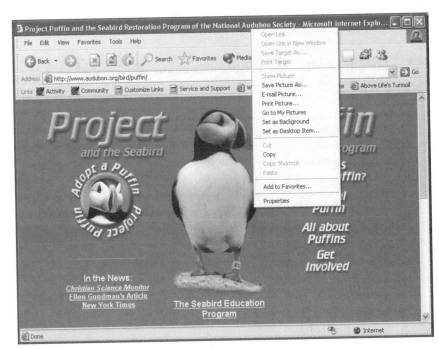

Figure 4.24

When you right-click the photo, a context menu appears.

TIP Don't forget the new "hover menu" that appears over most images. Just hover your mouse over an image on the Web, and you get several choices, including Copy to My Pictures.

Now, on to the question of legality. Early on, computer users were having a heyday gathering up photos and clips on the Web and using them to their heart's content. But you need to know that, unless you create a photo or image yourself, it doesn't belong to you. Most sites don't mind (unless it's posted otherwise) if you use an image for your own use—on *your* computer, to show your kids, to use as your background. But if you use that image in something you circulate—or worse, earn money for—chances are that the copyright police will be looking for you. To play it safe and smart, use the photos and images you create only if you're creating something to go outside the walls of your home computer.

Using the My Picture Folder

After you save an image—whether it's from the Web or from your scanner or digital camera—Windows XP wants to put it in your My Pictures folder by default. The My Picture folder is located in the My Documents folder. To open it, simply double-click it (see Figure 4.25).

The My Picture folder looks quite a bit like My Documents—in fact, after yesterday's session, this topic may seem like *déjà vu*. But notice one set of differences: In the choices under Picture Tasks, at the top of the tasks panel on the left side of the window, you see the following choices:

- ✿ Get pictures from camera or scanner
- ✿ View as a slide show
- ✿ Order prints online
- ✿ Print pictures
- ✿ Copy all items to CD

OTHER PICTURE CHOICES

Although this example shows you how to save a picture to your hard disk so that you can use it again later, as you can see from the menu, you have a number of other simple choices:

- **E-mail Picture** opens a new e-mail message so that you can send the picture to another person.

- **Print Picture** sends the picture right to your printer.

- **Go to My Pictures** opens your My Pictures folder.

- **Set as Background** sets up the new photo automatically as the background for your Windows XP desktop.

- **Set as Desktop Item** adds the item to your desktop as an Active Desktop item.

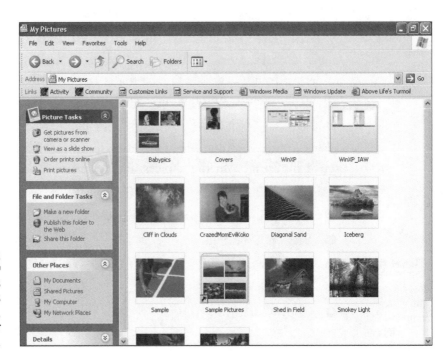

Figure 4.25

The My Pictures folder stores photos, pictures, and other objets d'art.

The sections that follow go into each of these tasks in detail.

Scanning Photos and Gathering Images

Sometimes, scanning photos can be a pain. If you're working with a scanner for the first time or you aren't sure whether your operating system will know what to do with it, you can spend an hour toying with the software and cables, trying to get everything talking to everything else. Likewise, if you've got a digital camera and you've installed the software but you can't find the instructions on what to push when, you're in for a good, long evening of trial-and-error (and probably *lots* of error).

Windows XP steps in and does a really nice thing by taking the coordination off your shoulders. By supplying the Scanning and Camera Wizard, Windows XP enables you to gather photos from your scanner or camera by simply answering a few questions. Want to try it? Here's the process:

1. In the My Pictures window, click Get pictures from camera or scanner. The Select Device dialog box appears (see Figure 4.26).

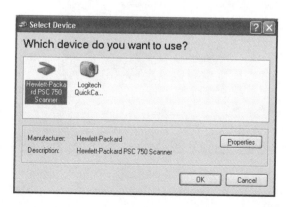

Figure 4.26

Choose the device you're using to scan or download images.

2. Click your selection and then click OK. That choice launches the Scanner and Camera Wizard. At the opening page, click Next. You are then asked to choose the type of picture you are scanning. Your choices are these:

- ✿ Color picture
- ✿ Grayscale picture
- ✿ Black-and-white picture or text
- ✿ Custom

After you make your selection, click Preview. The scanner reads the document you've put in the bed and shows you a preliminary image on the screen (see Figure 4.27). If you're happy with what you see, click Next to continue. If you need to make an adjustment to the way the image is placed, make the change and click Preview again to make sure the photo is positioned the way you want. Then click Next.

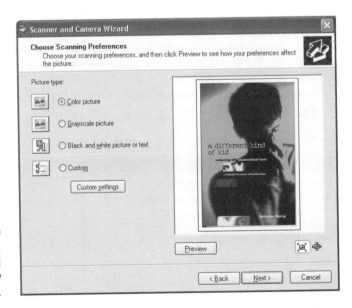

Figure 4.27

The Scanner and Camera Wizard does a preliminary scan of your image.

TIP ■■

If your image takes up only a portion of the scanner's surface, you can enlarge the image to fill the preview window by clicking the Enlarge button in the lower-right corner of the wizard page.

■■

3. The next page of the wizard asks you to name the group of pictures you are creating. Notice that as you type a name, the folder name in the entry in item 3 also changes to match the name you type. Choose a graphics file type for the image (BMP, JPG, TIF, or PNG), and then specify the folder in which you want to save the file. Click Next to continue.

4. The Scanner and Camera Wizard now does its thing and copies the image to the folder you specified. The last page of the wizard gives you the following options:

   ✪ Publish the image to a Web site

   ✪ Order prints of the image from a photo-printing Web site

   ✪ Quit working with pictures

5. Leave the last option selected and click Next. That's it! You're done. Now you can click the link the final page gives you to go to My Pictures and take a look at the image you just scanned.

Viewing Pictures as a Slide Show

If you really love those photos you've copied to your hard drive, you can create a continually running slide show that displays them over...and over...and over again. How? Simply click the folder you want to use (I selected Babypics, 'cause who gets tired of looking at baby pictures?) and then click View as slide show in the Pictures Tasks area of the My Pictures window. The slide show launches, showing the pictures at full-screen size.

At first, you don't see any keys to press or buttons to click, but don't be alarmed: You can display a navigational toolbar by moving the mouse pointer up toward the top of the screen (see Figure 4.28). The toolbar gives you give five choices:

- Start Slide Show
- Pause Slide Show
- Previous Picture
- Next Picture
- Stop

To stop the slide show by using the keyboard, press Esc. You then are returned to the My Pictures window.

Figure 4.28

You can put your favorite pictures in a continuous slide show. Great screensaver idea!

Creating a Photo Album

If you're like most people, keeping your photos in order is a huge challenge. You love to take photos, and you enjoy looking at them, but how do you keep them straight? What happened when? Did you take the trip to Lake Michigan *before* the trip to Myrtle Beach, or was it vice versa? How old were the kids in those pictures?

You can create a photo album to help keep your digital photos and images straight. This isn't exactly the same kind of photo album that you pore over on Grandma and Grandpa's 50th wedding anniversary—not one with captions and dates and macaroni-salad stains. This type of album is more of an organizing mechanism, and to use it, you begin in the My Pictures folder:

1. Open My Documents; then double-click My Pictures. The My Pictures folder opens.

2. In the File and Folder Tasks area, click the Make a new folder option. A new folder is placed in the display area.

3. Type the name you want to assign to the album and click outside the folder.

4. Right-click on the folder and choose Properties. The Properties dialog box appears.

5. Click the Customize tab and click the down-arrow at the end of the Use this folder type as a template option. A list of folder types appears.

6. Choose Photo Album.

7. Choose Picture to place a photo on the front of the folder.

8. Click Apply and then OK.

Getting "Real" Prints of Your Photos

One of the big complaints about digital photographs is that you can't have that same put-'em-in-the-album joy you can have with the *real* photos you have developed at Wal-Mart. Windows XP tries to solve that problem with the Online Print Ordering Wizard. This wizard walks you through the process of ordering prints online: You choose the company you want and tell it the particulars of your order, and then the photos arrive in the mail just a few days later. Here are the steps for ordering prints of your scanned photos or digital camera images:

1. In the My Picture folder (or the folder in which you have saved the photo or image you want to use), click Order prints online. The Online Print Ordering Wizard starts. Click Next.

2. In the Selection page, click the boxes of the photos you want to order. If you choose, you can click Select All to select all images in the current folder. When you've made your selection, click Next.

3. The wizard displays the Connect dialog box so that you can go online (if you aren't already). After the connection is made, a list of photo-printing companies is displayed. Click your choice (I chose Ofoto for this example) and click Next.

4. The wizard then downloads information about the company you selected. The photos you selected are then displayed in a window, along with size, quantity, and pricing choices (see Figure 4.29).

5. Make your choices and click Next. (Remember that you can stop the order at any time by pressing Cancel to end the wizard.)

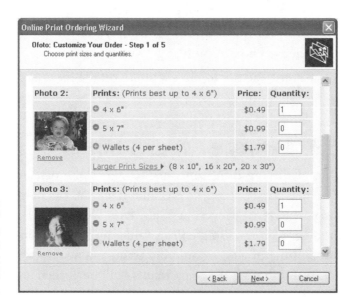

Figure 4.29

When you choose a photo-printing vendor, you select the size and quantity you want.

6. Next, you need to enter your shipping address. Just fill in the form as you would any order; then click Next.

7. Verify the shipping address, choose the postal carrier (U.S. Postal Service, FedEx 2Day, or FedEx Priority). If you want to add a message with your order (a nice touch if you're sending photos to Grandma), click in the message box and type your note. Click Next.

8. Finally, verify the order with tax and shipping charges; then click Next. You are taken to a secure site, where you can enter your credit card information.

The photos are then copied to the printing company (which could take a few minutes, depending on the speed of your connection and the number of photos you're sending). The last page displays your order confirmation numbers and lets you know that you'll be receiving a confirmation e-mail as well. Click Next and then Finish. Now all you have to do is wait for your package to arrive in the mail.

TIP If you have a modern inkjet printer, you also can buy photo paper and make your own prints.

Sending Photos via E-mail

One other fun thing you want to do with your photos is send them to countless interested people by e-mail. Because the image is already saved in an electronic file, the process of sending a photo over the Internet is as simple as sending any other type of file. Here are the steps:

1. Display the My Pictures window and choose the file you want to send.

2. In the File and Folder Tasks pane, click E-mail this file. Windows XP displays a small dialog box telling you that the photo can be resized so that it can be sent faster.

3. If you want to make the pictures smaller, leave the current option selected; otherwise, click the second option.

4. Click OK. Windows launches your e-mail program and attaches the photo automatically (see Figure 4.30). Fill in the necessary information and click Send.

 NOTE Keep an eye on the file size of your attached photos. Because digital images generally create large files, you should zip photo files whenever possible to reduce file size and save transmission time.

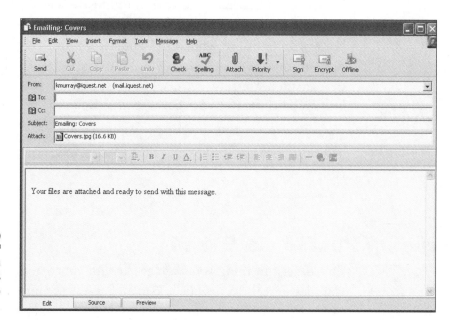

Figure 4.30

When you e-mail a photo, it is sent as an attachment to your message.

Directing Your Own Show with Windows Movie Maker

Windows Movie Maker is an amazing little media tool that was originally introduced with Windows Me. With Movie Maker, you can mix a variety of input—from your camcorder, for example, your TV, or the

Web—and then use it to create a unique video all your own. You can then use your movie to tell your parents what's going on in your neck of the woods, send a video report to your partner in Des Moines, run a product video announcing your newest release, or simply send something funny to your friends.

To start Windows Movie Maker, click Start and choose All Programs. When the program list appears, click Accessories and then click Windows Movie Maker. When the window first appears, it resembles Figure 4.31.

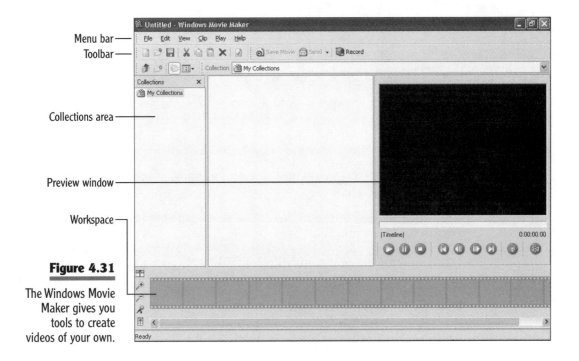

Menu bar
Toolbar

Collections area

Preview window

Workspace

Figure 4.31

The Windows Movie Maker gives you tools to create videos of your own.

The Windows Movie Maker window is quite a bit different from the other screens you've been seeing in this session. Across the top, you see the familiar menu bar and toolbar, but beneath that you see what's known as the *collections area,* the place on the screen where you assemble the different files you plan to work into your movie. The Preview window displays the video for the current project, and the workspace, at the bottom of the screen, shows you either the timeline or the storyboard and enables you to build, add to, and edit the movies you create.

NOTE Windows Movie Maker doesn't insist that you be a video producer—in fact, you can use the program even if all you have is a built-in microphone. Movie Maker gives you the option of choosing audio only, if you like, so that you can still create voiceovers even without the video to go along with them. Also, because you can use still photographs, VCR input, or Web video for your movies, you don't need to have a digital camcorder or Webcam to record your own video.

Recording a Simple Movie Clip

The process for recording a simple movie in Windows Movie Maker goes like this:

1. Open the File menu and click New; then click Project.

2. Open the View menu and choose Timeline. The view at the bottom of the window changes to show the movie timeline.

3. Click Record in the toolbar. The Record dialog box appears, as Figure 4.32 shows.

4. Choose what you want to record. Your choices are Video and audio, Video only, and Audio only.

5. If you want to change the device shown as the video or audio devices, click the Change Device button and choose the devices you want; then click OK.

6. The default recording time is two minutes. If you want to change the default, specify a new time.

7. The setting is set to Medium quality, which is the suggested setting. For now, leave this setting as it is. (You can play with it later, if you like.)

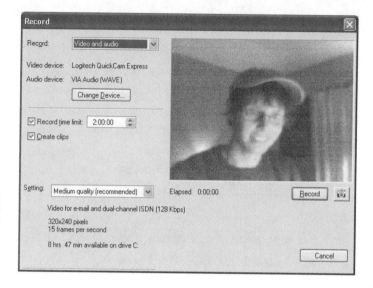

Figure 4.32

Recording a video
involves choosing
your devices and
clicking Record.

8. Click Record to begin recording your video. After a moment, the
   Record button changes to a Stop button and the flashing letters let
   you know that you are being recorded. Do your bit and, when
   you're ready, click Stop.

9. Windows Movie Maker offers a dialog box so that you can name
   and save the clip you just generated. You are returned to the main
   Movie Maker window so that you can add sound, edit, save, and
   send your movie.

TIP

You can use Windows Movie Maker to take a picture using a Webcam or other recording
device. When the Record dialog box is displayed, position the camera and set up the shot
the way you want it; then click the Take Photo button, just beneath the video display
window. Windows XP then opens the Save As dialog box so that you can enter a name
and choose a folder for the photo you've just taken (the default folder is My Pictures).
Enter a name and choose a folder, if necessary, and click Save. That action captures
the photo.

Adding Narration

Some of your projects might be collections of video from a variety of sources—perhaps a family collection of clips from the previous year, all pulled together in a nice, narrated storyline. Windows Media Maker gives you the means to add voiceover narration to the movie you're creating. The sound is saved as a separate object and is placed on the timeline as a separate entity, meaning that you can edit, loop, extend, or move the sound object anywhere in the movie you want it to go. To add narration to a movie clip, follow these steps:

1. With your movie project open in the Timeline window, open the File menu and choose Record Narration. The Record Narration Track dialog box appears (see Figure 4.33).

Figure 4.33

Recording a narration creates a soundtrack for your movie.

2. Verify that the correct audio device is being used; if it's not, click the Change button and choose the right device.

3. If your video has a soundtrack you want to mute so that your voiceover will be heard, click the Mute video soundtrack button.

4. If necessary, increase or decrease the Record level by moving the slider up or down.

5. Click Record to begin recording. The marker on the timeline ticks off the seconds, and the video in the display plays while you record the narration.

6. When you're finished, click Stop. The Save Narration Track Sound File dialog box appears.

7. Enter a name for the sound file and click Save. Windows Movie Maker saves the sound file and places its icon in the Movie Maker file area in the center of the screen.

Saving Your Movie

When you're ready to save what you've done, simply click the Save Movie button in the Windows Movie Maker toolbar. The Save Movie dialog box appears. Again, you have the option of choosing the playback quality setting (Medium should be fine). You also can enter information that is displayed whenever the file is sent or played (see Figure 4.34).

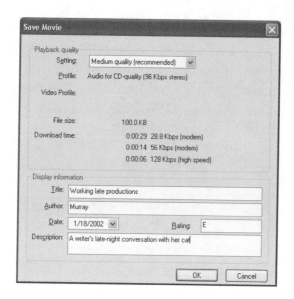

Figure 4.34

Your last step in creating the movie clip is to save it.

After you click Save, Windows Movie Maker saves the file in the folder you specified and then asks whether you want to watch it now. If you click Yes, the Windows Media Player launches, and there's your video, appearing in the Now Playing screen!

Now it seems we've come 'round full circle, and we're back where we started in this session, with the Windows Media Player. I'll bet you're ready to call it a night!

What's Next?

This session has taken you on a Saturday-night-fevered tour of media opportunities that are available to your through Windows XP. You've learned first about Windows Media Player—a multifunction utility that mixes the capabilities of a VCR, radio, and CD player all in one. You also learned about various ways you can play music on the Web and change your own computer's sounds. From sound, this session moved to games, where you discovered how you can enjoy the media features that are available—both sound and graphics—by yourself or with others. Finally, you learned about graphics—clip art, scanned photos, and slides—and found out how to make your own movies with Windows Movie Maker. That's lots of creativity for one session! You're probably spent. See you in the morning, when we tackle a more practical topic in Sunday morning's session, "Mastering Windows XP Tools & Accessories."

Working with Windows XP Accessories

- ✿ An Accessories overview
- ✿ Working with the Calculator
- ✿ Simple text with Notepad and WordPad
- ✿ Brushing up with Windows Paint
- ✿ Using the Character Map
- ✿ Cleaning up your hard disk
- ✿ No more file fragments
- ✿ Automating tasks
- ✿ Knowing your computer info
- ✿ Games, games, and more games

ood morning! And welcome to the last day in your trek through Windows XP. We start out this morning by exploring some of the important system accessories you use to enhance your use of Windows and ensure that your system is working the way it should. If you've got your coffee and Danish (remember, mouse buttons don't respond well to icing), let's get started.

An Accessories Overview

In this session, you learn about two different kinds of programs that are often referred to as *accessories* in Windows XP. The first type of program, a *system tool,* is generally a utility that in some way helps you organize, clean up, maintain, or fix your computer system. The second type of program might be referred to as an accessory or an application program. It is an add-on utility that enables you to perform a specific task—such as touch up photos, do some quick math, or dash off a note to someone. The accessory programs are pretty limited in what they can do—you don't find in Notepad, for example, the same range of features you find in a larger word processing program, like Microsoft Word.

Windows XP includes a number of these special tools, all tucked away in the Accessories menu selection. Let's take a look. Display the list of system tools by clicking Start and then choosing All Programs, Accessories, and System Tools. The submenu shown in Figure 5.1 appears.

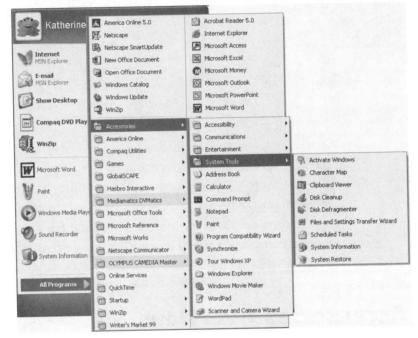

 NOTE

In the Accessories submenu, you see a number of categories—Accessibility, Communications, Entertainment, and System Tools—as well as other programs shown in the list below the category folders. Throughout this session, you work with the accessories in both the main Accessories menu and the System Tools submenu.

In this session, we focus on the accessories you are most likely to need and use as you work with Windows XP. The following list briefly introduces the accessories you will be using:

✪ Calculator is a simple calculator that can perform basic math functions (and even scientific notation, if you're willing to go hunting for it).

✪ Notepad is your basic text editor that enables you to write notes, memos, and more.

- Paint is a graphics program you can use to touch up photos, create drawings, and design logos.

- Character Map enables you to see all the characters in various fonts and copy them to other Windows applications.

- Disk Cleanup removes unneeded files on your computer, giving you more free space.

- Disk Defragmenter runs a utility that consolidates file storage and removes file fragments.

- Scheduled Tasks enables you to schedule regular maintenance tasks.

- System Information displays information about the hardware and software on your system.

Working with the Calculator

Have you seen those little $2.99 calculators for sale in checkout lines? The Windows Calculator looks like an electronic version of those liquid-crystal gems. The Calculator is actually a handy tool for those times when you need to figure something quickly—simple math is its forte, although you can do even scientific notation if you have the patience and the know-how. In fact, Calculator can handle all these tasks:

- Addition and subtraction
- Multiplication and division
- Square roots
- Percentages
- Scientific calculations
- Converting to a different number system
- Calculations with numbers in hexadecimal, octal, decimal, or binary format

Okay, so maybe that's more than your average $2.99 dime-store calculator can do.

To launch the Calculator, follow these steps:

1. Click Start to open the Start menu; then choose All Programs.

2. Click Accessories and choose Calculator. The Calculator appears, as Figure 5.2 shows.

3. To start a calculation, enter the first number by clicking the appropriate buttons.

4. Click the operator (+, -, /, or *) you need.

5. Enter the second number and click = or press Enter. The result appears in the display area at the top of the Calculator.

Figure 5.2

The Windows XP Calculator lets you perform simple math with the standard calculator.

TIP You can easily copy the result of your calculations to the Windows Clipboard so that you can paste it in other open applications. To copy the result, open the Edit menu and choose Copy (or press Ctrl+C).

You can display the Calculator in Scientific Calculation mode by opening the View menu and choosing Scientific. The Calculator expands to almost twice its size and includes all kinds of buttons that make no sense at all to English majors like me (see Figure 5.3).

When you want to return to the normal Calculator display, open the View menu and choose Standard. When you're finished using the Calculator, you can click Minimize to reduce the window to the Taskbar or exit the program by clicking the close button.

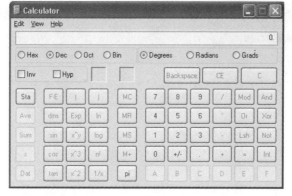

Figure 5.3

If you need more complex calculations, the Scientific version may be of help.

TIP

After you use one of the Windows XP accessories, like Notepad or Calculator, it appears in the Start menu so that you can select it easily the next time you want to use it.

Simple Text with Notepad and WordPad

Windows XP includes two different tools for word processing: Notepad and WordPad. Each one enables you to create simple text documents—letters, memos, lists, scripts, and more—and each one enables you to save the files you create in formats that other word processing programs can read. To start either program, click Start and choose All Programs, Accessories and then either Notepad or WordPad.

A Look at Notepad

The big difference between Notepad and WordPad is the number of features you find in each program. Notepad is truly a bare-bones word processor. In fact, unless you choose the Format option Word Wrap, as you can see in Figure 5.4, or press Enter where you want the line to break, the text you enter appears in Notepad as one long, continuous line. You won't find any bells and whistles here—including extras like the ability to control formatting and style changes (you won't be able to indent a list, for example, or boldface a heading).

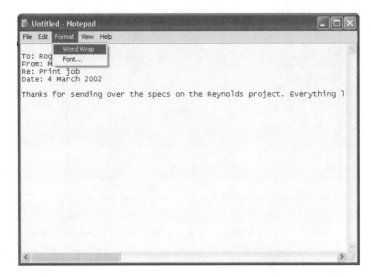

Figure 5.4

Notepad is your basic text editor—to wrap the text so that it's all visible in the display, select Word Wrap.

Let's try a word processing example with Notepad. Follow these steps:

1. Click Start, All Programs, Accessories, and Notepad to launch the program. The cursor is positioned in the upper-left corner of the window.

2. Type the following text (don't press Enter to make the text stay within the window—just let it extend off the right edge):

   I've never seen a purple cow; I guess I'll never see one. But I can tell you anyhow, I'd rather see than be one.

3. Click Format to open the menu and choose Word Wrap. Notepad wraps the text so that it is all visible within the margins of the screen.

4. To save the file, click File and choose Save (see Figure 5.5). The Save As dialog box appears.

5. Navigate to the folder in which you want to save the file, type a name for the file, and click Save. The file is saved with the default .txt extension, which means it can be imported by any program that supports text files.

6. Close Notepad by clicking the File menu and choosing Exit or by simply clicking the Close box.

TIP Working in a stripped-down word processor like Notepad isn't a bad thing if all you need is to capture a thought or a memo or write a quick piece of code for a Web page you're working on.

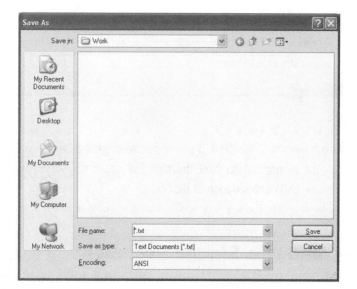

Figure 5.5

Notepad saves the file as a .txt file, which can be used easily by other word processing programs.

The Weightier WordPad

WordPad, on the other hand, is a fairly full-featured word processing utility. As you can see in Figure 5.6, WordPad includes the extras Notepad lacks: the ruler across the top of the work area; font and formatting options; text-alignment options, and more.

You won't use WordPad to do anything complicated, like newsletters or dissertations, but if you need to create a report with basic headings, indents, and even an imported chart or two, WordPad can handle it for you. If you want to change the color of text, create a bullet list, boldface and italicize text, and make other run-of-the-mill formatting changes, WordPad can swing it. The sections that follow give you a few things to try as you put WordPad through its paces.

Menus —
Standard toolbar —
Formatting toolbar —

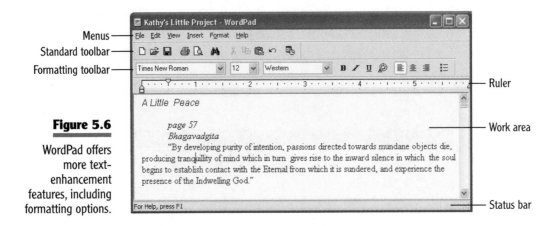

Ruler
Work area
Status bar

Figure 5.6

WordPad offers
more text-
enhancement
features, including
formatting options.

TIP

As you work with WordPad, if you're unsure of what a particular tool does, simply position the mouse pointer over the tool. The status bar, at the bottom of the WordPad window, gives a description of the tool.

Creating a Simple Document

When you first start WordPad, the cursor blinks patiently in the upper-left corner of the work area, awaiting your text entry. Simply type anything you want in the open area. If you want some sample text to use as a starter, type the following (without pressing Enter):

> **Welcome to our new spring Web site! We hope you'll enjoy the new articles, product descriptions, and customer raves and suggestions we've included in our new design. Be sure to visit our Events! page to check out our upcoming celebrity auctions. The next auction, hosted by the one-and-only Britney Spears, will be held on...**

Yes, go ahead and leave that last line incomplete. You finish the thought in the next section.

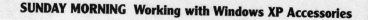

TIP Save your document quickly by opening the File menu and choosing Save. When the Save As dialog box appears, navigate to the folder you want, type a file name, and click Save. This action saves the file and returns you to the document.

Inserting the Date and Time

WordPad includes a feature that enables you to insert the date and time right in the document you are creating. That's the step you want to take here. With the cursor still positioned at the end of the text block you just entered, click the Date/Time tool in the toolbar. (If you prefer, you can open the Insert menu and choose Date and Time.) The Date and Time dialog box appears, as shown in Figure 5.7.

Figure 5.7

You use the Date and Time dialog box to insert the date or time in WordPad.

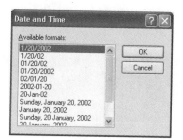

Scroll through the list until you see the date style you like. The last two formats are time styles. Click the format you like and click OK. Word-Pad inserts your selection at the cursor position.

NOTE Of course, the date and time stamps are based on the current date, so they are most often used in the heading of a letter or inserted at the start or end of a report.

Changing the Font

Not all text is created equal. You know from reading the paper, visiting Web pages, and watching television that typefaces—the formation and style of individual characters—have much to do with how easy text is to read and how effective it is in delivering its message.

NOTE A **typeface** is a family of type, such as Times New Roman, Arial, or Garamond. A **font** is one size and style of a particular typeface.

WordPad enables you to change the font of the text in your document (unlike its less-well-endowed cousin, Notepad). To change the font of text in your sample WordPad document, follow these steps:

1. Select the text you want to change. (If you're following along with this example, highlight the opening phrase, "Welcome to our new spring Web site!")

2. Open the Format menu and choose Font. The Font dialog box, as shown in Figure 5.8, is displayed.

3. To change the font, scroll down through the fonts list until you see the font you want to use. Click the font, and the Sample window shows what you've selected. For this example, choose Arial Black.

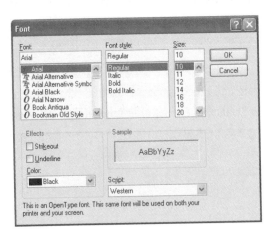

Figure 5.8

You can change the font, style, size, color, and effects in the Font dialog box.

4. In the Size list, click 14.

5. Click the Color down-arrow to display the list of colors, and click Blue.

6. Click OK to close the Font dialog box. The changes are reflected in the WordPad document.

TIP

If you don't like the changes you made, you can reverse them by opening the Edit menu and choosing Undo.

Creating a Bullet List

Bullet lists come in handy when you have several information items you want to call attention to—and you're hoping your readers will be able to find them easily. You can add bullets to existing text or create bullet lists by typing them as you go.

To create a bullet point in the sample document in WordPad, follow these steps:

1. At the end of the sample paragraph, press Enter twice to start a new paragraph and leave a blank line.

2. Click the Bullets tool at the end of the formatting toolbar. A bullet character is inserted and the cursor is indented, ready for you to type text.

3. Type the following line:

   March celebrity auction hosted by Lauren Hutton.

4. Press Enter and type the following line:

   April celebrity auction hosted by Julianne Moore.

   Notice what happened? When you pressed Enter, WordPad started a new line and added another bullet. Bullets appear each time you press Enter until you disable the feature by clicking the Bullets button a second time. The WordPad example should look something like Figure 5.9.

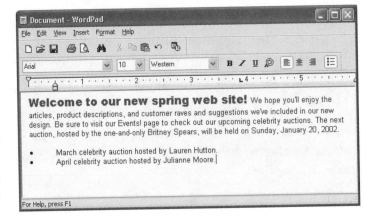

Figure 5.9

Adding a bullet
is as simple
as clicking the
Bullets tool.

TIP You can remove the bullets from existing bulleted text by clicking in the paragraph and clicking the Bullets tool. This action removes the bullet and formats the paragraph to align with the left margin of the page. Or, if you prefer, you can turn off bullets by pressing Enter twice at the end of a list.

Previewing and Printing the Document

One last stop in WordPad before we move on to other Windows XP accessories. After you've been adding and formatting text in WordPad, sooner or later you're ready to print. Before you send the document to the printer, however, you should take a look and see how it will appear in print. To preview the document, follow these steps:

1. Open the File menu and click Print Preview. The document is shown in Preview mode, as you see in Figure 5.10.

2. If you like, you can click the Zoom In button to enlarge the display of the document. If you were working with a multipage document, you could use Next Page, Prev Page, and Two Page to display different pages (and multiple pages) in the preview window.

3. If you need to make changes to the document, click Close and make your changes; then return to Print Preview mode.

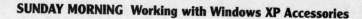

4. When you are ready to print the document, click Print. The Print dialog box appears, as Figure 5.11 shows. Choose the printer you want to use and the number of copies to print, and then click Print to send the file to the printer.

NOTE Print Preview isn't the only place you can print. If you want to print without going into Print Preview mode, open the File menu and choose Print. This action displays the Print dialog box, and you can print as usual.

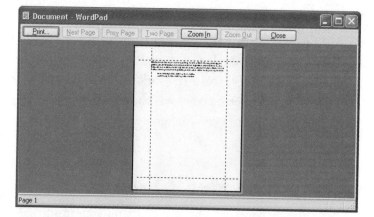

Figure 5.10

Print Preview shows you how the document will look when printed.

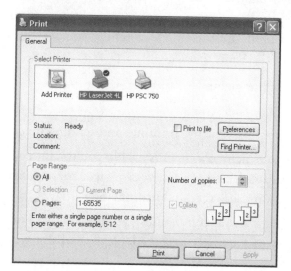

Figure 5.11

In the Print dialog box, choose your printer, select the number of copies, and click Print.

NOTE Fancy stuff—like headers and footers, section breaks, and automatic pagination—you still need to do in the high-powered programs, like Microsoft Word.

Brushing Up with Paint

Paint is a graphics tool you can use to do all kinds of things. Design a logo for your company stationary. Create a button for your Web page. Touch up the photos from your digital camera. Design a new background for Windows XP.

Although Paint isn't as complicated or as full-featured as some graphics or paint programs, like Paint Shop Pro, it is surprisingly good as an image editor. Paint enables you to work with individual pixels—the dots that comprise the larger image—which means you can shade, edit, remove, or change the color of even the most subtle points in the image you're working with.

Understanding the Paint Window

You launch paint by clicking Start and choosing All Programs, Accessories, Paint. The Paint window is straightforward, as you can see in Figure 5.12. At the top of the window, you see the familiar title bar; below that, the Paint menus.

Here's what the menus in Paint enable you to do:

- The File menu contains commands for starting, opening, saving, scanning, previewing, printing, and sending images.

- The Edit menu commands enable you to cut, copy, paste, select, and clear selected areas of your image. You can also reverse your last operation using the Undo command.

- The View menu commands give you what you need to control the display of the image and the look of the Paint window. You can

display the Tool box, Color box, status bar, and Text toolbar. You can also zoom (magnify) the display and choose View Bitmap, which displays the individual pixels of the image.

✿ The Image menu commands let you work with the image as a whole. You can flip, rotate, stretch, skew, invert the colors, and change the attributes of the image. You can also clear the image entirely or elect to make it opaque.

✿ The Colors menu contains only one command: Edit Colors. This important command enables you to create your own color palette for the selected image and modify the colors of individual pixels throughout the image.

✿ The Help menu gives you two commands: Help Topics and About Paint. You use Help Topics to display information you want to learn about Paint; About Paint simply gives you the version number and registration information.

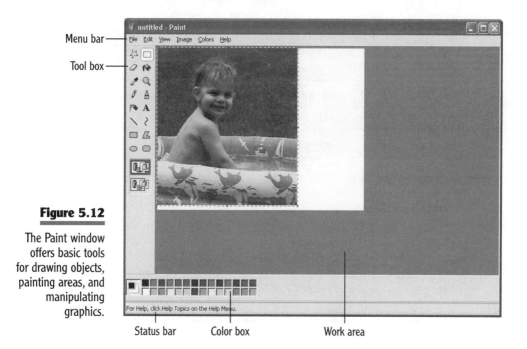

Figure 5.12

The Paint window offers basic tools for drawing objects, painting areas, and manipulating graphics.

The Tool box, along the left edge of the Paint window, contains the selection, paint, shape, and layering tools you need to work with your files. Table 5.1 lists the paint tools and gives you a description of each one.

TABLE 5.1 PAINT TOOLS

Tool	Name	Description
	Free-Form Select	Use to draw a line around the part of the image you want to select
	Select	Use to draw a rectangle around the image section you want to select
	Eraser/Color Eraser	Erases pixels at the cursor position (if Color Eraser is selected, erases in the selected color)
	Fill With Color	Fills the current area with the selected color
	Pick Color	Enables you to choose the color you want to use
	Magnifier	Magnifies the view at the cursor position
	Pencil	Draws a line as you drag the mouse
	Brush	Displays a brush palette so you can choose brush size
	Airbrush	Displays an airbrush palette so you can choose spray density
	Text	Enables you to add text to the image

TABLE 5.1 CONTINUED		
Tool	**Name**	**Description**
\	Line	Draws a straight line
?	Curve	Creates a curve in the image
▢	Rectangle	Draws a rectangle
◿	Polygon	Creates a polygon
◯	Ellipse	Creates an ellipse
▢	Rounded Rectangle	Draws a rounded rectangle

TIP Several of the Paint tools—such as Selection, Brush, Airbrush, and Rectangle—offer additional options in the palette area below the Tool box when they are selected. You can choose the selection style, brush width, airbrush density, or rectangle style (open, filled, or unbordered). Watch the palette area to see what your options are for individual tools.

A Few Painting Exercises

The next sections walk you through some common tasks you are likely to try in Paint. Even though Paint is a simple program to learn and use, you can use it for a number of interesting—and fun—tasks. Paint is also one of those surprising programs: The more you explore, the more you find. When you have a spare afternoon, come back and experiment with fun and photos in Paint.

Drawing Shapes in Paint

Shapes are simple and predictable. You don't need any artistic talent to draw a good solid shape. Let's give it a shot:

1. In the Paint window, choose the Rectangle tool in the Tool box on the right. The palette area shows three rectangle options:

   ✿ Clear shape with line border
   ✿ White filled shape with line border
   ✿ Color-filled shape

2. Click the third option, Color filled shape.

3. Move the mouse pointer to the center of the work area. Click and drag the mouse pointer down and to the right. A rectangle appears on the work area (see Figure 5.13).

TIP

When you first start Paint, the Color box is not displayed. You can display it by opening the View menu and choosing Color box. To choose a different color for filled shapes, click the color you want before you draw the shape.

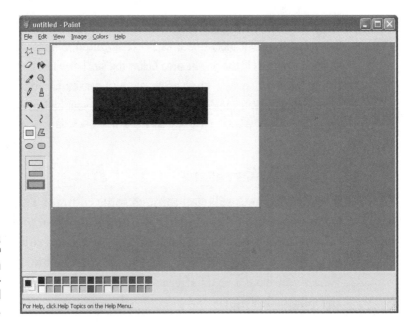

Figure 5.13

A basic shape in basic black— choose your tool and draw.

Selecting and Modifying Images

Paint includes two different tools you can use to select and move, copy, or erase items in your image. These tools are the Free-Form Select tool and the Select tool. Free-Form Select allows you to drag around an irregular shape and select it. Select draws a selection rectangle around the shape.

To use either tool, simply click it and drag around the portion of the shape you want to work with. You can select the entire document or any portion of it. Figure 5.14 shows a portion of the shape selected and moved away with the Free-Form Select tool. After you select the image, you can do any of the following tasks:

- Drag the selection to another point on-screen.
- Delete the selection by pressing Del.
- Copy the selection to the Windows Clipboard by opening the Edit menu and choosing Copy.
- Flip, rotate, or recolor the selection by opening the Image menu and choosing the option you want.

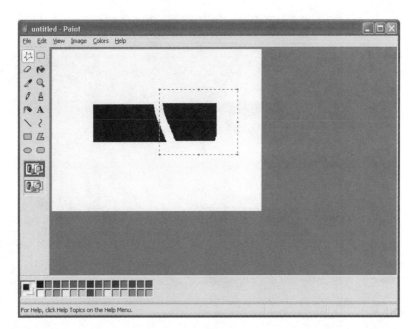

Figure 5.14

The rectangle section was selected with the Free-Form Select tool.

Erasing Paint Selections

The eraser is a talented little tool that can both remove pixels and leave whatever color you want in their place. Sound confusing? It's easier to see the process in action. Let's start with the easiest task first. When you want to erase a portion of your image, follow these steps:

1. Click the eraser tool in the Paint Tool box. A palette of four different eraser sizes appears beneath the Tool box area.

2. In the palette, select the eraser size you want by clicking your choice.

3. Position the eraser pointer on the image at the point you want to begin erasing. Press and hold the mouse button while you drag the eraser, and the image is erased as you drag (see Figure 5.15).

 TIP If you notice that you need your bifocals—or a magnifying glass—to get a good look at what you're trying to delete, don't worry. You learn how to enlarge the view in the next exercise.

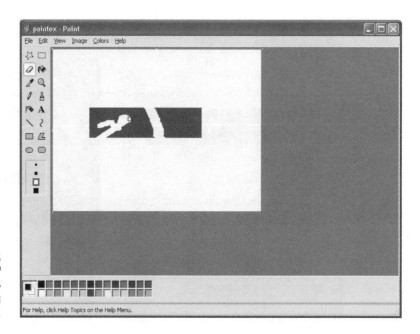

Figure 5.15

The image is erased as you drag the eraser tool.

Suppose that you're working with an image that has a background color—yellow, for example. If you erase a portion of your image with a white eraser, it leaves a white spot in your colored background. Then you wind up repainting the background with the missing color. You can fix this problem by simply choosing a color for the eraser. You can make the eraser yellow so that when you erase, the background of the picture looks right. Here's how you do it:

1. Select the eraser tool in the Tool box.
2. Display the Color box, if necessary, by pressing Ctrl+L.
3. Right-click the color you want to assign to the eraser. (For example, if you want to erase on a yellow background, right-click yellow.)
4. Erase the portion of the image you want to erase. Paint erases as you drag the mouse and leaves the colored pixels in the erased pixels' place.

WHAT'S A BITMAP?

Every industry, technical or otherwise, has its own language, to some degree. **Bitmap** is one of those words that is used to refer to paint-type graphics—the images that, at their essence, are simply dots (or bits) on a screen. Individual colored dots make up the photos you scan, the shapes you draw in Paint, and many of the art images you see on the Web. A bitmap, then, is literally a "map of bits," a collection of dots in a file, arranged to look like the image you want to see.

Not all graphics files are bitmap files, however. **Vector-based** files use calculations to draw and resize shapes, curves, and polygons. The types of programs that create vector-based art files are typically called **draw** programs. Programs that produce bitmap graphic files are usually referred to as **paint** programs.

Changing the View

If you followed along with this little erasing exercise, you may have noticed that it's hard to be accurate when you're so big and the eraser tool is so small. And individual pixels are even smaller. To get a closer view so that you can ensure that you're erasing what you mean to erase, you have two different options:

✪ Zoom the display, which magnifies the image.

✪ Change to Bitmap view to see the individual pixels.

When you want to zoom the display so that you can get a closer view of your work, follow these steps:

1. Open the View menu and choose Zoom. A submenu appears, offering you a number of choices (most of which aren't available at first).

2. Choose Custom to see all available zoom percentages. The Custom choices are 100%, 200%, 400%, 600%, and 800%.

3. Click your choice and click OK. The display is magnified so that you can see the individual pixels that make up the image (see Figure 5.16).

4. Make any necessary changes (the tools all work the same way as they do in the smaller view), and then choose View, Zoom, Normal Size (or press Ctrl+PgUp) to return to the normal display.

 TIP
When you are working in an enlarged view—larger than 200 percent, for example—you have the option of turning on the grid to help line things up properly. To turn on the grid, open the View menu, choose Zoom, and click Show Grid. To turn off the grid later, repeat the process or simply choose a view smaller than 200 percent.

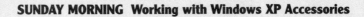

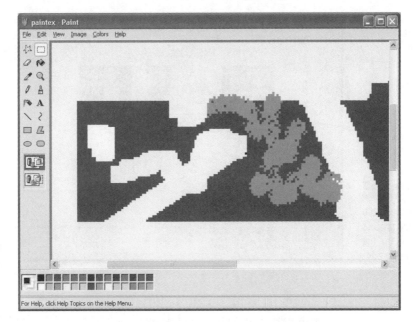

Figure 5.16

When you zoom the display, you can see the individual pixels.

Touching Up a Photo in Paint

Because Paint allows you to work with the individual pixels on the screen, and because digital images are also patterns of dots, you can use Paint to edit photos you've imported into Paint. Here's a quick process that shows you how to do just that:

1. Open the photo you want to use by clicking File and choosing Open. The Open dialog box appears, as Figure 5.17 shows.

2. Navigate to the folder storing the photo you want to edit.

3. Select the file and click Open. The photo opens in Paint.

NOTE The photo opens in the default image viewer or editor, so if your system uses another paint program by default, that program is used. To ensure that Paint is used, you can open the File menu and choose Open With, Paint.

Figure 5.17

Begin the photo touch-up process by choosing the file you want to edit.

4. Zoom in using the procedures in the preceding section to locate the item you want to change (see Figure 5.18). Let's say that you want to take the "red eye" out of a photo you want to send.

5. Click the appropriate tools to make the change to the photo. (To take the red out, I selected the Brush tool, chose the second-to-the-smallest brush, clicked black, and covered the red spot in the eye with the black paint.)

6. Return to Normal view by pressing Ctrl+PgUp.

7. Save your work by opening the File menu and choosing Save if you want to save the changed file to replace the earlier version. If you want to save the file and preserve the earlier version, choose Save As and enter a new file name for the touch-up photo. Click Save to save the new file.

TIP By default, Windows XP places in your My Pictures folder the photos you scan or download from your digital camera. Unless you've selected a different folder to store the photos, you'll probably find them there.

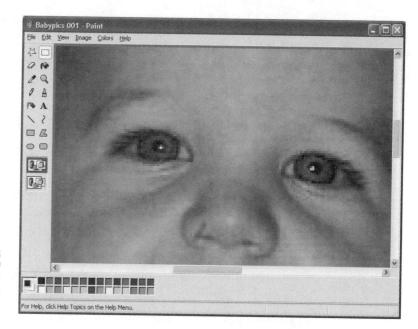

Figure 5.18

Zooming and editing enable you to get the red out.

TIP You can also scan photos and art right into Paint, if you choose. To scan a photo, put the photo in your scanner and then open the File menu and choose From Scanner or Camera. This action launches the Scanner and Camera Wizard, which scans the image and places it in your Paint window.

Adding Text to Your Images

The last stop we make in this quick tour through Paint is the text tool. If you're designing a logo or adding captions to a favorite photograph that you plan to send via e-mail, you need to have some way of adding text to your image. The text tool allows you to do just that.

NOTE Be forewarned, however, that adding text in Paint isn't like adding text in WordPad or Notepad—after you enter it and put away the text tool, you can't delete the text by simply backspacing and typing the characters you want, because the text becomes pixels, just like everything else in Paint. After you add the text, it is part of the graphic image; to get rid of it, you have to use the eraser tool.

• •

To add text to your image, follow these steps:

1. Display the image you want to work with.

2. Click the text tool in the Tool box. The mouse pointer changes to a cross-hair pointer.

3. Decide whether you want the text box to be opaque (a white box appears and blocks out what's behind it) or transparent (you can read the text, but the background of the image is visible behind the text). The text box is opaque by default, so to make the box transparent, open the Image menu and choose Draw Opaque so that the check mark is removed.

4. Drag a rectangle on the screen that will serve as the text box. (For this example, I turned off Draw Opaque so that you can see the photo background through the text box.) The Fonts toolbar appears, giving you choices about the font, size, and style you use for text (see Figure 5.19).

5. Click the Fonts down-arrow and make your choice; select the size and a style, if desired.

6. Choose the color you want the text to be by clicking it in the Color box at the bottom of the window.

7. Finally, type the text. The text appears in the font, size, and color you selected.

There's *so much* more to do with Paint—we didn't even get into flipping or stretching images, using the different paintbrushes, picking up a color with the eyedropper tool, or spraying it on with the airbrush tool. There's lots of room for creativity, so be sure to come back and play a while when you have the time. Paint is something your kids (or coworkers) might like to experiment with, so if you get the chance, use your newfound know-how to show them the basics so that they can get started!

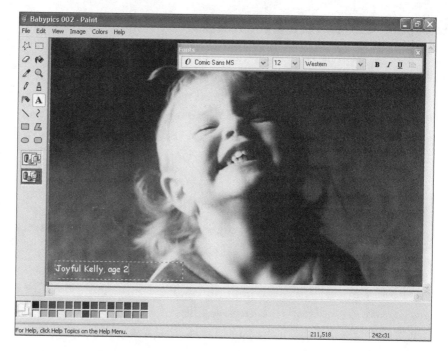

Figure 5.19

The Fonts toolbar appears so that you can choose options for the text in your image.

Take a Break

Up to this point in this session, you've learned about four of the biggest add-on programs you're likely to use with Windows XP. You can see that you've got tools for crunching numbers (Calculator), turning a literary phrase (Notepad and WordPad), and letting your artistic spirit soar (Paint). Hopefully, this exercise has been an inspiring one for a Sunday morning. As the day edges on toward noon, we look at the more practical matters: working with the Character Map, cleaning up your hard drive, finding system information, and more. This session winds up on a fun note once again by taking you on a gaming trip. So take a break, stretch your legs, and come on back when you're ready to wrap up our coverage of tools and accessories in the remainder of this morning's session.

Using Character Map

The Character Map comes in handy when you want to see all the characters available in a particular font. You might use the Character Map, for example, when you need to find a copyright symbol or a Greek character and insert it into a document or drawing. After you find the character you want, you can paste it to the Windows Clipboard and then paste it into whatever file you're working on. To use the Character Map, follow these steps:

1. Click Start to open the Start menu.
2. Choose All Programs, Accessories, System Tools, and Character Map. The Character Map dialog box appears, as shown in Figure 5.20.
3. Click the Font down-arrow and choose the font you want to use from the displayed list.
4. Scroll through the character area to find the characters you want to use.
5. Click the first character you want to add. The character enlarges so that you can see it more closely.

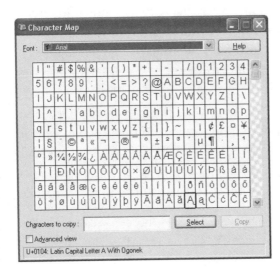

Figure 5.20

You can use the Character Map to see all characters in the selected font.

6. If this is the character you want to add, click Select, and it is added to the Characters to copy box.

7. Repeat steps 5 and 6 until you have selected all the characters you want to copy.

8. Click the Copy button to copy the chosen characters to the Windows Clipboard.

   Now that you've copied the characters to the Clipboard, you can paste them into the application you are using.

TIP   You also can open the Character Map over the document into which you want to paste the characters and drag them directly from the Map into the target document.

Cleaning Up Your Hard Disk

Everybody needs a little cleanup now and then. Your computer is no different. Windows XP includes the Disk Cleanup utility, which gives you a way of removing unneeded files from your computer's hard disk. Disk Cleanup doesn't make any tough judgment calls—you don't have to worry about the utility erasing a copy of that report you were really meaning to hang on to. Instead, Disk Cleanup erases files that get deposited in temporary Internet storage, installed items you don't need any longer, and discarded items that are now in the Recycle Bin.

NOTE   You may be wondering why Windows creates such things as temporary files. Temporary Internet files—and other Windows temporary files, such as those created when you're working on a word processing document—speed access to some files and Web pages by storing information that is needed only for a short period, perhaps until you save the document or until an application has downloaded and been installed on your computer. When the files are no longer needed, they can be discarded. Windows XP generally takes care of deleting unneeded files for you—the oldest files are removed as new files are added—but you may want to do some housecleaning and start fresh. Unless you know that the files are there, how do you know to delete them? Windows Disk Cleanup knows just what kinds of files to look for—and where to find them. When you run Disk Cleanup, all these unneeded files are gathered up and removed, leaving you with sometimes considerably more free space than you had before.

To start Disk Cleanup, follow these steps:

1. Click Start to open the Start menu, and choose All Programs, Accessories, System Tools, and Disk Cleanup. The Select Drive dialog box appears, as Figure 5.21 shows.

Figure 5.21

Your first choice involves selecting the drive you want to clean.

2. Click the Drives down-arrow and choose the drive you want to clean up.

3. Click OK to start the cleanup. After a moment, the Disk Cleanup dialog box appears, as shown in Figure 5.22. There, you can review all the files that Disk Cleanup has marked for deletion. The Description area tells you what the marked files are for and explains why they are no longer needed.

TIP   If you would feel better taking a look at the files to be deleted before you let Disk Cleanup do away with them, click the View Files button to display them in traditional folder style. When you're satisfied that you can let the files go, click the folder's Close box and continue with Disk Cleanup.

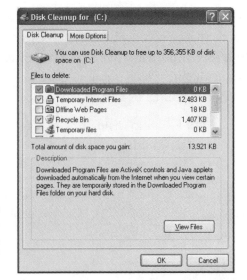

Figure 5.22

Disk Cleanup shows you the files marked for deletion.

4. Click the More Options tab in the Disk Cleanup dialog box. On this page, you find three more ways in which you can clean up your computer storage space:

○ **Windows components.** When you click the Clean up button in this section, Windows XP Setup launches the Windows Components Wizard so that you can add or remove programs in Windows XP (see Figure 5.23). To remove components you no longer need, scroll through the list and click the check box to remove the check mark. Click Next to continue. The Configuring Components window appears and shows you the status as the components are removed.

○ **Installed programs.** Clicking the Clean up button in this section displays the Add or Remove Programs window, which enables you to remove programs you do not use or need.

○ **System Restore.** Windows XP enables you to use the System Restore feature to set restore points that enable you to return your system to a previous configuration at a certain point. These restore points take up memory, so you can let Disk

Cleanup remove all but the most recent restore point in an effort to save space. When you click the Clean up button in this area, Disk Cleanup asks whether you're sure you want to delete all but the most recent point. Click Yes to continue and delete the earlier points; otherwise, click No.

5. Click OK in the Disk Cleanup dialog box to start the procedure. A confirmation box appears, asking whether you want to proceed. Click Yes to start the cleanup.

Disk Cleanup displays a status message telling you what's being cleaned and how far it has to go (see Figure 5.24). You can stop the operation at any time, if you choose, by clicking Cancel.

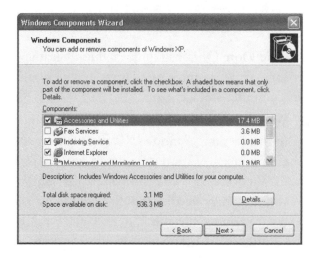

Figure 5.23

You can use the Windows Components Wizard to remove in Windows XP any items you don't use.

Figure 5.24

Disk Cleanup shows you the status of the operation for each file type it deletes.

PROTECTING YOUR PROGRAMS AND FILES

Although Windows XP doesn't have a virus-checker built into the program as part of the System Tools, you **must** have some sort of utility that scans your disk for viruses and corrects any problems it finds.

A virus is a computer program that spreads to files and folders on your computer and can do serious damage to the data stored on your computer. Unfortunately, viruses are intentionally created and accidentally passed along (one of the most embarrassing viruses gets into your Address Book and e-mails itself to all the people on your contact list).

When you first install Windows XP, depending on the manufacturer of your computer system and the arrangements it made with third-party vendors, you may have McAfee, Norton Antivirus, or another antivirus program icon positioned on your desktop. You can double-click the icon to launch a free trial of the software. If you don't see an icon for a free trial, check out one of the following sites to see whether trial versions are available:

•http://www.mcafee.com

•http://www.symantec.com (the company that produces Norton Utilities)

When you install a virus-checking utility, it can scan for viruses periodically (in most checkers, you can set this option for once a day, once a week, or once a month, as you prefer). The utility also evaluates any new files you download and open, and even tests your e-mail before you send it.

Antivirus programs also provide regular updates so that the program knows to check for the newest viruses (which, unfortunately, are being developed and circulated all the time). You should check often for updates for your antivirus software so that you can be sure to be inoculated against the latest viruses.

No More File Fragments

Over time, as you use your computer, creating, saving, and moving files; downloading files from the Internet; and deleting files you no longer need, the files and folders on your hard disk can become fragmented. Because of the way a computer stores information, it may store saved information in various places on your hard drive, even though it looks to you as though the data is all in one place.

The Disk Defragmenter utility consolidates the file and folder fragments that may be scattered on your hard disk. Defragmentation is subtle but important because it decreases hard drive wear (which means less seeking all over the drive) and speeds file access (for the same reason). When you run the Disk Defragmenter, the program analyzes your hard disk and then defragments the disk. Finally, it displays a report showing you what has been done.

Starting Defragmenter and Analyzing Your Disk Storage

Launch Disk Defragmenter by clicking Start and choosing All Programs, Accessories, System Tools, and Disk Defragmenter. To analyze your hard disk and determine whether you need to run the defragmenter, open the Action menu and choose Analyze. The Defragmenter begins to analyze the disk, as Figure 5.25 shows.

In the Estimated disk usage before defragmentation area, colored lines begin to appear during the analysis. This display gives you a visual sense of how files are organized on your hard disk. Use the key at the bottom of the Disk Defragmenter window to read the color coding on your machine:

- ♦ Red lines indicate fragmented files.
- ♦ Blue lines indicate contiguous files (files saved sequentially).
- ♦ Green lines indicate unmovable files.
- ♦ White lines indicate free space available on your hard disk.

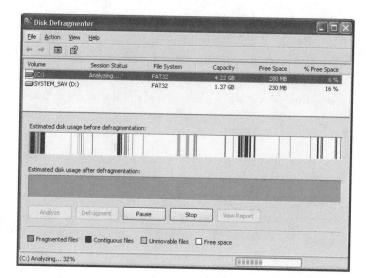

Figure 5.25

Disk Defragmenter analyzes your hard disk to see whether files and folders are fragmented.

After the analysis is finished, the Disk Defragmenter displays a pop-up box telling you whether your hard disk needs defragmenting (see Figure 5.26). To continue with the process, click the Defragment button.

Figure 5.26

After the Defragmenter analyzes your hard disk, it lets you know whether the process needs to be run.

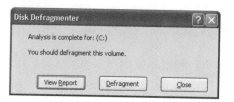

Defragmenting Your Hard Disk

If you decide to go ahead and run the Defragmenter, you can start the process by clicking the Defragment button. The Analysis begins again and displays the color patterning in the top and bottom bars showing the before and after affects of defragmentation.

TIP

If you don't have anything better to do, you can sit and watch the colors change while defragging is going on—but because the process could take 30 minutes or longer, you might want to start the defragment process as you're getting ready to go get some lunch.

Reviewing the Report

When the process is complete, the Disk Defragmenter displays a message box telling you that the defragmentation is complete and asking whether you want to view the report. You can click Close or View Report. If you choose to see the report, it is displayed in the Defragmentation Report window, as shown in Figure 5.27. You can scroll through the information items in the report and then choose one of three options:

- Click Print to display the Print dialog box and create a printed copy of the report.

- Click Save As to save the report as a file on your hard disk.

- Click Close to close the Defragmentation Report window.

To exit the Disk Defragmenter, click the Close box and return to the Windows desktop.

Figure 5.27

The Disk Defragmenter report tells you the status of your hard disk and reports on fragments that were not consolidated.

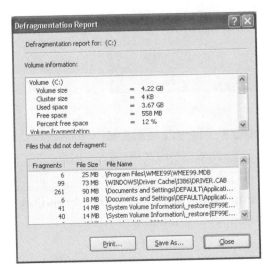

Automating Tasks

With all these different processes and utilities to worry about, you may be relieved to know that you can have Windows XP perform some of them for you automatically. By using the Scheduled Tasks utility in the Windows XP System Tools, you can schedule, arrange, and customize the order in which the tasks are carried out. Creating a scheduled task involves these steps:

1. Create a new task.
2. Link the task to the program that will execute at the given time.
3. Schedule the time you want the task to execute.
4. Choose task management options.

Display the Scheduled Tasks folder by clicking Start and choosing All Programs, Accessories, System Tools, and Scheduled Tasks. The folder opens, as you see in Figure 5.28.

Most of the Scheduled Task window will look familiar to you—it's not much different from My Computer and My Pictures. Another menu is added for Scheduled Tasks, however: the Advanced menu. In the Advanced menu, you find the following options related to scheduling automated tasks:

- ⚙ Stop/Start Using Task Scheduler stops and starts the scheduler.
- ⚙ Pause Task Scheduler pauses the use of the Scheduler.
- ⚙ Notify Me of Missed Tasks lets you know when scheduled tasks cannot be completed.
- ⚙ AT Service Account displays a dialog box you can use to set up another account that can run AT commands (scheduling commands available in versions of Windows before Windows XP).
- ⚙ View Log displays a log of attempts to carry out the scheduled tasks.

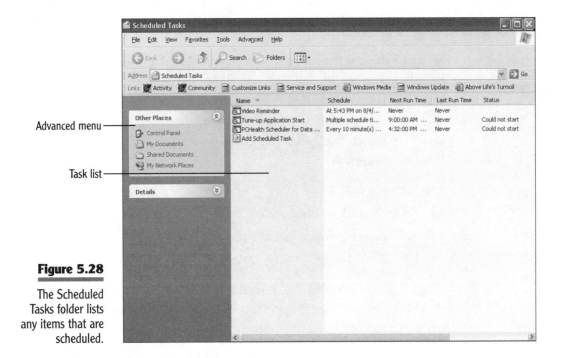

Advanced menu

Task list

Figure 5.28

The Scheduled Tasks folder lists any items that are scheduled.

Creating a New Scheduled Task

When you want to add a new task to the ones already scheduled, open the File menu and choose New, Scheduled Task. A new task appears in the task list. Double-click the new task icon to open the New Task dialog box (see Figure 5.29).

To set up the new task, follow these steps:

1. In the Run text box, type the file name of the program you want to run at a scheduled time. If you prefer, you can click Browse, navigate to the file name, and choose it in the Browse dialog box.

2. In the Start in box, enter the folder name in which the program and its related files are stored.

3. In the Comments box, you can add a note about the scheduled task (this step is optional).

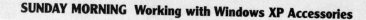

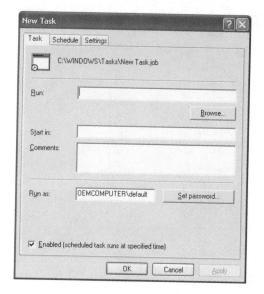

Figure 5.29

You set up a task in the New Tasks dialog box.

4. If you are working with multiple accounts, you can choose to assign the scheduled tasks to a specific user and password. In the Run as box, enter the username; click Set Password to assign a password to the task.

TIP

If you are creating scheduled tasks on a multiuser system, remember that only the administrator has scheduling permissions. Others who use your computer—kids, spouse, in-laws—cannot set scheduled tasks without permission.

Setting the Schedule

Next, you need to tell the Task Scheduler when you want to carry out the scheduled task. By default, Windows XP arranges to carry out the task at 9 a.m. every day, beginning on the current date. You use the options in the Schedule tab of the New Task dialog box to customize the schedule the way you want it. To set the schedule, follow these steps:

1. Click the Schedule tab in the New Task dialog box (see Figure 5.30).

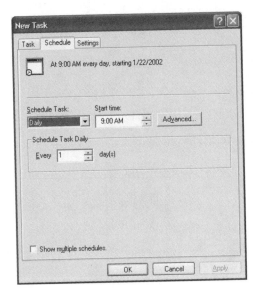

Figure 5.30

You set the schedule for the task on the Schedule tab.

2. Click the Schedule/Task down-arrow and choose how often you want to execute the task. Your choices are the following:

   ○ Daily (you can arrange to skip days by changing the entry in the Schedule Task Daily option)

   ○ Weekly

   ○ Monthly

   ○ Once

   ○ At System Startup

   ○ At Logon

   ○ When idle

3. Click in the Start time box and use the up or down buttons to set the time.

4. Click Apply to accept the settings and click OK to close the New Task dialog box.

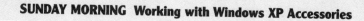

5. When the Set Account Information appears, enter and confirm a password (be sure to write the password in a place you can find later) and click OK.

TIP

If you want to set the task for a definite period with a start date and end date, click the Advanced button and specify the dates and settings for the task. When might you want to do this? Suppose that you are working on a project that requires weekly project meetings, one each week for the next eight weeks. Your team, which is spread virtually all over the country, meets via NetMeeting (the online conferencing tool included with Windows XP). You can schedule a task to launch NetMeeting at the desired time—and determine the end date for that task eight weeks in the future.

Knowing Your Computer Info

The final system tool we take a look at in this morning's session is System Information. When you click Start and then choose All Programs, Accessories, System Tools, and System Information, the screen shown in Figure 5.31 appears.

Figure 5.31

The System Information dialog box tells you everything you need to know about your computer—and then some.

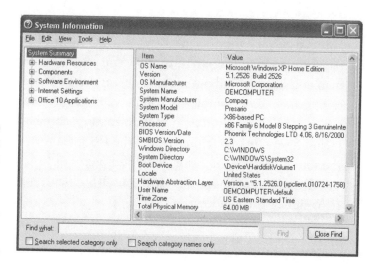

As you can see in the panel on the left, System Information collects and displays all kinds of facts about your computer system in general and these items in particular:

- ✿ Hardware Resources
- ✿ Components
- ✿ Software Environment
- ✿ Internet Settings
- ✿ Office Applications

Displaying System Information

The first page displayed is the System Summary page. This page lists all the major information items that a tech-support person might want to know—what version of Windows you're using; what type of system you have; what processor you're using, and so on. To review all the information in the System Summary page, slide the vertical scroll bar down.

TIP You learn about System Restore, a feature that enables you to return your system configuration to previous settings, in Appendix A.

You can display the subcategories beneath each of the items in the left panel by clicking the + sign to the left of the item name. Then click the item you want to find out more about, and the details are displayed in the right panel. For example, in Figure 5.32, I selected Components, followed by Sound Devices. The information about the sound device—including the manufacturer name, the IRQ channel, and the location of the sound driver (which are all helpful pieces of information if you need to call technical support about a sound problem)—are displayed in the right side of the window.

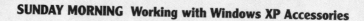

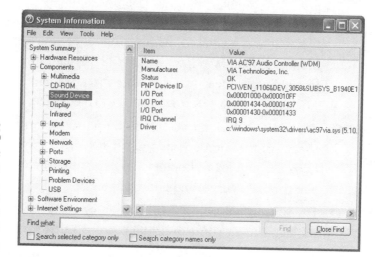

Figure 5.32

Navigate to the item you want to know more about, and the information is displayed in the right side of the window.

TIP

If you are searching for something specific, such as the name of a driver or a model number, you can enter the information in the Find what box in the bottom of the System Information dialog box. You can then click Find to search for the information, and the results of the search appear in the right panel.

Using Diagnostic Tools

In the Tools menu of the System Information window, you find a number of tools you can use to sleuth out problems you may be having with your computer:

○ Net Diagnostics gathers information about hardware and software settings and checks the network. You can also use Net Diagnostics to troubleshoot network problems.

○ System Restore enables you to restore your system to a previous configuration. To find out more about System Restore, see Appendix A.

- The File Signature Verification Utility checks to make sure that files that are integral to the functioning of your system have not been modified. Windows XP uses file signatures to ensure that key files maintain their integrity. This check searches for files to make sure they have not been damaged or changed in any way.

- The DirectX Diagnostic Tool is a sophisticated diagnostic tool that checks all the components and drivers on your system that use DirectX, a media technology developed by Microsoft that enables you to work with sound and graphics.

- Dr. Watson is a utility that keeps an eye on your system and logs problems in an effort to debug problems that occur.

When you're finished working with the components and tools in System Information, click the Close box to return to the Windows XP desktop.

Games, Games, and More Games

This session ends on a light note, with a closer look at the games included with Windows XP. Have you heard about the Minesweeper craze that keeps bleary-eyed computer users at their systems for hours on end? Have you heard about the marathon Solitaire games that keep players searching for that magical good deal? Windows XP games are simple but addictive—be sure to explore them *after* you've finished your more pressing work. These games are included with Windows XP:

- FreeCell
- Hearts
- Internet Backgammon
- Internet Checkers
- Internet Hearts
- Internet Reversi
- Internet Spades

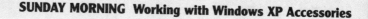

- Minesweeper
- Pinball
- Solitaire
- Spider Solitaire

Several games in Windows XP—FreeCell, Hearts, Minesweeper, Pinball, and Solitaire—have been around in previous versions of Windows. The new Internet offerings—Backgammon, Checkers, Hearts, Reversi, and Spades—take you online to **http://www.zone.com**, where you can play against other Internet users. In this section, you get to try out a few games and see which you like best.

TIP

This section focuses only on the games that come with Windows XP, but rest assured—the Internet has thousands of games (freeware, shareware, and retail) that you can download and install on your computer.

Single-Player Games

Windows XP includes games of different types—some card games, some skill games, some luck games—to entertain you in different ways. You can find all the Windows XP games by clicking Start and choosing All Programs, Games. This section takes a look at some of the different games and gives you a little nudge to try a couple.

FreeCell

The FreeCell card game is similar to old-fashioned Solitaire. The idea here is a bit different in that you have holding spaces, or "free cells," at the top of the play area, where you can place cards temporarily. As with Solitaire, the object of FreeCell is to return all the cards to their suit stacks, arranged from ace to king. Figure 5.33 shows you the opening screen of FreeCell.

Figure 5.33

FreeCell is a form of Solitaire in which you can use free cells as temporary holding areas.

Minesweeper

The object of Minesweeper is to find all the mines as quickly as possible without stepping on any of them in the process. This game is known to be highly addictive—especially among computer book editors. The upside is that it's short, it's fun, and it's simple. Let's give it a try:

1. Click the Start menu and choose All Programs.

2. Choose Games and click Minesweeper. Minesweeper opens on your desktop (see Figure 5.34).

Figure 5.34

Minesweeper is a fast and surprisingly addictive game.

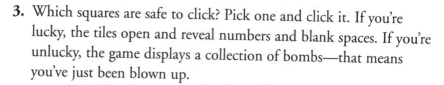
3. Which squares are safe to click? Pick one and click it. If you're lucky, the tiles open and reveal numbers and blank spaces. If you're unlucky, the game displays a collection of bombs—that means you've just been blown up.

Don't worry—winning at Minesweeper is nearly impossible. But you can delay the inevitable if you're lucky and perhaps a little psychic.

3D Pinball

3D Pinball is one of my favorites, simply because real-life pinball was always a favorite game at video arcades, even after Pong and Atari took the gaming world by storm. The Microsoft version of Pinball is really quite good, with terrific graphics, good action, and realistic sound.

Want to play a game? Launch Pinball by following these steps:

1. Click Start and choose All Programs, Games, and Pinball. The Pinball game launches (see Figure 5.35).

Figure 5.35

The sound effects and graphics make the game real enough to tilt.

2. Use the arrow keys on your keyboard to shoot the ball and begin to play. Here are the keys you use:

   ✿ The left arrow is the Left Flipper.

   ✿ The right arrow is the Right Flipper.

   ✿ The down arrow is the Left Table Bumper.

   ✿ The Enter key is the Right Table Bumper.

   ✿ The up arrow is the Bottom Table Bumper.

   ✿ The spacebar is the Plunger.

3. To launch the ball, hold down the space bar and then release it. The left and right arrow keys serve as your flippers.

4. If you score high enough, you're asked to add your name to the hall-of-famers list.

When you're ready to exit the game, click Game and then Exit.

Solitaire

Solitaire is that old-time favorite based on a simple objective: Just put the cards in order, according to their suits from ace to king. As part of the game play, you layer the cards in sequence in the playing area, alternating black and red suits. To start Solitaire, click Start and choose All Programs, Games, Solitaire. The Solitaire window opens, as you see in Figure 5.36.

Start playing by seeing which cards can be played on other cards—or, if possible, place cards in the suit area across the top of the playing area. When you've finished arranging the cards already on the desktop, click the top of the desk to turn over three more cards. Play any cards possible from the deck; then click to turn over three more cards.

TIP You can change the look of the deck by opening the Game menu and choosing Deck. The Select Card Back dialog box appears, offering 12 additional card styles. Click the style you want and click OK.

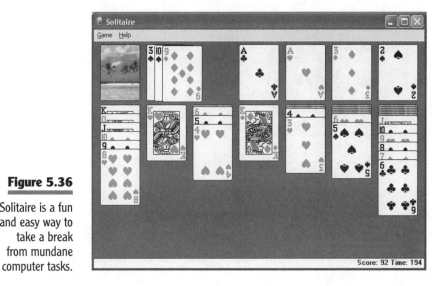

Figure 5.36

Solitaire is a fun
and easy way to
take a break
from mundane
computer tasks.

Internet Games

Windows XP also includes a number of games you can play online—
because working online doesn't have to be a lonely undertaking. A number of different online games are included, but I selected Checkers to
illustrate the process of playing games on the Internet.

Windows XP works with MSN and Zone.com to provide an enjoyable,
easy-to-use, and safe gaming interface. To start Internet Checkers and
play a game, follow these steps:

1. Click Start and choose All Programs, Games, and Internet Checkers. The opening window for Checkers appears, as Figure 5.37
   shows.

2. If you are not online, the Network Connections dialog box opens
   so that you can choose your connection and click Connect. This
   step displays the Connect dialog box so that you can check the settings and click Connect again.

3. After the Internet connection is made, Windows XP makes a connection with the game server.

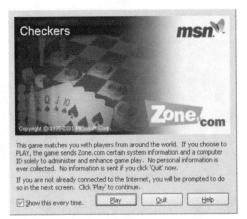

Figure 5.37

Windows XP teams up with zone.com and MSN to offer Internet game services.

4. As soon as the connection is made and another beginning-level player is found, the game begins (see Figure 5.38). Quick—you're red! It's your move!

5. To move a checker piece, click it and drag it to the new location. Next, it's your opponent's turn.

6. Continue playing the game until someone wins.

7. When you want to exit the game, open the File menu and click Game to open the menu; then choose Exit.

If you like, you can pseudo-chat while you play. The Internet Checkers game (and the other Internet games) include a chat feature that enables you to say encouraging or friendly things, but it's not an "open chat" in which you can say anything you want. Instead, you can choose from a list of "prefab" sayings to send to your opponent (see Figure 5.39).

TIP

If you're a parent and want to ensure that your kids are safe while playing against an online gamer, this restricted chat feature enables them to play while still keeping real-time contact to a minimum.

Figure 5.38

The Internet
Checkers game
appears in a
window on your
desktop; everything
is set up for you
and it's time
to play.

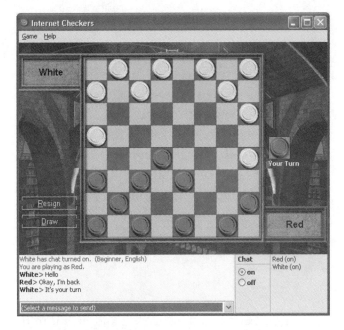

Figure 5.39

The game chat
feature is limited to
a selection of
common phrases.

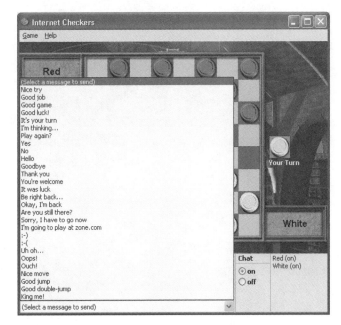

What's Next?

Is it past noon yet? This session may have run longer than some of the others, depending on how long you play the games in Windows XP. In this session, you worked with most of the tools and utilities you are likely to use in Windows XP. As you saw, all kinds of things are available, from the Calculator to WordPad to Paint to a number of system helpers and diagnostic tools. This afternoon's session winds up the book by showing you how to personalize Windows XP by setting your own preferences, creating multiuser accounts, and more.

SUNDAY AFTERNOON

Sharing and Personalizing Windows XP

- ✪ Sharing Windows XP with other users
- ✪ Personalizing your workspace
- ✪ Customizing your Windows XP experience
- ✪ Controlling mouse and keyboard behaviors
- ✪ Changing the date and time settings
- ✪ Using handwriting and speech features

Good afternoon! And welcome to your final session in *Learn Windows XP in a Weekend*. This afternoon, you learn about ways you can tailor Windows XP to look, act, and perform the way it suits you best. You also learn how to set up and work with multiple user accounts and find out about the various accessibility features that make using Windows XP possible for users of all types.

Sharing Windows XP

We all learned, as kids that sharing is a good thing. But when sharing means you have a 15-year-old hanging over your shoulder saying, "Aren't you done sending that e-mail *yet?*" or you have a line forming in the family room for who gets to play games next, that sharing can get a little tiring.

Luckily, Windows XP offers an easy way for you to coordinate and control the sharing that goes on at your computer. You can set up multiple user accounts, each with its own preferences, so that everybody gets what he wants. In fact, when you set up user accounts, it's almost like giving each person his own computer (that you have to time-share, of course). You can do the following things with user accounts:

✿ Create a user account for each person who uses your computer.

✿ Define a unique screen name and password for each user.

✿ Allow each user to keep a separate list of Favorites.

- Enable each user to customize her Windows XP desktop.

- Save music, document, and video files in separate My Documents folder.

An Overview of User Accounts

Different kinds of user accounts allow you to do different tasks in Windows XP. Before you set up user accounts, you can do everything that needs to be done—from installing programs to working with programs to setting Windows preferences, and so on. When you create a new user account, you—as the computer administrator—can still perform all those tasks. The user accounts you create, however, are a bit more limited in what they can do. You work with these three different kinds of user accounts in Windows XP:

- The *computer administrator* account is the primary account on your computer—the one you are most likely using.

- A *limited account* is an account you create that enables the user to have access to all programs and resources but does not allow administrator-level privileges, such as creating and deleting accounts, accessing all files (even in other accounts), and installing and removing hardware and software.

- A *guest account* is an account you can set up so that users who do not have an account on your computer can use it. A guest account is limited to using programs as they are and cannot make any system or program changes.

Setting Up Multiple Users

You begin the process of setting up multiple users in the Control Panel. Here are the steps:

1. Click Start and choose Control Panel. The Control Panel window appears.

2. In the Pick a category list, click User Accounts. The User Accounts window opens, as you see in Figure 6.1.

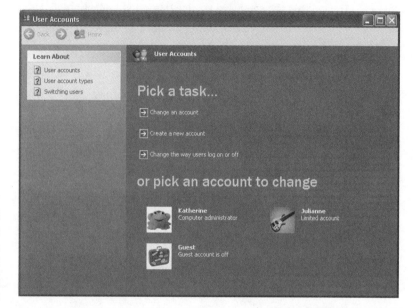

Figure 6.1

To create a new user account, begin by choosing User Accounts in the Control Panel.

NOTE The User Accounts window, shown in Figure 6.1, shows three different user accounts: the computer administrator account, one limited account, and one guest account. The guest account is turned off for now.

In the User Accounts window, the Pick a task area displays three options you use regularly: Change an account enables you to make changes to existing accounts; Create a new account is the option you use to create a new limited account; and Change the way users log on or off enables you to make changes in the way you change control from one user to another. Throughout this section, you learn how to use each of these options to work with user accounts.

ACCOUNT RESPONSIBILITIES FOR SHARED ACCOUNTS

Both the computer administrator and limited account types have different lists of responsibilities. Here's an overview of the tasks each account type can perform.

The computer administrator can:

- Create, modify, and delete new user accounts.
- Change system settings.
- Change and delete passwords on all accounts.
- Install and remove programs.
- View, move, modify, and delete all files (even those in limited user accounts).

The limited account user can:

- Create a unique background and theme.
- Customize desktop icons.
- Change or delete the account password.
- Access files the user has created or downloaded.
- Create unique Favorites.
- View and work with files in the Shared Documents folder.

Creating a New Account

When you want to create another user account, start in the User Accounts window (choose Control Panel and click User Accounts). In the Pick a task area, click Create a new account. Windows XP asks you to enter a name for the new account (see Figure 6.2).

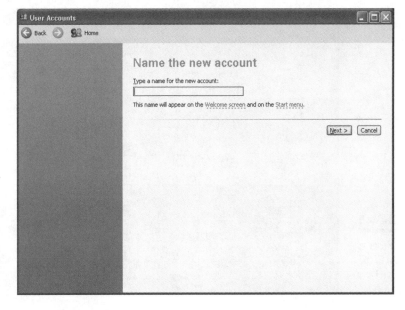

Figure 6.2

The first step in creating a user account is entering a username.

Type the username for the new account. A name can be a person's first name, a screen name or handle, or even a number (but who wants to be a number?). Type the name and click Next.

The next window asks you to choose an account type. Windows XP offers two account types: computer administrator and limited account. Even though you already have one computer administrator account on the system (the one you're using now), you can create another account with the same privileges, if you choose. Click the account type you want and click Create Account. The new account is shown in the bottom of the User Accounts window (see Figure 6.3).

Creating a Guest Account

If you want to create a guest account on your computer (suppose that the babysitter is coming over and has asked whether she can play Internet Checkers after the kids are asleep), you can activate the Guest account by starting in the User Accounts window.

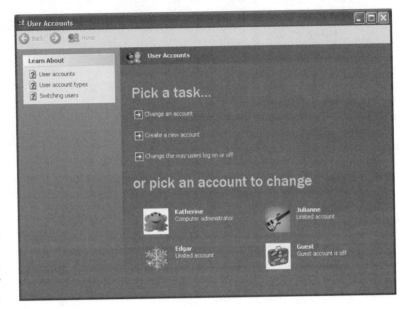

Figure 6.3

The new user is added in the bottom of the User Accounts window.

By default, the Guest account is turned off, and a computer administrator must be the person to enable it. Simply click the Guest icon. Windows XP displays a window asking whether you want to turn on the account. Click the Turn On the Guest Account button to make the account active. The Guest account is now available in the logon screen.

Logging On and Logging Off

So, now that you have different user accounts, how do you use them? Moving from user to user involves logging one user off and logging another on. It's a pretty simple task, but it requires a few keystrokes. Here are the steps:

1. Click Start to display the Start menu. The menu opens on the screen. In the bottom of the menu, you see the Log Off button (see Figure 6.4).

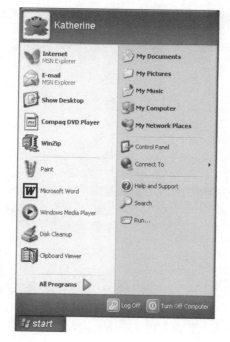

Figure 6.4

The Log Off button in the bottom of the Start menu enables you to switch users easily.

2. Click the Log Off button. A small message box appears, asking you to confirm that you want to log off. Click Log Off to continue.

NOTE Any programs you are using—such as Paint or WordPad—are closed down automatically if you had left them open when you began the logoff procedure.

3. Windows goes through a typical shutdown sequence (you even hear the Windows theme). After a moment, the logon screen appears, as Figure 6.5 shows.

4. Click a username, and Windows displays a welcome window and tells you that it's loading your personal settings. The next window is your Windows XP desktop, waiting and ready for you to use.

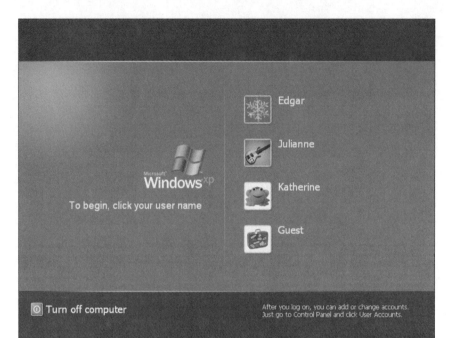

Figure 6.5

The new user is
added in the
bottom of the User
Accounts window.

Changing Accounts

After you create and work with user accounts a while, you're sure to want to make some changes. You might want to do the following:

- Rename an account.
- Add a password.
- Choose a new picture.
- Change the account type.
- Delete the account.

The sections that follow describe each of these different processes. To get to the point in Windows XP where you can make your account changes, follow these steps:

1. Click Start, choose control Panel, and select User Accounts. The User Accounts window appears.

2. In the Pick a task window, click Change an account. The Pick an account to change window appears so that you can select the account you want to change. (*Note:* This step is available only to those users who have computer administrator privileges.)

3. Click the user account you want to use. A list of options appears, showing you which items you can change on the selected account (see Figure 6.6). The sections that follow explain more about completing each of these tasks.

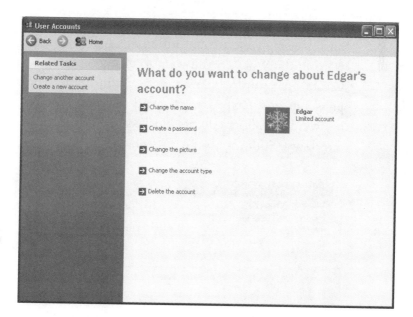

Figure 6.6

The new user is added in the bottom of the User Accounts window.

Renaming the Account

This stuff is about as easy as it gets. When you want to rename your account, you simply display the User Accounts window (by choosing Start, Control Panel, and User Accounts) and click Change an account. Choose the account you want to rename and then click Change my name. When prompted, type a new name for the account and click Change Name. Yes, it really is that simple.

TIP

A good name says it all. You may not worry about using your chat room handle, Snookums, on your computer administrator account, but won't you get tired of your 12-year-old son razzing you about it? Whatever screen name you choose is visible to everyone else using your computer, so you may want to put some thought into the nickname or proper name you use.

Adding a Password

You can create a password for your account to ensure that you're the only one accessing your account information. To do that, click Create a password in the What do you want to change about your account? list. The Create a password window appears, and you can type the new password, press Tab, and retype the password a second time (see Figure 6.7). The password you enter appears blocked out (so that anyone looking at the screen over your shoulder can't see).

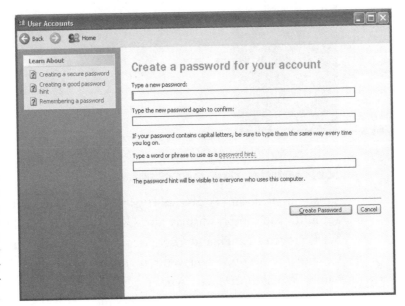

Figure 6.7

As the administrator, you can set up passwords for your own account or for other user accounts.

NOTE If you are adding a password for a limited user, Windows XP warns you that any personal certificates or stored passwords the user may have created will be lost.

In the third line, enter a word or phrase that will give you a hint if you ever forget the password. Be sure that the hint you enter isn't too obvious, however; anyone who uses the computer can see the hint and maybe guess at your password before you do. After you enter the hint, click the Create Password button to finalize the password.

WHAT MAKES A GOOD PASSWORD GOOD?

Here are a few ideas for creating a password that works for you:

- A good password is memorable—to you. Create a password you will remember later, something that the hint can help you recall.

- A good password is confusing to others. Avoid choosing something obvious (like your dog's name, your office extension, or your first name).

- A good password doesn't demand that you enter it in a certain way. Use all lowercase (so that your password won't be rejected if and when you forget to enter that capital letter).

- A good password mixes letters and characters. Mixing letters and numbers makes the password harder to figure out.

- A good password is not too short and not too long. Create a password of between five and seven characters.

Remember: A bad password can be changed.

Choosing a New Picture

Windows XP includes a number of fun pictures you can assign to your own user account (and, if you're the computer administrator, you can assign pictures to other peoples' accounts). You can easily change the images Windows chooses for you by following these steps:

1. Click Start and choose Control Panel.

2. Click User Accounts. The User Accounts window appears.

3. Select Change an account. The Pick an account to change window appears.

4. Choose the account you want to change. (Notice that the images already applied to the individual user accounts are displayed in this window.)

5. When Windows asks which item you want to change, click Change my picture. A window with 23 different account images appears (see Figure 6.8).

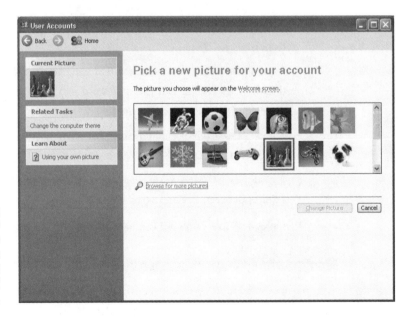

Figure 6.8

You can choose a new picture for your account or add one of your own.

6. Scroll through the list to find a new picture. Click the one you want and click the Click Picture button. The picture is applied to your account.

The new user account picture appears to the left of your username when you log on or off or perform other account-maintenance operations.

TIP If you don't see a picture that you feel captures the essence of who you are, you can click Browse for more pictures and use an image from your My Pictures folder. Windows displays the Open dialog box so that you can choose the file and click Open. The picture is then automatically resized and applied to your account.

Changing the Account Type

Another job for the computer administrator involves being able to change the type of account from administrator to limited and back again. When you want to change the type of account (perhaps you're going on a friends-only vacation and you want to make sure your college-age daughter can do everything she needs to do without you there), you simply display User Accounts again (you know the routine—click Start, choose Control Panel, and click User Accounts). Then choose Change an account, choose the account you want to change, and select Change the account type. The screen shown in Figure 6.9 appears, showing you what the account is set to handle and giving you the option of changing the account.

Click the account type you want to assign to the user account or click Cancel to abandon the change. You are returned to the previous window, and you can continue making account changes, if you like.

Removing the Account

When you no longer need an account you've created, you can delete it if you have computer administrator privileges. To remove the account, display the Users Accounts window by choosing Start, Control Panel, and

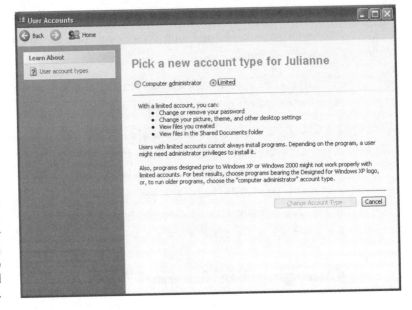

Figure 6.9

You can change the type of user accounts from limited to administrator and back again.

User Accounts. In the Pick a task list, choose Change an account; then choose the user account you want to change. Finally, click Delete the account, and the window shown in Figure 6.10 is displayed.

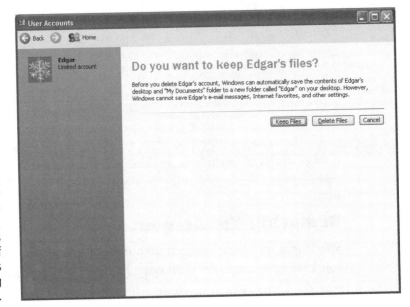

Figure 6.10

When you delete an account, Windows XP gives you the option of keeping the user's files or discarding them.

You can choose whether you want to save the user's files (the ones that were stored in his My Documents folder) or delete them. Click the Keep Files button to store the files; click Delete Files if you want to remove them.

Personalizing Your Workspace

Now that you know how to set up individual user accounts so that everyone can have her own, special preferences when using the computer, you need to know how to set those special preferences. You can do all kinds of things in Windows XP to personalize your computer experience. Here are just a few:

- ✿ Choose a different Windows background for the desktop—or use your own favorite photo.
- ✿ Select a theme (the look of the background, windows, sounds, and icons) for your computer.
- ✿ Change the colors used on your screen.
- ✿ Add Web elements to your desktop.
- ✿ Select a screen saver (or create your own).

These items can all be done for each individual user on your system. That's lots of personalization! The sections that follow show you how to make the changes you want to change. They all begin with the Display Properties dialog box, which you find in the Control Panel window.

An Overview of Display Properties

To set all these personal preferences for your user account, start by displaying the Display Properties dialog box. Follow these steps to get there:

1. Click Start and choose Control Panel.
2. In the Control Panel window, choose Appearance and Themes.
3. Click Display. The Display Properties dialog box appears, as you see in Figure 6.11.

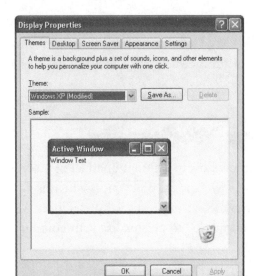

Figure 6.11

In the Display
Properties dialog
box, you choose
the way you
want Windows XP
to look.

The Display Properties dialog box includes five different tabs, each of which controls a different aspect of the interface design. The following list gives you a brief introduction to each of the tabs, and you use the various settings in the upcoming sections:

○ Themes shows you the current display theme selected for your computer.

○ Desktop allows you to choose the background for your desktop and customize the appearance of icons.

○ Screen Saver enables you to add a screen saver to your system and adjust the power settings for your monitor.

○ Appearance enables you to choose a style, color scheme, and font size for the windows and buttons in the interface.

○ Settings enables you to set the screen resolution, control colors, and configure your system to work on multiple monitors.

The Background You Want

Windows comes with a number of backgrounds you can substitute in place of the one set up on your system by default. To change the background, follow these steps:

1. Click Start and choose Control Panel. The Control Panel window opens.

2. Click Appearance and Themes; then click Display. The Display dialog box appears.

3. Click the Desktop tab. In the Background list, scroll through all the different backgrounds to find one that suits you.

4. If you don't find one you like and you would rather use an image of your own, click the Browse button. The Browse dialog box appears so that you can navigate to and select the file you want to use as a background. Find it, click it, and click Open. The Browse dialog box closes and the image is added to the preview monitor in the Desktop tab (see Figure 6.12).

Figure 6.12

You can use one of your own photos as a background. Just click Browse and select the file you want to use.

TIP   You can use Windows background files plus HTML documents and files in the formats .bmp, .gif, .jpg, .dib, and .png for your background images.

And Now, for an Entirely New Theme

What is a *theme?* It's a combination of elements that create your Windows XP experience. The background, icons, and the sounds you hear all contribute to the theme effect. If you're not particularly attached to an image on your desktop, you may want to ditch the previous settings and choose a new theme. Windows XP comes with several different themes, and you can choose one by following these steps:

1. Click Start and choose Control Panel. The Control Panel window opens.

2. Click Appearance and Themes; then click Display. The Display dialog box appears.

3. Click the Themes tab. Click the Themes down-arrow to display your choices (see Figure 6.13).

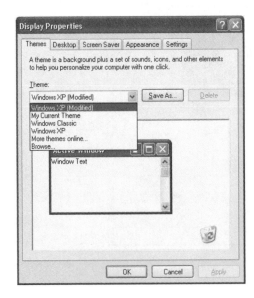

Figure 6.13

You can set in the Themes tab a different theme for the Windows XP desktop.

TIP You can get additional themes by choosing the More themes online selection in the Themes drop-down list—but be prepared to get out your charge card because these themes aren't free. The Web site is **http://www.microsoft.com/Windows/Plus,** and the themes offered are part of Microsoft Plus! For Windows XP. In Plus! you get digital media tools, new 3-D games and graphics, themes, backgrounds, and more.

Your Icons, the Way You Want Them

When you first begin working with Windows XP, you're more interested in learning where everything is than you are in changing it. But after you've had a chance to find your way around, you may start to notice things you want to change. Perhaps you would change some of the icons, if you could. Or you would hide the icons you rarely or never use. You make these changes, and more, in the General tab of the Desktop Items dialog box.

To customize the items on your desktop, follow these steps:

1. Click Start and choose Control Panel.

2. In the Control Panel, choose Appearance and Themes; then click Display. The Display Properties dialog box appears.

3. Click the Desktop tab; then click Customize Desktop near the bottom of the tab. The Desktop Items dialog box appears (see Figure 6.14). In this dialog box, you can make changes to the following elements:

   - **Desktop icons.** You can remove the icons for My Documents, My Computer, My Network Places, or Internet Explorer by clicking their respective check boxes.

   - **Change icons.** You can change the icon used for the common desktop icons, if you choose.

   - **Desktop cleanup.** You can click the Clean Desktop Now button to have the Desktop Cleanup Wizard remove unused icons and file them in a folder in case you want to use them later.

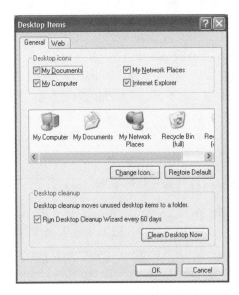

Figure 6.14

In the General tab of the Desktop Items dialog box, you can change the icons displayed on your desktop.

Setting a Web Page as Your Desktop

If you have a Web page you particularly like—so much so that you want to start and end your day looking at it—you can choose it over the default Windows backgrounds or even your own art. You begin with the Display Properties dialog box. Here are the steps:

1. Click Start and choose Control Panel.

2. In the Control Panel, choose Appearance and Themes; then click Display. The Display Properties dialog box appears.

3. Click the Desktop tab; then click Customize Desktop near the bottom of the tab. Next, click the Web tab. The screen shown in Figure 6.15 appears.

4. Click the New button. The New Desktop Item dialog box appears. You can now choose one of the following:

   ❖ **Visit Gallery.** Clicking this button takes you online to the Internet Explorer Desktop Gallery, where you can sample the active desktop items, such as the Microsoft Investor Ticker,

CBS SportsLine, Weather Map from MSNBC, and J-Track Satellite Tracking. You can choose the Add to Active Desktop button to download this item to your system.

⚙ **Location.** To add the Web page of your choice, click in the Location box and type the URL.

⚙ **Browse.** If you want to use an HTML document on your desktop, click the Browse button and navigate to the HTML file you want to use; click Open to complete the operation.

5. Click OK to close the New Desktop Item dialog box. The new selection is added to the Web tab.

TIP If you want to safeguard your desktop against changes, click the Lock desktop items check box before clicking OK to close the Desktop Items dialog box.

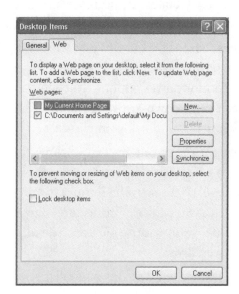

Figure 6.15

You can set a Web page to function as your desktop, if you choose.

Selecting a Screen Saver

Why do you need a screen saver? Especially if you're away from your computer for long periods of time—more than 30 minutes or so—the same image is being painted on your screen, over and over again. On older model monitors, this process caused wear-and-tear on a screen that you could avoid by keeping things moving. Screen savers were designed to do just that: Keep things moving on the screen. Although newer monitors aren't affected by the same "screen burn" problem, it's still nice to see something moving on your screen (even when your mind is at a standstill).

Windows XP comes with a number of different screen savers. You can choose one and set both the amount of time after which you want the screen saver to begin and any options that apply to the screen saver you selected. To choose a screen saver, follow these steps:

1. Click Start and choose Control Panel.

2. In the Control Panel, choose Appearance and Themes; then click Display. The Display Properties dialog box appears.

3. Click the Screen Saver tab. On this tab, you see a preview monitor that shows the screen saver you select; you also see Screen saver options and Monitor power options. To choose a new screen saver, click the Screen saver down-arrow. A list of screen savers is displayed (see Figure 6.16). Click your choice.

NEW IN ▶
WINDOWS XP

4. Set the options for the screen saver by clicking the Settings button. Different screen savers have different settings. The dialog box shown in Figure 6.17 displays the settings for the My Pictures Slideshow screen saver choice. This feature, new in Windows XP, enables you to use your favorite pictures (stored in My Pictures) as a slide show screen saver.

5. Set the options as needed. For this particular screen saver, you can elect how often you want the images to change, how large you want the images to be, which folder you want to use, and whether you want to use transitions between images. You can also elect to move through the pictures by pressing the spacebar.

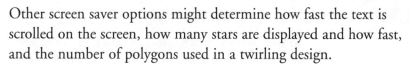

Other screen saver options might determine how fast the text is scrolled on the screen, how many stars are displayed and how fast, and the number of polygons used in a twirling design.

6. Click OK to return to the Display Properties dialog box. Click Apply and then OK to apply the changes and close the dialog box.

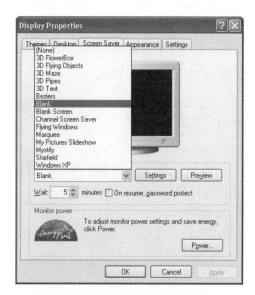

Figure 6.16

Windows XP offers a variety of different screen savers to try.

Figure 6.17

Remember those digital photos you scanned earlier this weekend? You can make them into a screen saver for your Windows XP desktop.

Changing Color Schemes

So you've been making lots of changes to the way Windows XP was originally configured. Are you happy with the effects you're creating? Another change that touches virtually every level of your work with Windows involves the color schemes used for dialog and message boxes. In the Appearance tab of the Display Properties dialog box, you can choose the color scheme and font size you want to use for all windows and buttons used throughout Windows XP and its application programs.

To change the color scheme, follow these steps:

1. Display the Display Properties dialog box by choosing the Control Panel and clicking Display.

2. Click the Appearance tab. In the top portion of the Appearance tab, a preview window shows the current color sections.

3. Click the Windows and buttons down-arrow if you want to change to Windows classic style.

4. Click the Color scheme down-arrow to select either the olive green or silver color scheme.

NOTE   If you don't see any color schemes you like, you can further customize the colors and appearance by clicking the Advanced button in the Appearance tab.

5. Click the Font size down-arrow if you want to change the size of the fonts used in menus and windows.

6. When you have set the color scheme and font the way you want them, click Apply and then click OK to close the dialog box.

TIP   Click the Effects button in the Appearance tab if you want to change additional settings about the appearance of menus (such as whether the menus fade or scroll and whether they display shadows) and windows (whether the contents appear while they are being dragged). Choose the settings you want to use and click OK to close the dialog box.

Take a Break

How are you doing? Ready to take a break? Now that you've finished tailoring the way you want your Windows XP desktop and menus to look, take a 15-minute break, get a snack, do a Sunday-afternoon kind of thing (no, don't take a nap—you still have half a session to go!). Then come on back and we'll talk about other items you can customize—such as mouse and keyboard settings—that enable you to further personalize your experience with Windows XP.

Customizing Your Windows XP Experience

Now that you know how to change the way things *look,* you might be interested in changing the way things *work.* Windows XP enables you to make changes that relate to the all-important Start menu and Taskbar, the way your mouse moves and your keyboard clicks, and the display of the date and time on your computer. This section helps you customize these various tasks and create the working environment you want in Windows XP.

Choosing Taskbar Settings

You learned about the Taskbar in an earlier session, so you already know that you use the Taskbar to move between open applications. In addition, you find the Start button in the Taskbar, you launch applications from the Taskbar, and you get important system information—such as the time, date, and system utilities that are in use—from the Taskbar. Use these steps to display the Taskbar tab of the Taskbar and Start Menu Properties dialog box:

1. Click Start and choose Control Panel. In the Control Panel window, choose Appearance and Themes.

2. In the Appearance and Themes window, click the Taskbar and Start Menu option.

3. You can then choose the option you want to change (see Figure 6.18). The following sections explain those options.

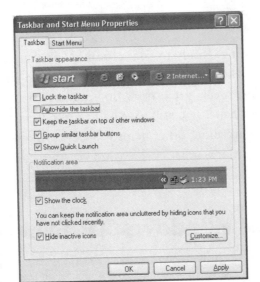

Figure 6.18

The Taskbar tab offers a number of settings that enable you to customize the Taskbar display.

Auto-Hide and Always Show

You can change several things about the Taskbar, if you choose. You can decide to auto-hide the Taskbar, which in effect "puts it away" when you aren't using it, giving you more room on-screen. You also can do the opposite, if you like, making sure that the Taskbar always stays visible, even on top of open applications. The option for this task is Keep the taskbar on top of other windows.

Grouping Buttons

You also can elect to group similar buttons on the Taskbar so that they are shown one atop the other in a Taskbar selection. By choosing the Group similar taskbar buttons option, you tell Windows XP to display all similar programs (such as Internet applications, for example) in a single button on the Taskbar. When you click that button, a small pop-up menu appears, and you can click the program you want (see Figure 6.19).

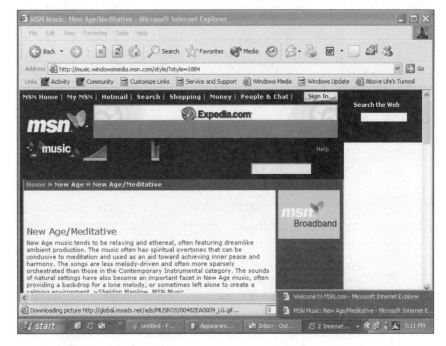

Figure 6.19

Grouping similar
tasks enables you
to have more room
on the Taskbar.

Locking the Taskbar

After you make the changes you want to the Taskbar and get it just the
way you like it, you may want to lock it so that it can't be inadvertently
or purposely changed. The option to do the trick is Lock the taskbar: Just
click it to enable the feature. After you click Apply and click Close, the
current settings for the Taskbar are locked into place.

Changing the Notification Area

The items in the lower half of the Taskbar tab offer choices about the
notification area, the area on the far right side of the Taskbar that displays
the clock and other system icons. The two options offered you are these:

○ Show the clock, which displays the system clock.

○ Hide inactive icons, which suppresses the display of icons that are
   not in use.

Both these options are enabled by default, which means that the system clock is always showing and any icons that are not in use are hidden. If you want to change either of these settings, simply click the check mark to remove it.

You can customize the icons used for the notification area by changing when they are displayed and when they are hidden. To make the change, click the Customize button. The Customize Notification dialog box appears. The list of current and past items is displayed. To change the status of an item, select it and then click the down-arrow that appears to the right of the current selection (see Figure 6.20). Choose the setting you want (your choices are Hide when inactive, Always hide, or Always show); then click OK. Windows XP makes the change, and that icon is displayed (or hidden) in the notification area according to your selection.

TIP

If you make changes to the notifications and then decide that you liked them better the way they were, you can return the icons to their normal settings by displaying the Customize Notification dialog box and clicking Restore Defaults.

Figure 6.20

You can change the way icons are displayed in the notification area.

Customizing the Start Menu

The Start menu is likely to become the most-often-used menu on your computer. You use it to start programs, to log on and off, to shut down your computer, and to do lots of tasks in between. As your experience with Windows XP grows, you may discover a few things you want to change about the Start menu. You make those changes in the Start Menu tab of the Taskbar and Start Menu Properties dialog box, as shown in Figure 6.21.

Figure 6.21

You can customize the Start menu as it is or choose a retro Start menu instead.

Display the dialog box by following these steps:

1. Click Start and choose Control Panel. In the Control Panel window, choose Appearance and Themes.

2. In the Appearance and Themes window, click the Taskbar and Start Menu.

3. Click the Start Menu tab. This is where it all begins. Click Customize to begin setting options. The Customize Start Menu dialog box appears.

TIP

If you want to see what the classic Start menu looks like without going to the trouble of changing it, click the Classic Start menu button. The display changes to show you the style. Want to return to the Start menu? Just click its button.

Changing the Way the Start Menu Looks

The General tab of the Customize Start Menu dialog box, as shown in Figure 6.22, gives you a number of ways to control the display of the items offered. Your first choice has to do with the size of the icons used. By default, Windows XP displays large icons (or maybe that setting is only for those of us over 40); you can change to small icons by clicking the Small icons button.

The Programs area of the General tab enables you to choose the number of program shortcuts that you include on the Start menu. This is an automatic feature of Windows XP that adds to the Start menu the programs you use most often—it's a convenient addition to the Start menu. But if you want to keep your Start menu from being cluttered, you can reduce the number of program shortcuts you include there. To reduce

Figure 6.22

The General tab offers options for changing the way the Start menu looks.

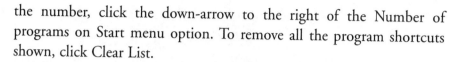
the number, click the down-arrow to the right of the Number of programs on Start menu option. To remove all the program shortcuts shown, click Clear List.

Finally, in the Show on Start menu area of the General tab, you can choose the program you want to be displayed for your Internet and e-mail choices. If you've installed MSN Explorer, that choice is entered by default in both selections. If you want to change to Internet Explorer, Outlook Express, or some other programs you use as a matter of course, simply click the down-arrow and choose the program you want to use.

Modifying What the Start Menu Does

How the Start menu behaves is another matter—and you can make the changes for those behaviors in the Advanced tab of the Customize Start Menu dialog box (see Figure 6.23).

In the Start menu settings area, you make decisions about whether you want submenus to open automatically when you point to them or whether you want to require a click before they open. By default, point-ing does the trick. Additionally, the Highlight newly installed programs check box causes any new programs to be highlighted so that you can find

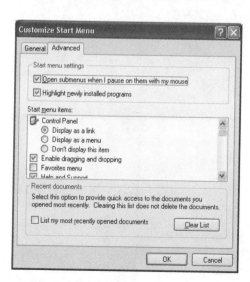

Figure 6.23

You can change in the Advanced tab the way the Start menu acts.

them easily the first time you go looking for them. If you want to change either of these settings, simply click the check box to turn them off.

The Start menu items area lists all the different items you could possibly display on the Start menu and lets you decide whether you want to display them and, if so, *how* you want them to be displayed on the menu. Scroll through the list and read them one by one; click those you want to include and click (to deselect) any displayed items that you don't want to display. Some items, such as My Documents, give you three options:

- ✪ Display as a link.
- ✪ Display as a menu.
- ✪ Don't display this item.

The first option places the selection on the Start menu as a link, meaning that you can click it to simply move to the item as usual. If you choose the second option, Display as a menu, the item is shown as a menu and you can select items from it, as Figure 6.24 shows.

Figure 6.24

You can opt to display items on the Start menu as menu selections so that they display submenus when clicked.

The final option on the Advanced tab has to do with Recent documents. If you used earlier versions of Windows, you are familiar with this feature—it lists the files you used most recently so that you can select them again later. This is another convenience item that can really be a help if you work routinely in the same files.

To display recently used documents on the Start menu, click the List my most recently opened documents check box. If you want to erase the documents on the list so that you can start again, click the Clear List button. Finally, click OK to close the Customize Start Menu dialog box; click Apply and then OK to close the Taskbar and Start Menu Properties dialog box. Windows XP makes the changes you selected, and the Start menu and the Taskbar should reflect your custom choices.

Controlling Mouse and Keyboard Behaviors

Another setting that often drives users nuts until they change it to work the way they want it to has to do with input devices—specifically, the mouse and the keyboard. If the mouse leaves a little trail of arrows stretching across your screen, you may find it annoying. Similarly, if your keyboard feels sluggish, if the letters appear slowly instead of almost instantly, as you type, it may bug you. This section shows you how to experiment with the settings that affect your mouse and keyboard and shows you how to change them if needed.

Making Mouse Changes

The mouse options are all tucked away in the Mouse selection on the Control Panel. Get there by following these steps:

1. Click Start and choose Control Panel.
2. In the Pick a category area, click Printers and Other Hardware.
3. Next, click Mouse. The Mouse Properties dialog box appears, as you see in Figure 6.25.

Figure 6.25

The Mouse
Properties dialog
box gives you
everything you
need to set mouse
options.

The Mouse Properties dialog box includes five different tabs that each
provide a different set of options related to the way your mouse works:

○ Buttons enables you to choose primary and secondary buttons,
control the double-click speed, and use the ClickLock feature.

○ Pointers allows you to choose the way you want the pointer to
look.

○ Pointer Options sets the motion, control, and look of the pointer
as you move it across the screen.

○ Wheel helps you choose scrolling options.

○ Hardware enables you to see which mouse is installed on your system and test it to make sure that it is working properly.

Two items that most mouse users are interested in are the double-click
speed of the mouse and the appearance of the mouse pointer. The following exercises walk you through the process of changing both those
options.

Changing the Double-Click Speed

You use double-clicking frequently. When you want to launch a program on your desktop, you double-click the icon. When you want to open a file in your My Music folder, you double-click it.

But a little finesse is involved in double-clicking. If you wait too long between clicks, Windows XP thinks that you're simply clicking twice and doesn't open the file or launch the program the way you want it to. Similarly, if you double-click it too fast, Windows XP might miss it completely and your program icon just sits there on your desktop, looking at you.

To check and change the double-click speed, display the Mouse Properties dialog box. In the center of the Buttons tab, start by double-clicking the folder that is displayed. What did it do? If the folder didn't open, try dragging the slider toward Slow on the Speed bar. Alternatively, if you feel that the mouse is responding too slowly, you can adjust the slider toward the Fast end. Experiment with the setting until you can click the folder and have it open or close in a manner that feels comfortable for you.

When you've got the speed the way you want it, click Apply; then click Close to close the dialog box.

Changing Pointer Options

But wait—before you close Mouse Properties, you might want to stop by the Pointer Options tab. The Pointer Options tab contains just about everything you might want to change related to the way the mouse pointer moves on the screen.

This issue might not be something you're conscious of, but the pointer on the screen is an important element in the way you use your computer. If the pointer moves slowly across the screen or drags a tail after it, you might feel like you're having to struggle to get your work done. If the pointer is too responsive, or skittish, it may seem jumpy and unpredictably—and you may spend time looking for it on your screen, which can make *you* jumpy. Why fuss with these things when you can correct them instead? That's what the Pointer Options tab can help you do.

Display the Pointer Options tab by displaying Mouse Properties (choose Start, Control Panel, Printers and Other Hardware, and Mouse). Then click the Pointer Options tab (see Figure 6.26).

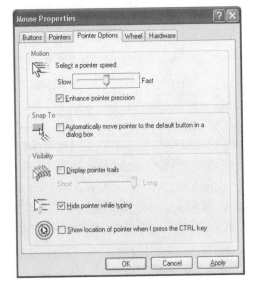

Figure 6.26

Setting Pointer Options is an important part of getting comfortable with your mouse.

You can then look over and set the options as follows:

○ Select a pointer speed enables you to control how quickly the pointer moves across the screen. The trick here is to get as close to your own speed as possible so that when you move the mouse, you feel that the pointer is moving seamlessly with you.

○ Enhance pointer precision helps position the pointer accurately so that it's not dancing around an option but rather placed directly on it.

○ Automatically move pointer to the default button in a dialog box is an option that is turned off by default. If you choose to enable it by clicking its check box, the pointer is positioned on the default

option automatically. (This can be confusing to those of us who always like to know where we left our mouse pointers.)

✪ Display pointer trails is another option that is turned off by default. This one shows you a trail of pointers when you move the pointer on the screen. If you have trouble finding the mouse pointer on the screen, this option can help you keep track of the mouse position.

✪ Hide pointer while typing is an option that is turned on at first. This option suppresses the display of the pointer when you are typing.

✪ Show location of pointer when I press the Ctrl key is one of those items that helps you locate the pointer on the screen. It is turned off by default.

After you review the options, make any changes you want by clicking the check box or dragging the slider (for the pointer speed and pointer-trails options). When you've made your changes, click Apply to put the changes into effect.

Keyboard Considerations

Your keyboard is another device you spend lots of time with. If you find yourself accidentally including double characters in your typing—that is, if you repeat letters in words without meaning to—you can change the repeat rate on your keyboard to correct the problem.

Using the keyboard options, you also can change the rate at which the cursor blinks, if that's something that catches your attention regularly. Some people like a faster cursor rate than Windows XP provides because it helps them remember where the cursor is on the screen. Others of us find that a too-fast cursor blink rate raises our blood pressure, like the computer is saying "Well? Are you going to type something or not? Don't you see me waiting here?"

To display the Keyboard Properties dialog box, click Start and then choose Control Panel, Printers and Other Hardware, and Keyboard (see Figure 6.27).

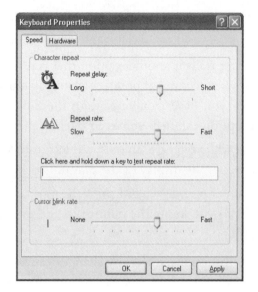

Figure 6.27

You can set the repeat delay, repeat rate, and cursor blink rate in the Keyboard Properties dialog box.

First, a few definitions. The *repeat delay* is the momentary pause that happens when you first press and hold a key. You can see what I mean if you click in the test box and press and hold the letter *M*. The first *M* appears, and then there's a pause, and then a whole line of *M*s begins to extend across the box. That pause is known as the repeat delay.

In contrast, the short time between the repeating *M*s is known as the *repeat rate*. You control both the delay and the rate by adjusting the sliders in the Character repeat section of the Keyboard Properties dialog box. Experiment with the different rates and test them out in the test box until you get a speed you are comfortable with.

The Cursor blink rate is another setting you control using a slider. This one determines how fast or slow the cursor blinks. Move the slide to Fast if you want to increase the speed, or drag it toward None to slow the blinker down.

When you're finished setting keyboard options, click Apply and then click OK to close the Keyboard Properties dialog box.

TIP The Hardware tab displays information about the specific keyboard on your system. You can click it to discover the make and model of your keyboard and to troubleshoot any keyboard problems you may be having.

Changing the Date and Time Settings

Chances are that you don't need to change the date and time too often, unless something almost unheard of happens, like the battery in your system wears out or your computer is zapped by lightning and lives to tell the tale. But in case you need to set your date and time (perhaps you just moved across country or you purchased your computer over the Internet and it just arrived from the west coast), here are the steps:

1. Click Start and choose Control Panel.

2. In the Pick a category window, choose Date, Time, Language, and Regional Options.

3. In the Pick a task window, choose the Date and Time selection. This step displays the Date and Time Properties dialog box (see Figure 6.28).

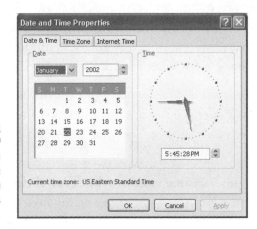

Figure 6.28

Correct the date and time in the Date and Time Properties dialog box.

After you display the Date and Time Properties dialog box, you can do several different things:

- Synchronize the time on your system with reliable Internet time.
- Select a different time zone (that's the move-across-the-country part).
- Change the date and time.

The sections that follow show you the particulars of performing each of these tasks.

Setting Internet Time

The Internet Time tab of the Date and Time Properties dialog box enables you to set your system clock according to a reliable international time. You have two choices of time server:

- **http://time.windows.com**
- **http://time.nist.gov**

To choose a different time server, simply click the Server down-arrow; then click Update Now. This action synchronizes the time.

TIP By default, Windows XP synchronizes the time once a week without any intervention from you. If you want to turn off the automatic synchronization, click the check box in the Internet Time tab to deselect it.

Choosing Your Time Zone

Setting the time zone in Windows XP isn't something you do often. In fact, if you do it once—or maybe twice—the whole time you have your current computer system, you may be doing it twice as often as the rest of us.

To set the time zone, display the Time Zone tab and click the down-arrow to the right of the selected time zone. A long list of choices appears. Click the item that reflects your place on the planet, and Windows XP displays it in the time zone entry. Now that you've got the right zone, you can move on to setting the date and time.

Setting the Date and Time

The Date & Time tab contains the settings you need in order to change the current day and the current time. (Of course, if accuracy is important to you, you allow the Internet time clock to establish the time setting for you.)

If you need to change the date, click the month down-arrow and choose the correct month; click the up- or down-arrows to change the year; and click the correct date in the displayed calendar to choose today's date.

 NOTE If you synchronize your system with Internet time to ensure the accuracy of the system clock, you need to keep the date set at the current date. If you set the date ahead or behind, Internet time can't synchronize with your machine.

Using Handwriting and Speech Features

NEW IN ▶ WINDOWS XP The final personalization option we cover in this session is about as personal as they get—using *your* handwriting and *your* voice to interact with Windows XP. The handwriting features in Windows XP enables you to literally write your own ticket—in Internet Explorer, in Outlook Express, and in other Windows-compatible applications.

These features are a little different from those discussed earlier in this chapter in that they are shared features with Office XP and other compatible programs. Although you set up the Language bar options from within Windows XP, you use the features when you are dictating text into

Word, for example, or using dictation commands to open and close Excel spreadsheets. Before the speech and language features are available in Windows XP, you must have enabled them in an application program, such as Office XP.

The speech feature in Windows XP enables you to teach your programs to recognize your voice. You can "speak" windows open, choose dialog box options, enter data, and run the spelling checker, all by the power of your voice. This section wraps up your Windows XP in-a-weekend tour with a closer look at these new, exciting features.

Checking Out the Language Bar

Both the handwriting and the speech features are part of the Language bar, a new feature with Windows XP (see Figure 6.29).

Figure 6.29

The Language bar provides the commands and options you need to work with speech and handwriting features.

The Language bar includes tools that enable you to do the following things:

- Change input languages.
- Turn on the microphone.
- Dictate text.
- Use voice commands to work with application programs.
- Set speech and handwriting options.
- Turn on handwriting features.
- Display the Drawing Pad.

Displaying the Language Bar

To display the Language bar, follow these steps:

1. Click Start and choose Control Panel.

2. Choose Date, Time, Regional, and Language Options; then choose Regional and Language Options.

3. Click the Language tab and, in the Text services and input languages section, click Details. The Settings tab appears, as you can see in Figure 6.30.

Figure 6.30

You can check the speech and handwriting features and configure the Language bar in the Settings tab of the Text Services and Input Languages.

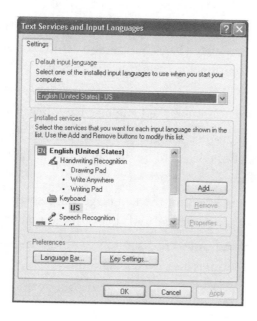

4. Review the items shown in the Installed services window. If your system has handwriting recognition and speech recognition features installed, they appear in this window. If they do not appear, use your Office XP installation CD to install them.

5. Click the Language Bar button to display the Language Bar Settings dialog box (see Figure 6.31).

Figure 6.31

Language bar
display options
enable you to
control the way the
bar looks.

6. Click the Turn off advanced text services check box to remove the check mark so that text services can be used.

7. Click the first option, Show the Language bar on the desktop, to display the Language bar. You can also set the following options to further customize your Language bar choices:

   ✪ Show the Language bar as transparent when inactive enables you to see through the Language bar when it is not being used.

   ✪ Show additional Language bar icons in the Notification area causes all the icons to be displayed in the Taskbar area, to the left of the system clock.

   ✪ Show text labels on the Language bar displays the names of the various Language bar tools beneath their icons.

   ✪ Turn off advanced text services disables handwriting and speech features and makes them unavailable to your programs.

8. Select any additional settings and click OK. Click OK to close the Text Services and Input Languages dialog box.

9. Click Apply in the Languages tab of the Regional and Language Options dialog box; then click OK to close the dialog box.

The Language bar is available when you next launch the application program that will be using it. The next time you open Word 2002, for example, the Language bar appears along the upper-right edge of your work window.

Hiding the Language Bar

When you're ready to minimize the Language bar, simply click the Minimize button in the upper-right corner of the bar. A dialog box appears, telling you that the Language bar icon will be displayed in the notification area. Click OK to continue. The bar is reduced to an icon on the Taskbar. You can redisplay the bar by clicking the Restore button.

Working with Handwriting

The handwriting features in Windows XP enable you to add your signature, jot a few notes, and sketch a diagram, directly in your application program, such as Microsoft Word 2002. You start handwriting from the Language bar by clicking the Handwriting button. A submenu appears, offering three options:

- ✪ Writing Pad
- ✪ Write Anywhere
- ✪ Drawing Pad

If you choose Writing Pad, a pop-up window appears, in which you can write the characters you want (see Figure 6.32). Simply use the pointer or the pen on your graphics tablet to write the letters you want to appear. When you release the mouse button or lift the pen, the character is inserted at the cursor position. Close the Writing Pad by clicking the Close box in the upper-right corner.

Choosing Write Anywhere displays the writing toolset (the same tools that are available on the right side of the Writing Pad) as a small palette you can position anywhere on-screen. You can then use the mouse pointer to

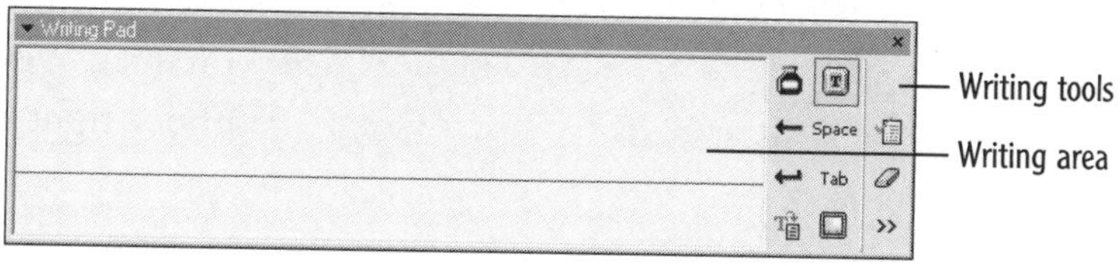

Figure 6.32

You can enter notes using the Writing Pad.

Writing tools

Writing area

write your notes as needed, and Word interprets the characters and places them at the cursor position. To close the tool palette, click the Close box.

Clicking Drawing Pad opens the Drawing Pad as a sketch box in the center of your screen (see Figure 6.33). You can sketch the image you want to add and use the Drawing tools on the right side of the Drawing Pad to copy, paste, or erase the image or return to the Writing Pad.

Figure 6.33

The Drawing Pad enables you to sketch out a thought without leaving your document.

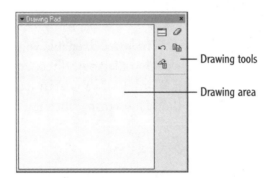

Drawing tools

Drawing area

WHAT DO YOU NEED IN ORDER TO USE HANDWRITING FEATURES?

Handwriting recognition requires that you have something to write on—something like a digital pen and tablet, a writing tablet, or a CAD tablet. You can even write using your mouse on your mouse pad, if you're willing to practice a bit. And, when push comes to shove, even a touchpad can be a writing device if you're patient enough to keep trying until you get something legible. For best results, however, a computer device, such as a writing tablet, is the best bet—you spend less time squinting and wondering what you meant to write after the text is entered.

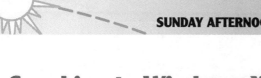

Speaking to Windows XP

The speech features in Windows XP are also part of the Language bar and become available when you install them using your Office XP installation CD. Getting the speech features to a point that they really save you time and trouble takes an investment of time and effort: you use the training session to teach Windows XP to recognize your voice and interpret your words properly.

TIP Windows XP enables you to create a different profile for each user on your computer. Each person can do a training session so that Windows XP recognizes the words, inflections, and phrasing of each individual user.

Training the Speech Tool

The first stop in working with the speech features in Windows XP involves teaching the program how to understand and interpret the words you speak. Each voice has its own fluctuation, intonation, and dynamics. We each phrase words differently, we breathe differently, we speak at different volumes, and we pronounce words using regional dialects we might not even notice. For this reason, you need to train Windows XP to recognize your words the way you speak them. To do this, you need about 20 minutes, a good microphone, and the patience to read and restate words Windows doesn't understand.

To launch the training tool, follow these steps:

1. Display the Language bar, if necessary.
2. Click the Tools button. A submenu appears.
3. Click Training. The Microsoft Speech Recognition Training Wizard launches (see Figure 6.34).
4. Click Next. Tell the wizard whether you are male or female and click the button that best represents your age. Click Next.

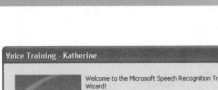

Figure 6.34

The Microsoft Speech Recognition Training Wizard helps you help Windows understand your words.

5. After two more preliminary screens (click Next on each one), the training begins. Read the text you see on-screen. The wizard highlights the words as it hears them (see Figure 6.35).

6. The wizard advances the pages as you complete each one. When the process is completed, the wizard builds a user profile and offers you the choice of doing more training. If you want to continue teaching speech to recognize your voice, click the More Training button.

7. Click Finish to end the training and return to your document.

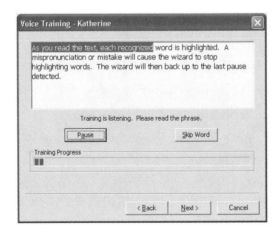

Figure 6.35

The wizard asks you to read each word clearly as it makes a record of your voice patterns.

Using Voice Commands

After Windows XP knows how to interpret the words you speak, you can use your voice to order the program around. Are you ready to save a document file? You can use Voice Commands to work with menus, toolbar, and dialog box options. Rather than open the File menu and choose Save, for example, you can follow these steps:

1. Say "voice command" to select the option in the Language bar.
2. Say "file." The File menu opens.
3. Say "save." The Save As dialog box appears. You can now use the mouse to choose the folder in which you want to save the file and type the new file name; then speak "save."

TIP Office XP applications and the speech-recognition features enable you to switch seamlessly between using voice commands, the mouse, and the keyboard.

Windows XP Dictation

Dictation is one of those things you learn only by experience. It would be nice if we could simply talk in our normal voices, at our normal speed, and have Windows XP simply record and display the information as we talk. Dictation isn't quite as seamless as that, although you may find it helpful, or at least fun. The challenge of dictation is in teaching it to recognize your words accurately—and that takes lots of training.

To switch to Dictation mode, you can click Dictation in the Language bar or simply say "dictation." Now speak clearly into the microphone, and the speech-recognition feature inserts at the cursor position the words it thinks you said.

TIP Chances are that it will take lots of practice to get this working right. If you want to do additional training to help Windows XP better understand your words, click Tools, Training in the Language bar.

What's Next?

This final session introduced you to the various ways you can tailor Windows XP to work and look just the way you want it. From a beginning discussion of setting up and maintaining multiple user accounts to a step-by-step exploration of various system preferences, this session topped off your Windows XP weekend intensive by showing you how to make it your own.

The next steps are up to you. I hope that as you use Windows XP to run your programs, organize files, browse the Internet, and maintain your system, you also remember to have some fun with the extras: media, messaging, and more.

Thanks for spending the weekend with me, and enjoy your time with Windows XP!

A Windows XP Install-and-Update Guide

- ✪ Updating or restoring Windows XP
- ✪ Before you install
- ✪ Installing and removing programs
- ✪ Adding hardware

Congratulations! You've made it through your whirlwind weekend with Windows XP. Hopefully, you've learned everything you need to know in order to get comfortable with the operating system and to take advantage of the features that make your computing life easier.

This appendix is meant to serve as a reference for you whenever you need to install a new program, add a piece of hardware, or update (or restore) your version of Windows XP. Let's start with what you need to do to prepare for making major changes to your system.

Updating or Restoring Windows XP

When you purchased your system, one version of Windows was already installed on it. If your system is a few years old, you might have started out with Windows 98 or Windows Me. If your system is new, you already have Windows XP (which means that you don't need to use this appendix to install it). First, let's establish what you need to do, and when, as far as Windows upgrading goes:

○ You can get periodic Windows updates to make sure you have the most current information possible.

○ You can restore Windows XP to its original settings if you are having trouble with the operating system and want to reverse changes you've made.

Updating Your Version of Windows

Software is always changing. New versions are released all the time; new patches (or "fixes") for programs are introduced. You can make sure that you're up-to-date by using the Windows Update feature in the Help and Support Center. Here are the steps:

1. Connect to the Internet.
2. Click Start and choose All Programs.

3. Click Windows Update. A window appears, telling you that Windows XP is checking for the latest version of Windows Update (see Figure A.1).

4. Click Scan for updates to begin the search for items you can download.

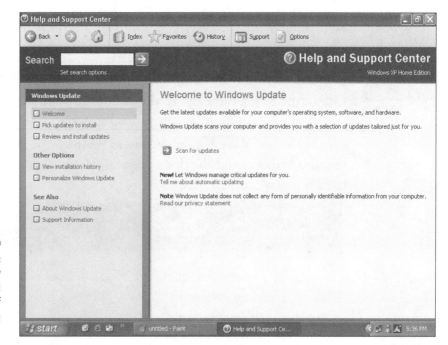

Figure A.1

Windows Update searches for any changes you need in your version of the operating system.

 TIP

If you have problems with the way a program operates after you upgrade to Windows XP, use the Program Compatibility Wizard to search for and resolve the program setting that is conflicting with Windows XP. To start the Program Compatibility Wizard, click Start to open the Start menu and choose Accessories, and then choose Program Compatibility Wizard. The wizard launches and walks you through the process of trying different setting configurations to resolve any conflicts your older program may have with Windows XP.

Restoring Windows

Windows XP includes a feature, called *System Restore*, that keeps track of the changes made to your computer so that if you need to return the system to its previous settings, you can do so. The utility can reverse changes without erasing any of your documents, e-mail, or favorites.

The System Restore utility functions like a wizard, leading you step-by-step through the process of restoring your computer. To start System Restore, follow these steps:

1. Click Start and when the Start menu appears, click Control Panel.

2. In the Pick a category window, click the Performance and Maintenance option in the Control Panel window.

3. In the See Also panel, click System Restore. The System Restore wizard launches and the first screen appears, as you see in Figure A.2.

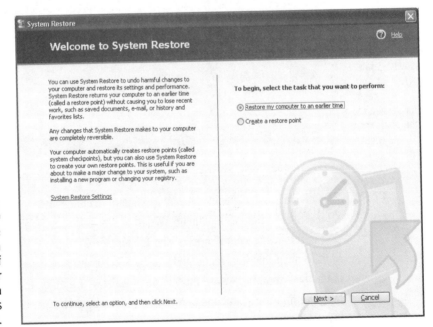

Figure A.2

System Restore leads you through the process of returning your computer to a previous configuration.

4. Choose one of the following options:

   ✿ Restore my computer to an earlier time.

   ✿ Create a restore point.

5. In the Select a Restore Point window, click a date on the calendar to choose a restore point on that day. Available days appear in bold. A list of available restore points appears in the list on the right.

6. Choose a restore point in the list on the right. Click Next to continue.

7. Windows displays the restore point and asks you to close all open programs. Click Next to complete the restore.

System Restore then shuts down and restarts Windows, using the settings saved on the day you selected as the restore point.

TIP You should create a restore point before you install a new program on your computer. This process makes returning to that point a simple matter if the program causes problems on your system.

Before You Install

As you learned in Sunday morning's session, "Working with Windows XP Accessories," you should get in the habit of backing up regularly. *Backing up* means to make copies of those files that are important to you—things you would miss if they were suddenly, accidentally wiped away. Before you install a new program on your computer, you should do the following things as a precaution:

✿ Back up all important files.

✿ Make a copy of your Windows Address Book.

✿ Create a restore point using System Restore so that you can return to previous computer settings if your system has trouble.

Backing Up Your Files

Depending on the method you choose to back up your information, you might work with a backup utility or simply use Windows Explorer to copy essential files to a safe place, such as a diskette, a recordable CD, or a Zip disk. The most important thing is to back up those files regularly just in case something happens when you install a new program and you can't get back to your data.

 TIP If you need a refresher on zipping up big files to make them smaller, see the section "Compressing and Extracting Files," in Saturday afternoon's session, "Handling Files and Folders."

Copying Your Address Book

One of the files you may not think about as something to preserve regularly is your Windows Address Book. But consider what it would mean to look up all those e-mail addresses and phone numbers—all that contact information. It's enough to make you have heart palpitations. You can avoid that crisis by following these steps:

1. Click Outlook Express icon in the Quick Launch bar. Outlook Express starts.

2. Click the Addresses tool to open the Windows Address Book.

3. In the Address Book window, click File and choose Export. The Select Address Book File to Export to dialog box appears (see Figure A.3).

4. Enter a name for the backup file and click Save. That saves the file—now you don't have to worry about it.

Now that you're covered, backup-wise, you're ready to install your programs or upgrade your version of Windows. The next section is about making changes to Windows, and after that you find out how to add first new programs and then hardware devices.

Figure A.3

You can back up your Windows Address Book to preserve it—just in case.

Installing and Removing Programs

Sooner or later, you want to install new programs on your computer. The new program might be a great new game your kids have been looking forward to, a new Web design program you've been wanting to try, or the latest copy of Microsoft Office. Whatever program you want to install, the process begins for you in the Control Panel.

Adding Programs

Begin by clicking Start and choosing Control Panel. In the Pick a category window, choose the Add or Remove Programs option. The Add or Remove Programs window appears, as Figure A.4 shows.

Click Add New Programs. The next window asks you to insert the CD or disk on which the program is packaged. Click the CD or Floppy button. This action launches the Install Program From Floppy Disk or CD-ROM wizard. Insert the disk or CD and click Next.

When the Run Installation Program window appears, click Finish. Windows installs the necessary software to walk you through the installation. Follow the prompts on-screen to read the license agreement for the

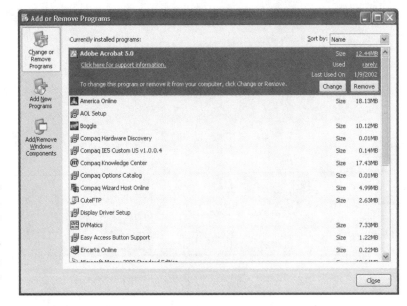

Figure A.4

Windows XP keeps track of all the programs you install on your computer in the Add or Remove Programs window.

program and choose where the files will be stored. The program then copies the necessary files to the folder you selected.

Removing Programs

The process for removing programs you no longer need is even easier than installing them. Follow the same basic process:

1. Click Start and choose Control Panel.

2. Click the Add or Remove Programs option. The Add or Remove Programs window appears.

3. Click the name of the program you want to remove. The program is highlighted, and a Change/Remove button appears, as you see in Figure A.5.

4. Click the Change/Remove button. The Confirm File Deletion message box appears, asking you to confirm that you want to remove the program you selected.

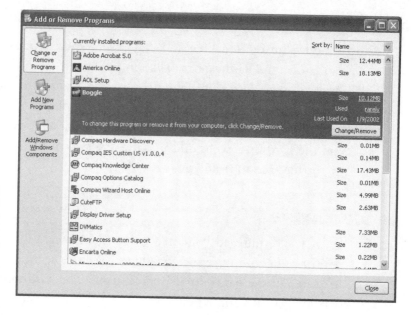

Figure A.5

You can easily remove a program by using Add or Remove Programs in the Control Panel.

5. Click Yes to delete the program.

6. Click the Close button to close the Add or Remove Programs window and return to the Control Panel.

NOTE To add or remove Windows XP components, click the Add/Remove Windows Components button on the left side of the Add or Remove Programs window. You can then choose to install Windows features or remove components you no longer need.

Adding Hardware

Remember that scanner you wanted for your birthday? Don't tell anyone I told you, but it's in the trunk of your spouse's car right now, waiting to be wrapped. After you blow out those birthday candles and let your family sing "Happy Birthday," you'll rush into the family room and want to plug it in and scan to your heart's content.

Introducing Plug and Play

Windows introduced Plug and Play several incarnations ago as a way to standardize the hardware installation process. It essentially makes things easier on you: Just plug your new printer, scanner, camera, or joystick into the appropriate port, and Windows recognizes it and knows what to do. If the hardware is Plug-and-Play compliant, Windows installs the drivers the hardware needs and updates the system automatically, without any further action from you.

Adding Hardware

So, if you've plugged your new piece of hardware into the appropriate port on your computer and Windows XP didn't seem to recognize it, you need to add the hardware drivers yourself. The hardware you purchased may have come with either diskettes or a CD with the appropriate install program. If so, follow these steps:

1. Insert the disk or the CD in the drive.

2. Click Start to display the Start menu and choose Run. The Run dialog box appears (see Figure A.6).

3. Click Browse and navigate to the drive or CD containing the hardware disk or CD.

Figure A.6

Use Run to launch the setup program to set up your hardware with Windows XP.

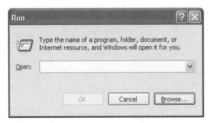

If your hardware didn't come with a CD or disk of its own, you can use the Add Hardware Wizard to let Windows XP help you set up the hardware. To run the Add Hardware Wizard, follow these steps:

1. Click Start to display the Start menu and choose Control Panel.

2. In the Control Panel window, select Printers and Other Hardware.

3. In the See Also box, the first option is Add Hardware. Click it to launch the Add Hardware Wizard (see Figure A.7).

Figure A.7

The Add Hardware Wizard walks you through the process of getting that new hardware set up.

4. Follow the prompts to complete the installation process for your new device.

5. Click Finish to complete the wizard—and your new hardware should be ready to use.

Windows XP Troubleshooting Tips

- ✪ Choose your troubleshooter
- ✪ Troubleshooting Q&A
- ✪ For more information

"Into every life a little rain must fall." The person who first penned that line had most likely never even used a computer—but somehow, mysteriously, it applies. Even the smoothest-running applications have glitches and klunks. Knowing a way around those problems—and whom to call on to help you when there's no way around but through—is a smart thing to include in your kit of computer knowledge.

Choose Your Troubleshooter

Windows XP offers a number of wizard-like troubleshooters that help you identify the problem you're having and try to resolve it with specific solutions. You'll find a troubleshooter ready to help with tasks related to the following topics:

- Digital video discs
- Display
- File and print sharing
- Hardware
- Home networking
- Input devices
- Internet connection sharing
- Internet Explorer
- Modem
- Multimedia and games
- Outlook Express (messaging)
- Printing
- Sound
- Start-up and shutdown
- System setup
- USB

So where do you find a troubleshooter when you need one? Suppose that your mouse is acting a little squirrelly. You're not sure what's going on, but the buttons don't seem to be functioning properly. What do you do? Here are the steps:

1. Press F1. The Help and Support Center dialog box appears.
2. Click in the Search box and type **mouse troubleshooter**. Press Enter. Windows XP finds the Input Devices Troubleshooter and highlights the statement that applies to you (see Figure B.1).

TIP You can also find troubleshooters by displaying the Control Panel and navigating to the Control Panel option that relates to the item you're trying to fix. You find troubleshooters in the Troubleshooters panel on the left side of the Control Panel window.

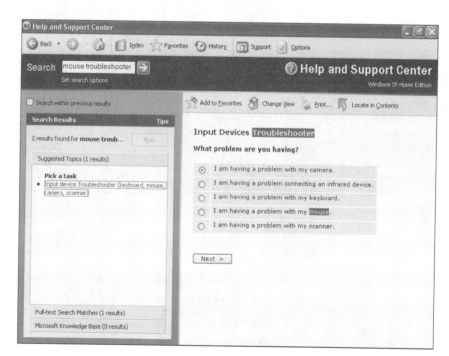

Figure B.1

Searching for mouse trouble-shooter brings up the Input Devices Troubleshooter.

3. Because the item you want is already selected, click Next. The troubleshooter asks whether you use a USB mouse or another type of device. Click Yes or No as appropriate and click Next.

4. The troubleshooter displays the first of the suggestions for ways to resolve the problem (see Figure B.2). To try the suggested solutions, click Mouse Properties and make the changes as noted.

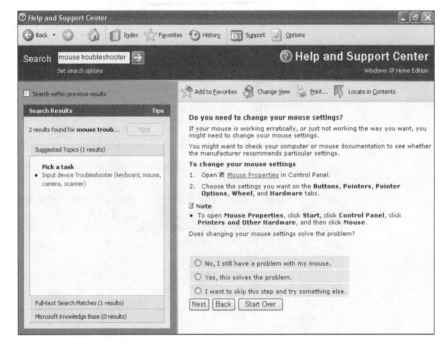

Figure B.2

The Troubleshooter suggests solutions one at a time and leads you through the process of sleuthing out the problem.

5. When you return to the troubleshooter, choose one of the following choices:

- ⚙ No, I still have a problem with my mouse. (This option takes you to the next step in the troubleshooter.)

- ⚙ Yes, this solves the problem. (This option closes the troubleshooter.)

- ⚙ I want to skip this step and try something else. (This option takes you to the next suggestion.)

6. Click Next, Back, or Start Over.

7. Continue through the suggested solutions until the problem is fixed or you have resolved what the problem *isn't* and have determined that you need to contact the hardware or software manufacturer for more information.

Troubleshooting Q&A

"I can't display all open windows at once." Sure you can. Right-click a blank area on the Taskbar and choose Tile Windows Horizontally or Tile Windows Vertically. This action arranges all open windows side-by-side on the desktop.

"My previous version of Windows displayed my most recently used documents in the Start menu, but Windows XP doesn't do that. Is there a way to display that feature?" You can add the feature to the Start menu, if you like. Right-click the Start button and then choose Properties. Select the Start Menu tab; click Start Menu first and then Customize. In the Advanced tab, click the List my most recently opened documents check box. Now you see My Recent Documents on the Start menu.

"I need to rename a whole list of files, but I don't want to click them one by one. Is there a faster way?" If all the names have certain letters or numbers in common, you can do this task with a search-and-replace procedure. Suppose that you have a list of files named CRE01, CRE02, CRE03, and so on and you want to rename them as REN01, REN02, REN03, and so on. Navigate to the folder in which the files are stored and select them. Then open the File menu and choose Rename. Enter the new name and press Enter. This action renames the files.

"I have a program that ran fine in Windows 95, but it locks up in Windows XP. What can I do?" The Windows XP Program Compatibility Wizard solves just this problem. The Program Compatibility Wizard

tests various program settings until it finds and resolves the conflict. You access this wizard by choosing Start, Help and Support, Find compatible hardware and software for Windows XP. In the See Also panel, select Program Compatibility Wizard.

"I can't hear any sound from my computer's speakers." First, check the obvious: Is the volume turned up? Is your microphone plugged into your headphone jack by mistake? If neither of those options is the problem, make sure that the CD is functioning properly and that (this would be embarrassing) it isn't in the drive upside-down. If none of these issues is the answer, you may have a problem with your sound card.

"The sound on my computer is choppy." Do you have any other programs running on your computer? Media programs need lots of system resources, and if you have another program that is running in the background, it could be struggling with your media program. Try closing any open programs and rerunning the sound application you are using. If that doesn't work, check practical matters, like making sure that the CD surface isn't scratched; you have the most recent driver for your sound card; and your speakers are turned up and functioning properly.

"Windows XP isn't seeing my digital camera." Before the Scanner and Camera Wizard can copy digital photos from your digital camera to your computer's hard disk, the wizard needs to be able to read what is stored on your camera's storage card. Different cameras have different settings for access. Does your camera need to be turned on? Check the manual that came with your camera to see whether specific settings need to be in place before files can be downloaded.

"The printouts of my photos are poor quality." This problem could be caused by printing on substandard paper. To get the best printed results, print photos on digital photography paper. You can tell Windows XP about the paper type before you print. To do this, display the Control Panel and choose Printers and Other Hardware. Then click Printers and

Faxes. In the display area, right-click your printer's icon, click Printing Preferences, and select the Paper/Quality tab. Choose Photo Paper or Glossy in the Media area. This process should improve the print quality you see. If blurring or uneven printing occurs, perform a print cartridge test or a cartridge cleaning on your printer to make sure your print cartridges are in the best working order.

"I can't establish a connection with my ISP." First things first: Check the clock. Is this a high-traffic time? If so, try again in an hour or so. If you still can't connect, check your username and password and make sure they are entered correctly. Also check the number your modem is dialing—and use the phone to listen to the dial tone. Do you hear static? If you can't find any problem with the line and you still have trouble connecting, call the tech support number of your ISP and find out whether it is having server problems.

"The animations on Web pages I visit don't work." The most common problem here is that the animation requires a certain media player, such as Flash, that is not installed. Most Web sites prompt you to display the necessary player if you cannot view the animations displayed on the page.

"Internet Explorer doesn't seem to be saving all my Favorites." One of the great features of Windows XP is that it customizes the choices it shows you according to the way you use them. One feature that takes advantage of this customization is the Personalized Favorites menu, which is turned on by default when you launch Internet Explorer. The Personalized Favorites menu displays only those Favorites you've used most recently, so Favorites you haven't used in a while aren't displayed in the menu. You can turn the Personalized feature off so that all your Favorites are displayed by opening the Control Panel and choosing Network and Internet Connections and then choosing Internet Options. The Internet Properties dialog box appears. In the Advanced tab, click the Enable Personalized Favorites menu to deselect the option.

For More Information

Although you find lots of information in Windows XP that can help you find answers to the problems you may be experiencing, even more answers are available. As part of the massive Microsoft online presence, you can get into the support area of Windows XP and read through the program's FAQs (Frequently Asked Questions) to see whether other users have been experiencing the problems you are having. You can also use the Microsoft Knowledge Base to find articles published on the issues you're struggling with.

Using the Microsoft Knowledge Base

Microsoft has a huge online database of articles that can give you additional insight into your hardware and software challenges. To get to the Microsoft Knowledge Base, follow these steps:

1. Establish your Internet connection.

2. Launch Internet Explorer.

3. Enter **www.microsoft.com** in the Address bar and press Enter.

4. Click the Support tab in the upper-right corner of the screen.

5. Select Knowledge Base. The Product Support Services page appears.

6. Click the Search down-arrow and choose Windows XP.

7. Enter the phrase or keyword in the Solutions box and click Search now. The results of the search are displayed in the Summaries section of the browser window (see Figure B.3).

8. Click the article title, and the whole article is displayed in a new browser window. You can copy the file to your hard disk, if you choose, or simply read through the article and discover techniques you can try.

9. You can repeat the search as often as you want to retrieve as many articles as you need.

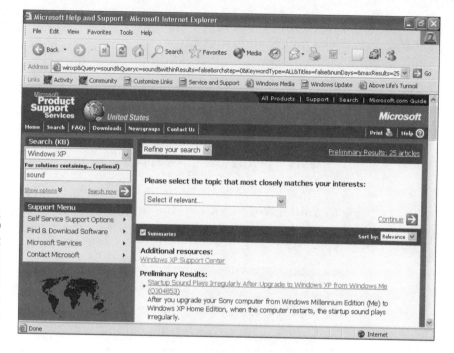

Figure B.3

The Microsoft Knowledge Base contains thousands of articles related to various solutions for Windows products.

TIP FAQs are another feature that can help you gather answers to troubleshoot hardware and software problems. FAQs list common questions and answers about various tasks. To display the FAQs, start in the Support Menu pane of the Product Support Services page and click Self Service Support Options. On the page that appears, click Product Support Center (FAQs and Highlights) to display a page full of FAQs related to various Windows XP topics.

Error Reporting

Windows XP also includes a built-in error-reporting feature that can automatically send error reports to Microsoft as well as to the manufacturers of your application programs when your system locks up or experiences a serious error. When an error occurs, a dialog box appears, asking whether you want to send an error report. Click Send to send the file; click Don't Send to cancel.

If you want to review or change the Error Reporting settings that are in effect on your system, follow these steps:

1. Click Start and choose Control Panel.

2. Click Performance and Maintenance; then choose System. The System Properties dialog box appears.

3. Click the Advanced tab.

4. Click Error Reporting, and the dialog box shown in Figure B.4 is displayed.

Figure B.4

You can choose to report errors that occur in Windows XP and in application programs.

5. If you want to turn off the reporting, click the Disable error reporting radio button.

6. Click OK to close the Error Reporting dialog box; click OK again to close the System Properties dialog box.

TIP

You can tell Windows XP to report on only selected programs by clicking the Choose Programs button. In the Choose Programs dialog box, click All programs in this list and then select only the programs you want to report on. Click OK to close the dialog box.

GLOSSARY

A

active content. Web page content that continually changes—such as a stock ticker, running headlines, and more.

ActiveX. A Microsoft-designed technology that enables computers to communicate with each other across platforms.

add-on. A small program or utility that extends the capabilities of another program or browser.

Address Book. The file in which you store e-mail addresses, phone numbers, and other contact information.

antivirus software. A program that checks files that are downloaded or saved to make sure that the files do not have viruses.

B

background. The screen color, pattern, or image behind the foreground images in a graphical interface.

bandwidth. The width of the data channel through which data is transmitted on the Internet and between networked computers.

baud rate. The speed at which your modem is capable of transmitting data.

bitmap. A graphics image formed from a collection of pixels (individual colored dots).

broadband connection. A high-speed Internet connection.

browser. A program designed to display Web pages. Internet Explorer is part of Windows XP, and MSN Explorer is another online service and Web browser available from Microsoft.

buffering. The process of downloading media files and storing them while other portions of the file are playing.

C

chat room. A virtual meeting room that enables users to gather and have online discussions.

codecs. A compression of the term compressor-decompressor; software used to compress and expand digital media.

compression. The task of reducing the size of files so that they can be sent over the Internet or copied to a disk. You compress files using a compression utility, such as WinZip.

Content Advisor. A security measure in Windows XP that enables you to set allowable standards for your system regarding language, obscene material, and more.

cookie. A small file created when you log on to a Web site that enables a site to identify you (or your system) when you return to the site at a later time.

D

default. A changeable system setting that is preset on your computer. For example, Windows XP puts in your My Music folder by default any music files you save.

default folder. The folder a program stores files in—unless you specify otherwise.

defragmenting. The process of consolidating file fragments and deleting unneeded data.

desktop. The main Windows work area.

device. A hardware component, such as a printer, scanner, joystick, graphics tablet, adapter, or modem.

Device Manager. A tool you can use to orchestrate the use of devices on your system.

diagnostics. An automated test that checks the status of a system device.

dial-up connection. The type of Internet or network connection that uses telephone lines.

digital media. Media files—including sound, photos, movies, and more—that are saved in electronic (digitized) form.

DirectX. A Microsoft-developed technology that enhances the multimedia capabilities of games and other programs that use media.

domain name. The portion of a Web address, or URL, that gives the name of the server on which the site resides.

downloading. The process of copying a file or program from the Web to your computer.

drag. To select an item by pressing and holding the mouse button and moving it to another location.

draw program. A graphics program that uses calculations to draw object-oriented files.

driver. A file of specifications that tells Windows how to work with a particular device.

E–F

e-mail. Electronic mail sent between computers on a local-area network or the Internet.

extracting. The process of expanding files that have been compressed by using a compression utility, such as WinZip.

FAQ. An acronym for frequently asked questions, a listing of questions and answers that users commonly ask about a specific topic.

file attachment. A file, such as a Microsoft Word document or photo file, added to an e-mail message so that both can be sent simultaneously.

filtering. The process of sifting out e-mail messages you do not want to receive.

folder. A basic storage container for files you create in Windows.

G–H

guest book. A form found on many Web sites that asks you to enter information about yourself so that the site owners know who has visited.

History folder. A feature included in Internet Explorer (and other browsers) that enables you to return to the Web sites you've visited recently.

home page. The page set as the default Web page where your computer opens when you first launch Internet Explorer or another browser.

HTML. An acronym for Hypertext Markup Language, a system of tags used to encode documents to prepare them for the Web.

hub. A connection device used to connect multiple segments of a network.

I–J

icon. An image displayed on the desktop or in folders, used to represent files or programs.

Internet. The worldwide network of computer systems.

Internet Connection Wizard. A wizard that walks you through the process of establishing a new connection on your computer.

ISDN. An acronym for Integrated Services Digital Network, a high-speed connection that enables fast transfer times online.

ISP. An acronym for Internet service provider, a services company that provides access to the Internet.

Java. A programming language developed by Sun Microsystems that is used to create animation in applications on the Web.

L–M

link. A connection on a Web page that takes you to another page or causes an action (such as opening a new e-mail message) to occur.

local-area network. A network of two or more local computers, linked together by network cabling.

magnifier. An accessibility tool that enables you to magnify a portion of the screen to enhance visibility.

Media bar. The panel that appears when you click the Media tool in Internet Explorer. You can listen to music, watch videos, hear radio broadcasts, and more using the Media bar.

messaging. The task of sending instant messages using Windows Messenger.

My Documents. The folder in which the documents you create in Windows XP are stored by default. My Music and My Pictures are stored within My Documents.

N–P

narrator. An accessibility tool that reads items and options in Windows XP, helping visually challenged users work with menus, choose dialog box options, and more.

NetMeeting. The online conferencing tool included with Windows XP that enables you to hold virtual meetings, share programs, have live discussions, transmit video, use a whiteboard, and more.

network. Two or more computers connected by physical cabling or via telephone line connections that can share resources and devices, such as printers, scanners, and more.

network adapter. The connector that makes your computer network-ready. Also may be called a network interface card.

Network Setup Wizard. A wizard that helps you configure a new network.

notification area. The section on the far right side of the Taskbar (close to the clock) that displays the icons of system devices in use (such as the Connect icon when you are online).

object-oriented. A graphics style that creates an image based on calculations so that it can be drawn, resized, and manipulated as a single object (as opposed to pixels).

on-screen keyboard. An accessibility tool that displays a keyboard on the screen so that users with mobility challenges can use a special input device for data entry.

paint program. A graphics program that creates bitmap images.

Plug and Play. An installation technology Windows uses to automatically sense and install devices you plug into your computer. The device might be a printer, scanner, digital videocamera, modem, or other type of device. Not all devices support Plug and Play, but most can be configured manually to work with Windows.

print queue. The list of print jobs in line to be printed.

Q–S

Quick Launch area. The segment of the Taskbar closest to the Start button in which icons of application programs appear.

RAM. An acronym for random access memory, the storage space in your system that holds data during the current worksession.

Recycle Bin. The area where Windows XP sends files you delete. The files are stored in the Recycle Bin until you intentionally empty the bin.

restore point. A point you set in System Restore that marks the way your system was configured so that you can return to that point, if necessary, with System Restore.

right-click. To click an object using the right mouse button.

Scanner and Camera Wizard. A wizard that leads you through the process of scanning a photo or loading a digital image.

screen saver. A program that runs automatically to reduce wear and tear on the monitor after your computer has been unused for a specified period.

search engine. An online tool that locates and displays information about a specific topic you enter.

shared folder. A folder that can be shared by one or more users or by different computers on a network.

shortcut. A link, usually on the desktop, that enables you to launch a program quickly.

synchronize. To compare and match versions of files on different computer systems and make sure that the most recent version is the one in use.

T–W

Task Manager. A tool that enables you to start and stop programs.

Taskbar. The bar across the bottom of the Windows XP desktop that includes the Start button and enables you to switch between programs.

thumbnail. A view in which small images are used to display files.

uploading. The process of copying a file or files from your computer to a computer at a remote location.

USB. An acronym for universal serial bus, a universal port that supports Plug and Play installation. USB enables you to connect printers, scanners, digital cameras, and more using the same connection.

username. The account name you are given by your ISP (or other online service provider). You enter your username and password when you first log on to the Internet.

URL. An acronym for Universal Resource Locator, the technical term for Web address. A typical Web address is **www.microsoft.com**.

Utility Manager. An accessibility tool in Windows XP that enables users to manage all accessibility tools, turning them on and off from one point.

videoconferencing. Conferencing by phone or on the Internet using a Webcam or digital camcorder to provide video input.

Windows Media Player. A multifaceted program that enables you to listen to a CD, watch a DVD, tune in to a radio broadcast, and copy and organize your favorite songs and media clips.

Windows Movie Maker. A program included in Windows XP that enables you to create your own movies using a variety of input from VCRs, digital camcorders, Web videos, and more.

wizard. An automated feature that walks you through a specific process by asking you a series of questions. You answer the question (usually by clicking an option) and click Next to move to the next step in the wizard. Windows XP uses wizards to help you set up many different elements—including Internet connections, automated tasks, home networks, and more.

INDEX